1ª d
5-

The Writer in Our World

with contributions by

Stanislaw Baranczak
Terrence Des Pres
Gloria Emerson
Leslie Epstein
Carolyn Forché
Michael S. Harper
Ward Just
Grace Paley
Mary Lee Settle
Robert Stone
Derek Walcott
C. K. Williams

with additional work by moderators
Angela Jackson and Bruce Weigl

Symposium Assistant Director:
Fred Shafer

The Writer in Our World

a symposium sponsored by *TriQuarterly* magazine

Edited by Reginald Gibbons

The Atlantic Monthly Press
Boston/New York

First Edition

This book first appeared as a special issue of *TriQuarterly*,
a publication of Northwestern University

Library of Congress Cataloging-in-Publication Data

The writer in our world.

"First appeared as a special issue of TriQuarterly
[Northwestern University]"—Verso of t.p.
    1. Literature and society—Congresses.   2. Politics
and literature—Congresses.   I. Gibbons, Reginald.
II. TriQuarterly.
PN51.W72   1986   306'.47   86-3317
ISBN 0-87113-092-0

Published simultaneously in Canada

PRINTED IN THE UNITED STATES OF AMERICA

Contents

Preface   9
Reginald Gibbons

I Political Reality and Imaginative Writing

Poetry and Politics 17
Terrence Des Pres

A Lesson in Commitment 30
Carolyn Forché

The Novel's Grip upon Reality 39
Leslie Epstein

Questions and Answers 46

II Poetry and History, Exile, Race

It is the Man/Woman Outside Who Judges:
The Minority Writer's Perspective on
Literature 57
Michael S. Harper

The Continental Drift: An Eastern European
in America 67
Stanislaw Baranczak

A Colonial's-Eye View of America 73
Derek Walcott

Questions and Answers 78

Special Section: New Work and Work in Progress

Three Poems 87
Stanislaw Baranczak

Equipment for Living (essay) 90
Terrence Des Pres

A Jew and Indians: A Discarded Excerpt from
a Work Far from Done 99
Leslie Epstein

Five Poems and an Interview 109
Michael S. Harper

Miz Rosa Rides the Bus (poem) 129
Angela Jackson

From *Treemont Stone* (excerpt from novel) .. 131
Angela Jackson

From *The American Ambassador* (excerpt
from novel) 141
Ward Just

Midrash on Happiness (story) 151
Grace Paley

From *Children of Light* (excerpt from novel) . 154
Robert Stone

Three Poems 173
Derek Walcott

Five Poems 181
Bruce Weigl

Nine Poems 188
C. K. Williams

III   Writing and War

Vietnam—Fiction and Fact 199
Ward Just

The Children in the Field 205
Gloria Emerson

Me and the Universe 213
Robert Stone

Questions and Answers 219

IV   The Writer's Work—
The Solitary and the Social

Of Poetry and Women and the World 231
Grace Paley

Of Poetry and Justice 239
C. K. Williams

Facets of Censorship 245
Mary Lee Settle

Questions and Answers 250

V Some Last Questions and Answers

Roundtable, November 10, 1984 . . . . **261**
Symposium and audience members

Contributors (includes identified speakers from audience) **294**

Cover design by Gini Kondziolka

All photographs were taken November 9 and 10, 1984 at Northwestern University by Susan Lukes and Jim Ziv. Lukes took the photographs on pages 31, 66, 74, 206, 232, 244, 266, 270, 275, 279, 283, 287, 291 and 293. Ziv took those on pages 19, 41, 58, 200, 214 and 238. All photographs copyright © 1986 by Northwestern University.

The quotations on page 8 from Milan Kundera's essay, "The Novel and Europe," are reprinted with permission from the New York Review of Books, *copyright © 1984 by Nyrev, Inc.; the essay appeared in the* Review's *July 19, 1984 issue. The quotations from Benjamin DeMott's essay, "Did the 1960's Damage Fiction?," are copyright © 1984 by the New York Times Company and reprinted by permission; the essay appeared in the* New York Times Book Review *of July 8, 1984.*

The rise of science propelled man into the tunnels of specialized knowledge. With every step forward in scientific knowledge, the less clearly he could see either the world as a whole or his own self, and he plunged further into what Husserl's pupil Heidegger called in a beautiful and almost magical phrase "the forgetting of being." . . . [T]he character of modern society . . . reduces man's life to its social function, the history of a people to a small set of events that are then themselves reduced to a tendentious interpretation; social life is reduced to political struggle, and that in turn is reduced to the confrontation of just two great global power blocs. Man is caught in a veritable whirlpool of reduction where Husserl's "world of concrete living" is fatally obscured and where being is progressively forgotten. Now if the novel's raison d'être is to keep the world of concrete living constantly before our eyes and to protect us from "the forgetting of being," is it not necessary today more than ever that the novel should exist? . . . But alas, the novel too is eaten by the beetles of reduction which diminish not only the sense of the world but also the meaning of works of art. . . . The novel's essence is complexity. Every novel says to the reader: "Things are not as simple as you think." That is the novel's eternal truth, but its voice grows ever fainter in a world based on easy, quick answers that come before and rule out the question. . . . Does this mean that the novel will disappear in a world "that is alien to it"? . . . All I think I know is that the novel cannot live in peace with the spirit of our times: if it is to carry on uncovering the undiscovered, to continue "progressing" as novel, it can only do so against the "progress" of the world.

Milan Kundera

The most interesting [writers nearing or into their 40's] sometimes seem actually to be secret collaborators bent on telling one and only one story, the changeless theme of which is human unresponsiveness. . . . In his second novel, "The Ultimate Good Luck" (1981), Richard Ford [writes]—"People watched each other with the expectation of diseased response." The unifying project of the group of writers I have in mind is just this: to show us—ceaselessly, unrelentingly—people watching each other with expectations of diseased response. . . . [E]arlier generations were not yet tyrannized by the notion, spawned by the sexual revolution, that the claims of public reality and long-term human connection were less significant than those of private ego and merely personal will. And . . . writers of the earlier generations began work when letters hadn't yet become completely marginalized, when the task of communicating the realities of war or mass joblessness or profound moral disruption still fell most immedi-ately to the writer . . . With power often comes the sense of responsibility to wholeness—belief that one must engage with the whole life of society. With feelings of marginality and powerlessness comes the sense that personal despair can't be tran-scended. . . . But this fidelity [to contemporary impassivity] is dehumanizing, crippling to the highest literary and moral value—responsiveness to life. Truthfully, one does not know how to speak to it. . . . It's never optimism that needs endorsement in this country; always it's the values of variousness, imaginative growth, individual respon-siveness. Without responsiveness, moral penetration is utterly inconceivable.

Benjamin DeMott

Preface

Three days after the 1984 presidential elections—a subject more than once mentioned in this book—a dozen writers of fiction, nonfiction and poetry gathered in the small American town of Evanston, just north of Chicago, to take part in a symposium sponsored by *TriQuarterly* magazine at Northwestern University. The topics they had been invited to address, in four panel discussions and one roundtable, had in common the relationship between imaginative writing and the larger social order in which it exists—and in which it is read or heeded or attended to. Or not. And which it therefore either influences or fails to influence. And further—how such influence as it has, or fails to have, may be variously considered as good or bad or irrelevant to the larger culture.

Although the writers were grouped in trios on the panels, to address certain topics, the range of subjects proposed to them all was vague, and not unintentionally so—to admit the largest range of responses. The format was intended not so much as a spur to opinion on the set topics, as to demonstrate that the views and beliefs of writers as artists and thinkers could and should have a place in debates regarding the whole of our culture. Whether imaginative writing could or should be expected to have any but a marginal place among us; who the readers of serious writing are and how they might increase or decrease in number; what the individual artist's relationship to the larger culture is or might be; what place history and contemporary events have or could have in contemporary fiction and poetry; whether some subjects of writing such as war or race or exile were to be regarded as essential and necessary or peripheral and of no privileged status; how a writer's responsibilities may be variously conceived (to himself or herself, or to readers past or hoped-for)—such were the sorts of issues in question.

9

The contributions to this volume are the proceedings of that symposium. To them have been added a number of excerpts and instances of new work and work in progress. The latter writings stand at the center of the book as a kind of validating evidence of the intimate engagement of these writers with large subjects in the work that is most important to them—be it poems, fiction or nonfiction—as well as in their opinion as individuals, citizens, artists.

Some participants brought prepared statements and read them; others spoke extemporaneously. The latter have been lightly edited, merely in order to remove the hesitations of spoken discourse and to clarify arguments and correct quotations. There were four panels, and the contents of this volume, divided in the middle by the central anthology of new work, reflect that order of presentation. The question-and-answer sessions at the end of each panel and at the roundtable conclusion of the symposium, when all twelve writers were on stage at once to respond to each other and to the audience, have been edited also—rather more carefully—leaving only the most interesting and pointed discussion for readers of this volume.

The panels were moderated by two younger writers who will be less known to readers than the twelve whose statements form the heart of this book and whose work needs far less introduction. One was the poet Bruce Weigl, whose two books contain work that seems—because of its intensely felt but also scrupulously clear attention to working-class American life, and experience of the war in Vietnam (and the later, civilian residue of that experience)—considerably larger than most new poetry. The other was the poet and novelist Angela Jackson, whose work in progress is a novel in which the everyday travail and violence of urban black life in Chicago are portrayed, richly, with many reminders of the powers and possibilities of love and dignity, as well. Although their voices are not heard in this published version of the presentations, new work by both of them appears in the anthology section.

It has taken more than a year to prepare the manuscript and set the book in type and print it, yet the concerns and problems which during the symposium were voiced, debated, argued—sometimes declaimed passionately, sometimes with a quiet eloquence—have of course found no alleviation or solution in that historically short interim. It's important to see clearly what those concerns and problems are, and are not: if these days we commonly read or hear that much contemporary writing lacks power or that it suffers from a claustrophobic narrowness of subject or a lack of strong feeling, it's also true that there are great and extraordinary exceptions to this general state of the vast (and yet insubstantial) body of undistinguished and even popular work. The complaint has no validity against the vigor, originality and accomplishment of works such as those by the writers in this volume. For this reason were they invited! What is the relationship, then—whether it is a burden or an irrelevancy to writers and readers—between this prevailing tone and the best work that rises above it?

It is clearly wrong to ask all writers to do the same thing, whatever that may be; or it's simply foolish, since even if they wanted to, they couldn't necessarily succeed in altering entirely their own temperaments and personal history and artistic gifts to suit the claims or demands of anyone else. But the purpose of this symposium was to get beyond the stage of complaint or exhortation, and to hear from the writers themselves how they regard the distinction and greatness of great works, and the questions of where the writer's responsibilities lie or don't lie, the way the literary artist works in this social context, or feels he or she *should* work.

In fact, it can seem that we have a great deal of wonderful and substantial contemporary writing and not enough *readers* to appreciate it—or not enough of the serious sort. One of the questions addressed, if sometimes only obliquely, by the participants in the symposium, was the nature and size of the audience for serious fiction and for poetry. And one hint at an answer was provided by the sessions themselves, for most of those attending—in a hall, often full, that seated over two hundred—were not from the academic environment in which we were meeting. There were a number of students, but few faculty, and many in the audience made clear, by the nature of their questions, that they were some of the very same Serious Readers—living and working in an ordinary world, the "our world" of the title of the gathering and of this book—whom the writers are seeking for their work. This was heartening, as was the intensity of their questions and exchanges with the writers—often and clearly implying by passionate tone of voice that such questions as these writers raised *do* matter, and the mere voicing of them was refreshing and renewing and exhilarating, and sent many listeners up to the stage after each session to ask about books and where they could be found.

It was especially interesting, and exciting, to sense what only rarely happens in symposia—that the themes of the conference were defining themselves and that as the sessions continued there was a sense of ongoing debate and refinement of ideas, especially in the conflicting opinions on what was called an "aesthetics of violence." If any consensus can be said to have come from the five sessions, it might be a challenge to two opposed assumptions: (1) that consciousness of the social sphere of human relations, beyond the private life, has no necessary place in the artist's deliberations—for many of these writers say that, for them, it does hold a place and must, if they are to respond to their own artistic impulse; (2) that the artist *must* respond to social or political reality in an explicit way in his or her work—for if it is proper and even necessary to exhort one's self and one's fellow artists, it is improper—and merely another form of censorship—for anyone to prescribe what an artist should do. The refutation of these two assumptions—both by statement and by example—both clears ground for the artist and narrows it.

There is such a thing as a citizen-artist, who may or may not have an intention to carry a cause through a piece of writing. An artist's goals as an artist arise partly out of his or her temperament, but also will show to greater or lesser degree the profundity of the artist's understanding of matters beyond the individual psyche. The issue is not "political" writing or even specific subjects of writing, but a way of responding as an artist to the reality beyond immediate experience. But this formulation is too crude, as well, for of course "immediate experience" can meet sensibilities as responsive as those of Dickens, Hardy, Stendhal, Baudelaire, Celan, or Kafka; or Dreiser, Williams Carlos Williams, even Eliot; to say nothing of more recent writers like Jarrell, Lowell, Patrick White, Nadine Gordimer, Alice Munro and all those participating in this symposium. If the writer's sensitivity to his or her "immediate experience" is of that sort, then the issue is not at all a "political" or "social" kind of writing but simply the largeness of the writer's response to worlds both large and small, to experience both material and spiritual, to realms both contemporary and imagined.

Grace Paley's serious and funny definition of the poet's responsibility is a case in point: it offers exhortation and liberty at once. It is a manifesto *for* the citizen-poet rather than a decree regarding what he or she should write about. It has to do with being and living before it has to do with writing. And its implicit assumption is that in the artistic work of a person of alert awareness and thoughtfulness the world will perforce make its entrance. Not in a mechanical or merely referential way, as when a poet attempts to prove his or her sensitivity by making sure the big subjects appear in a poem. But, as readers of Paley's stories will know, in a way that is achieved through a felt responsibility to understand—and a gift for understanding—how the playground holds already the drama of the battlefield or the courtroom, and sets the direction in which those later dramas will be played out. Tragically or, at times, with more hope.

The underlying common ground of all the presentations seems to lie in each writer's sense that a responsibility first of all to truthful and honest language is the only thing that can produce the honesty and even grandness of a literary work—no surprise, given such forbears as Conrad and Orwell. An abhorrence of deceitful language can be discerned in presentations as diverse as Stanislaw Baranczak's account of various surprises in the American scene and Robert Stone's self-accounting for what he felt when he found himself for the first time in the middle of the bloodshed of wartime, or C. K. Williams's meditation on the languages of poetry and politics and Gloria Emerson's comments on the need to attend to honest and accurate accounts of the real human experience of situations of extreme danger and suffering. Or Derek Walcott's comments on the way of the poet on whose words the history not only of *a* people, but of mankind, waits for expression, and on the careful distinction that must be preserved between poetry and journalistic writing—a care that can only arise out of a respect for the art of poetry that naturally strives to distinguish it from opinion. Or Leslie Epstein's insistence that violence against persons is not beautiful, and that to aestheticize it is dishonest. To say nothing of Carolyn Forché's accounts—corroborating in her very different way Walcott's sense of poetry—of how the contemporary reality of horror, once it impinges on the writer, leaves a burden of responsibility for the honest representation of that horror. Or Michael S. Harper's comments on the socially-inflicted double consciousness in the black artist in a white society, and the inevitable distortions and possibilities of language that result; Ward Just's moving acknowledgement of the compelling power of a single subject, war, and his understanding of the languages of reporting and of fiction; Mary Lee Settle's remarks on the destructiveness of censorship; or Terrence Des Pres's analysis of the mood of contemporary American poetry, which he diagnoses as inward and timid before dimensions—both frightening to acknowledge and necessary to strive against with hope—of reality which poetry, in pretending it does not see, falsifies.

Taken together, these statements form the most comprehensive contemporary assessment of the writer's place in our society that we have. And the stature and seriousness of these writers assure us that their experience and their comment are likely to remain the benchmark for discussion of these subjects for a long time to come.

Reginald Gibbons
January 1986

13

I Political Reality
and Imaginative Writing

Poetry and Politics

Terrence Des Pres

A moment of preface. This afternoon I'd like to talk about my response to the *example*, if I can put it this way, of Central European literature—a kind of writing that isn't, on the home front, much in evidence. It occurs to me, however, that the poets participating in this symposium make an important exception to the American rule of separation—that poetry and politics can't meet—and to poets who address the larger world I'm grateful. When I read Harper and Forché, Walcott, Baranczak and C. K. Williams, I find poems strong enough to handle history and not stay cowed within the halting world of self. I'm assuming, of course, that there is something more to life than solipsistic self-regard. Now I begin.

If the matter before us is "political reality and imaginative writing," then the subject is immense. I take it, though, that our immediate concern is less with the older notion of art politicized, and more with the kind of poem or novel that takes as its donnée the realm of political experience—and here at the start I'd like to avoid confusion by stressing the word *experience*.

By way of illustration, I might point, for example, to the awful emptying of personality that Nadezhda Mandelstam observed among her friends in the years of Stalin's terror. Or, less extreme but still real, the feeling of shame that comes over us when our own government supports regimes like the ones in South Africa or El Salvador. Or, finally and for everyone, the ruinous impact of living under nuclear threat. Political intrusion, in these cases, is feeling's occasion, the motive for metaphor. Politics twists the soul in vicious ways, and there are poems and novels that compute the cost. Writing of this kind is not so much grounded in ideology as in the concrete reactions of men and women who find themselves in history's path. This is one way, at least, to think about imaginative writing in relation to political reality.

Most of us have no trouble accepting fiction in which human behavior is at least partly determined by political pressures, novels like *Transit of Venus*, *A Flag for Sunrise* or *Waiting for the Barbarians*. With poetry, however, the situation is different. There is still plenty of resistance to the idea that poetry, especially the lyric, can have any truck with politics. This bias is perhaps strongest among academic critics and the sort of poet our ubiquitous "workshop" turns out. What especially interests me is the contradiction in American literary culture—I mean the fact that while we promote one sort of product at home, we invest deeply in work of a very different cast from other cultures and nations, as if we couldn't quite purge ourselves of interest in poetry not officially sanctioned, a circumstance revealed in part by the recent high regard for poetry in translation. This contradiction, it seems to me, was signaled by Roland Barthes when he said that critics talk endlessly about Desire (amorous) but almost never about Need (social). An interesting situation, it seems to me, and one to which I'll return.

But first an aside. Do any of us recall, I wonder, Carlyle's 1840 lectures on heroism, among which he included "The Poet as Hero"? I like Carlyle's designation, which was meant to publicize the Romantic estimate of the poet's importance. No doubt he had in mind Shelley's grand notion of unacknowledged legislation, but perhaps also Wordsworth's claim that the poet is "the rock of defense for human nature." In America, meanwhile, Emerson, who was Carlyle's transatlantic ally, spoke with equal emphasis about the poet's high office. In his essay "The Poet," Emerson refers to poets as "liberating gods," says that their job is "announcement and affirming," and after describing the United States as a poem "yet unsung," goes on to call for an American Homer. We know, I guess, who that would be. Walt Whitman took up Emerson's challenge, and, by way of introducing the author of *Leaves of Grass*, Whitman said of and to himself in his Preface: "Love the earth and sun and the animals, despise riches, give alms to every one that asks, stand up for the stupid and crazy, devote your income and labor to others, hate tyrants, argue not concerning God, have patience and indulgence toward the people, take off your hat to nothing known or unknown," and, in sum, "dismiss whatever insults your own soul."

That's an heroic program certainly, but that was in 1855 and may now sound too good to be true. A century later, in 1951, Lionel Trilling developed a more sobering view in his essay on Keats, which without irony he entitled "The Poet as Hero." Trilling is mainly concerned with

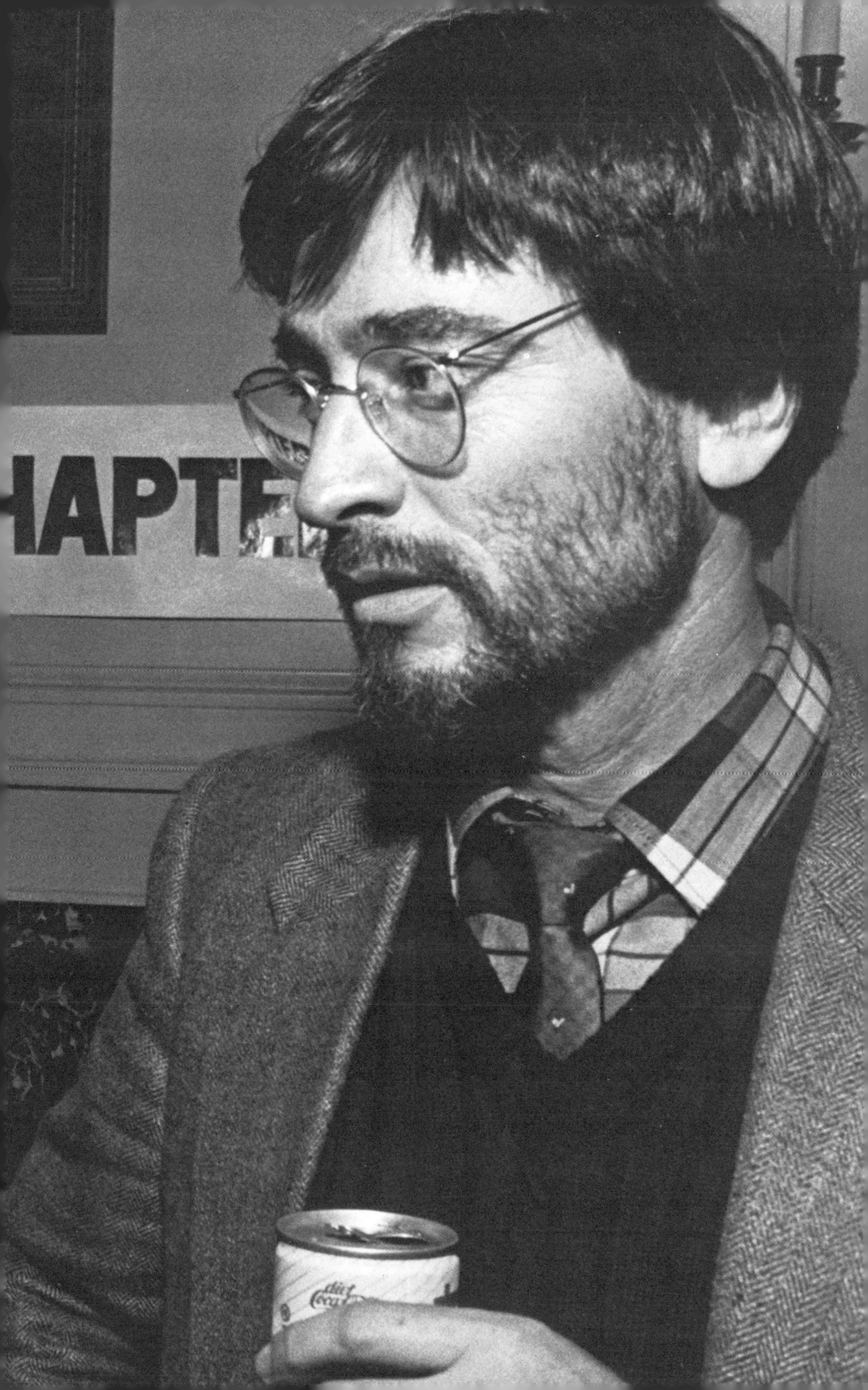
HAPTE

Keats's courage in adversity, the young poet's solid faith in his calling despite the fact that, as Trilling puts it, "Keats never deceived himself into believing that the power of imagination is sovereign, that it can make the power of circumstance of no account." Keats and Trilling shared a sense of the heroic that is essentially tragic. And if we should set the "power of imagination" in active opposition to "the power of circumstance," we'd soon enough find ourselves with W. B. Yeats in his aggressive realm of tower, sword and birthings of "terrible beauty." As Yeats saw it, the modern poet's stance is embattled. Poetry is worth the fight, but without clear victories, and precisely in this conflict—imagination against circumstance—the poet's task becomes heroic. Upon this Yeats insisted to the end.

I am not, then, without support if I wish to think of poets and poetry in heroic terms. Heroism is not necessarily a romantic notion. In our time it might mean simply standing firm amid adversity, the fighting of a losing war with the aim of losing less than everything. And perhaps, quietly, in secret, many of us harbor heroic sentiments about what poetry is or ought to be. Maybe, too, this is not wholly unreasonable or without ancient foundation. We still feel, I think, a sort of atavistic respect for the figure of the poet, and I'd like to suggest that this is not wholly a romantic or recent invention, but in fact goes back to the old and venerable tradition of the bard—the tribal poet, whose job was to celebrate and satirize, to praise and curse, and upon whom, in hard times, the tribe might really depend for its sense of identity and will to endure. Homer gives us a wonderful glimpse of such a poet in Book Eight of *The Odyssey*, and there is hard evidence, especially concerning the early bards of Ireland and Wales, to back up such claims.

In the case of Ireland and Wales, proud cultures were threatened by the English attempt to subdue the native populations. This was an early example of empire at work, and the fact that the British enacted actual laws against poets suggests something of the importance, or subversive potency, that imperial power attaches to the poets of conquered peoples. I might cite, here, T. S. Eliot's remark in his essay, "The Social Function of Poetry," that language is the root of communal identity and, as he puts it directly, "no art is more stubbornly national than poetry." Eliot normally avoided such unambiguous pronouncements, but this one slipped out in 1943, compelled, no doubt, by the terror of the Second World War. The same war instructed Czeslaw Milosz in a similar view, and in *The Witness to Poetry* (1983) he says straight out: "When an entire community is struck by misfortune, for instance, the Nazi occupation of Poland, then the 'schism between the poet and the great human family' disappears and poetry becomes as essential as bread." As essential as bread.

It seems that poetry's service to the body politic is most needful, and the poet's standing highest, when a nation or culture feels itself in danger. A voice from Prague adds substance to this surmise. Speaking of the bold outpour of films, novels, poetry and works of philosophy born in Central Europe after the Soviet takeover in 1945, Milan Kundera pits East against West and says in a recent essay:

> . . . it is a drama of the West—a West that, kidnapped, displaced, and brain-washed, nevertheless insists on defending its identity.
> The identity of a people or civilization is always reflected and concentrated in what has been created by the mind—in what is known as "culture." If this identity is threatened with extinction, cultural life grows correspondingly more intense, more important, until culture itself becomes the living value around which all people rally. That's why, in each of the revolts of Central Europe—in which the actual extinction of a people was feared—the collective cultural memory and the contemporary creative output assumed roles so great and so decisive. ("A Kidnapped West or Culture Bows Out," in *Granta*, No. 11, 1984, p. 97)

Milosz and Kundera know what they are talking about, and I'll return to them later. So far, however, my aim has been to call attention to the old connection between poetry and crisis and, against the backdrop of politics, to recall the figure of the poet as the man or woman whose force of language commands, or can command, heroic stature.

Keeping these ideas of poetry and poets in mind, I move on to my central concern, which I see this way: if in an increasingly Orwellian world the human spirit is more vulnerable than we usually admit; if global violence is on the rise and, up ahead at no great distance, we see ourselves mocked and unnerved by the nuclear option; then I presume that we turn where we can for sustenance, and that some of us take poetry seriously in exactly this way—as a spiritual resource from which we gather fortitude and nourishment. I don't mean the sort of bounce that takes us clear-eyed and laughing to the grave, but rather the kind of empowerment we gain when poetry gives us, as Wallace Stevens put it, a "pressure within" that can withstand and push back against the "pressure without." We do what we can as citizens, of course. But when it comes to the Bomb, or just to the prospect of empires in endless conflict (the U.S. and the S.U. wracking the world into two contending spheres of influence), it seems clear we cannot do very much very fast. So the immediate question isn't what to do but how to live, and some of us, at least, turn for help to poetry—we turn as once, maybe, a perishing tribe looked to its bards for resolve and renewal. The question thus becomes: Where, and to whom, do we turn?

To a degree, to a surprising degree, we turn *elsewhere*, not foremost or finally to poets of our own country, but to poets from abroad and mainly from cultures threatened by imperial takeover. We forego the pleasures of native voice and endure the indignity of translation in order to come upon an authority seldom apparent among the 4,000 or so poets now publishing or the 50,000 poems-per-year that flood our literary magazines. Despite this enormous industry at home, we increasingly turn elsewhere. Can this really be the case? It's difficult to tell, but consider the following questions. Which poets today do you see as heroic? Whose examples do you prize for sustaining excitement? Whose work seems truly exemplary?

There is, at the moment, this strange habit among us. We read American work to confirm and cheer, in an almost cliquish way, the American "poetry scene." But then, we go on to read *other* poetry to help us live our lives, to recompose the soul and fortify our sense of being in the world. In particular, we turn to poets who address the world at those unhappy points where self and history meet; where private and public realms collide; not, that is, connection with *a* world, transcendent and apart, but *the* world, unfree, murderous, surfeited with sorrow — political torment such as men and women know when events intrude to curtail or cancel the spirit's claims to self-determination. To speak of "the world" is necessarily to speak of politics, the array of impersonal forces playing havoc with our personal lives, the world of dread and savagery that, more and more, is getting us down. Beirut, San Salvador, the coming of our Latin Wars, it's a horror show nonstop, delivered to us daily on the evening news, the prospect of nuclear wipeout as well. The theater of war and cruelty spreads, and at very least, what others suffer we behold.

It seems to me that poetry in the Emersonian tradition, the poetics of self-and-nature that Keats once called the "egotistical sublime," no longer speaks *to* us, no longer even makes sense. Further adventures of the self-delighted self are not what's wanted. Rather, a poetry that, as Max Frisch said of Brecht, stands up to the world in which it is written. Poetry that does not retreat into the inconsequence of self but rather confronts the burden of the terrible world and announces against the sort of political torment that all of us suffer or witness. Poetry as the rock of defense? Not at home it isn't. For substance of this tougher kind we turn elsewhere.

I want to know why we go where we go for the poetry we feel we need. How, for example, shall we make sense of the extreme respect with which Czeslaw Milosz is received in our country? Until recently not much of his work was available to us, and what we did have was not, in translation, technically very profound. Yet it served. This poet's peculiar sense of being *in* history and yet in problematic ways beyond history merely, seems instantly to capture some similar sense, however distant, of our own situation, as when Milosz writes in his "Elegy for N.N.":

> We learned so much, this you know well:
> how, gradually, what could not be taken away
> is taken. People, countrysides.
> And the heart does not die when one thinks it should,
> we smile, there is tea and bread on the table.

The "first impulse," Milosz writes, is joy — song filling the valleys. But it is taken away. How to recover it, again to sing despite a spectacle of misery, is the predicament that Milosz sounds out with his art. And in the doing he defines poetry as "a passionate pursuit of the Real." How silly that sounds beneath the seminar's translucent light. How compelling, when darkness arrives.

Another example: among poets now writing in English, why does Seamus Heaney enjoy such manifest distinction? He writes magical verse, he's a wonderful person — a friend to many of us here today. Yet his art, judged solely by its inventiveness and craft, isn't superior to the best of his American contemporaries. His use of language is distinctive, of course, but that is not what lifts him above his peers. What counts is his vision of self in relation to history — "memory incubating the spilled blood" — that sets him apart and calls us to him. Here again political consciousness, obliquely active as in Heaney's sequence of bog poems, would seem to be the decisive factor.

And what, finally, are we to make of the near sainthood of the great Russians, Osip Mandelstam and Anna Akhmatova in particular? A mantle of reverence rests not only upon their poetry but upon their lives as well — although, of course, under Stalin their lives were implicated in and by their art. We know that Mandelstam was arrested, released, then hounded to his death by the Soviet secret police, and that he died in a Gulag transit camp. We know, too, that Akhmatova survived, her friends and husband dead, her son imprisoned, and that to this share of suffering she bore witness both stately and brave. The bare stories of poets like these seem almost allegorical of the poet in our time — or rather, of the poet heroically perceived. And maybe that is exactly their appeal. Thinking about Akhmatova and Mandelstam, we instinctively feel their harrowing experience to be the plight of poetry, and therefore of the human spirit, in this untoward century.

Here is an example, a short poem by Akhmatova, written about Mandelstam. It is entitled "Voronezh" after the place of Mandelstam's last exile. Akhmatova visited him there, in that town "locked in ice," the old atrocities still palpable. Notice especially, at the poem's conclusion, Akhmatova's emblem of poetry beseiged. We do not share the actual situation, for none of us has been there (almost none of us, excuse me), but I would suggest that we nonetheless partake of the complexity of feeling that the poem develops. Here is "Voronezh" (the Kunitz/ Hayward translation, slightly revised):

> And the town stands locked in ice:
> A paperweight of trees, wells, snow.
> Gingerly I tread on glass:
> the painted sleighs skid in their tracks.
> Peter's statue in the square points to
> crows and poplars, and a verdigris dome
> washed clean, in a cloud of sun-motes.
> Here the earth still shakes from the old battle
> where the Tartars were beaten to their knees.
> Let the poplars raise their chalices
> for a sky-erupting toast,
> like thousands of wedding guests drinking
> in jubilation at a feast.
> But in the room of the banished poet
> Fear and the Muse stand watch by turn,
> and the night comes down
> that has no hope of dawn.

The poem's authority cannot be doubted. Neither can its odd familiarity. The poem is a clear enactment of political torment, and if we should wonder why it appeals to *us*, calls our attention to an experience so seemingly alien, or why, finally, this valorization of poetic fate feels accurate, we should have to go beyond the mechanics of artifice merely.

There is, to begin with, the factor of *lyrical will* – the way the poem still sings, still pushes against its own negation. The situation, after all, might be expected to silence poetry, or turn it to bitterness and naysaying, or ruin its self-confidence. How much can poetry suffer, what degree of wounding can be sustained, without the death of song? One of the paradoxes of our destructive era is that we begin to know poetry's strength, its power to keep itself intact and us with it. Events occur, circumstances take hold which should, but do not, stop either the poem or the poet. Then too, there is the way Akhmatova's poem *announces against* the specific inhumanity of the poet's plight. This capacity to say "No" to political compulsion, and thereby say "Yes" to human worth, very much suggests that "rock of defense" Wordsworth spoke of at the dawn of the modern political age, when he conceived of the poet as "an upholder and preserver" of our humanness.

And there is, finally, the poem's fine management of its focal imagery, so that it gathers its energies into what Seamus Heaney, borrowing from Yeats, would call an "emblem of adversity." The poem, that is, incorporates the horror it stands up against — the world trapped in ice and history's tremor, and especially the image of tyranny implicit in Great Peter's statue, which after Pushkin's "Bronze Horseman" can only be a figure of oppression, under which the ceremonies of love and simple joy grow mute. Except, of course, that here they do not. The abridgement of joy is real, as real as the poet's fear, but neither the terror nor the hopelessness precludes homage to the Muse. What I am saying might sound like mindless rhetoric, if not for the evidence of Akhmatova's witnessing and our knowledge of the historical conditions under which she, like Mandelstam, served her art. It makes such powerful *sense*, this poem, and surely we must wonder how — how, as an emblem of adversity, poetry of this kind speaks to *us*, we who are so apparently removed and safe and also, as we like to say, helpless.

One of the literary oddities of our time is the frequency with which the writer singlehandedly, and with no power base except his or her own art, openly challenges the State. This lopsided feuding might seem ludicrous, and yet a Nazim Hikmet or a Breyten Breytenbach sets his art against injustice, willingly suffers the consequences, and we at home feel inspired to applaud. It's easy to suppose that thereby we applaud ourselves. Literature is, after all, an entrance to the experience of others, and this especial virtue of art is as likely to be exploited, to be reduced to consumerism, as anything else of value. Then too, the American cultural habit has always been to prefer the foreign to the homegrown brand in almost everything.

Our homage to the heroic poet might therefore be no more than snobbery and radical chic, and no doubt such stratagems play their tacky part. But to credit self-deception with the whole of it, to reduce an enormously important cultural shift to a mode of unearned indulgence, is itself a shabby stratagem, one defeated by its own reductiveness. Who will say that our fearful love for Kafka has been no more than a fad? Or that, for us, Solzhenitsyn's serious rage is only cold-war sop? Or that Breytenbach's Afrikaner poems of self-laceration are just another opportunity, for us, to wallow by remote control in liberal guilt? One can admit the grain of truth in such charges and still see that something more is at stake. Real care for poetry from politically embattled cultures has been growing steadily. To judge from the new authority of translation, the practice of *turning elsewhere* is becoming an active part of current literary behavior. A solution, perhaps, to mainstream deficiencies.

For some years my own turning to poets of endangered nations—especially the pull I've felt toward the art of Eastern Europe—has troubled me. Why *this* fascination? By way of answer, I wouldn't rule out anything, not snobbery, not packaged compassion, not empire's curiosity about colorful native customs. But also there is this: we live on a small planet getting smaller day by day. Thanks to high-tech miracles, our minds are wired, via the media, into all the earth's disasters, political disasters first of all. There is no part of the world from which I can feel wholly free, knowing that what happens anywhere abroad impinges on my life at home. As the superpowers lock into permanent battle formation, countless small political destinies must sooner or later add up to one—to this thing called *human destiny* that we have always talked about and might at least expect to see. The prevailing mood, in any case, is one of fearful expectation, and fear provokes prophetic habits, alertness to signs of the times. Akhmatova's emblem of adversity—the poet besieged—is one of the signs.

When did *geopolitics*, the word, become current? When did the fate of poets like Mandelstam begin to count for poets in America? To bring these questions into relation creates larger questions that until recently have been off-limits to literary intelligence. We don't know how politics and poetry interact, although we do know that power is the secret reference point for discourse of every kind. We don't know much about cultural transmission, either, although nobody denies that alien arts play a signal role in the development of modern culture. Most mysterious, perhaps, is the way we seem to develop forms of consciousness corresponding to events still to come. Our ignorance is the more complete if Milosz is right when he says of our century "that, while the list of dreaded apocalyptic events may change, what is constant is a certain state of mind. This state of mind precedes the perception of specific reasons for despair, which come later."

All around us, peoples, nations and cultures are under siege and failing. This global state of affairs, it seems to me, determines more and more our state of mind. This is, at least, the view I gather from Kundera. The threat of cultural extinction, very real and keenly felt in places like

Hungary and Poland and the land of the Czechs, threatens European culture in general. By European culture I don't mean Eurocentric hegemony or the older claims of empire, but the small core of shared values which, so far as I can tell, might well be universal, but which in any case includes Homer's high estimate of the bard, the Hebrew prophets' faith in the word, the valor of the poet's task in troubled times. When Kundera equates the "struggle of man against power" with "the struggle of memory against forgetting," he endorses a very old tradition. And from his position of exile, Kundera has a vantage worth considering. As with Prague or Warsaw, so, in time's fullness, with us. Precisely here, it seems to me, we come upon our hidden connection to the fate of writers as different, from each other and from us, as Akhmatova, Milosz and Kundera. Poetic fate is perhaps the most accessible instance of cultural fate, and Kundera seems exactly on target when he says:

> Actually, in our modern world where power has a tendency to become more and more concentrated in the hands of a few big countries, *all* European nations run the risk of becoming small nations and of sharing their fate. In this sense the destiny of Central Europe anticipates the destiny of Europe in general, and its culture assumes an enormous relevance. (*Granta*, No. 11, 1984, p. 109)

And he concludes: "All of this century's great Central European works of art, even up to our own day, can be understood as long meditations on the possible end of European humanity." Does this sound accurate? Do the primary poems of our time remind us, by the very conditions of their making, that time is running out?

The fate of "small nations" heralds, very possibly, the struggle of humanity against power—or the State against its human base— beginning to gear up everywhere. Increasingly we feel ourselves the distant recipients of a destiny already endured by others elsewhere. We don't throw in the towel, but neither do we hope overmuch. Meanwhile, we search out the work of men and women who have been forced to find "in the written word a *last rampart* against the loneliness of annihilation." The words "last rampart" are from Milosz's *The Witness of Poetry*. It is something, this discovery of poetry as last defense, that we are just beginning to hold dear. Of course we do not live in Prague or Gadansk or the black holes of South Africa. We do not live in such places. But imagination does, and we honor poets as we find them.

Coda: Added After the Symposium

I came across Kundera's ideas just as my own were taking shape and suddenly I felt I had a sort of key. But only, I now think, up to a point. Kundera stresses the notion of cultural continuity, the spiritual web that alerts those of us at the center to shattering events on the outskirts. From the outskirts, in turn, we take our bearings. I would like, however, to add a qualification: at some point what counts most is culture's discontinuities, and also the way any dominant culture functions to exclude or devalue subject cultures. One might argue (although I doubt it) that in the case of empire, colonies gradually absorb the values imposed upon them. But as soon as one goes further and introduces the notion of "interior colonies," then clearly the dominant culture contains islands of spirit not its own. Even in urbane situations – this symposium, for instance – discontinuous energies circulate, sometimes like ships in the night. Listening to other speakers, I have had to recognize and respect the divisions among us, where earlier I saw only our singleness of purpose.

In particular, when colleagues move from principles (on which there is general agreement) to the specific case, emphasis shifts from one predicament to another and then agreement stops. In one case the focus is Eastern Europe, but in another it is the plight of women, or blacks, or other minorities that compose our internal colonies. Then again the focus jumps to empire at large, and the new case is Nicaragua or South Africa. What I want to point out is that while all of us join in a single effort to define literature's relation to politics, each of us has in mind a different history of political experience, and each of these examples, furthermore, has the force and authority of a cause. Here we are not in accord. For while I may be chiefly distraught by the tragedy, say, of the Czechs, my colleagues are responding to political scenarios that, in their urgency, exclude mine as mine excludes theirs.

Is there, then, any sense in speaking of cultural continuity? Can I really believe that what happens in Prague touches me in America because we share a discourse that conveys a transmissable message? Or put it this way: Does the political torment of Central Europeans find a significant reverberation in Afro-American, or Central American, politics? This question is crucial if we, as a group of writers committed to a literature of political recognition, are to act and move together. We are united in our effort, that's clear enough. But to the extent that we come from different backgrounds and therefore have different notions of urgency, we are at odds. The heart, as usual, is in the right place. The hand, however, is less certain, and when it curls into a fist it can shake at, but not with, other fisted hands.

If I embrace a tradition that includes writers like Milosz, Kundera and Mandelstam, I must equally credit my colleagues' turning to different traditions for the substance of an art that finds its calling and its challenge in the political torment of the continuing Vietnam ordeal, the renewed subjugation of women, the steady savagery of Salvador. In the immediate sense, these experiences suppose different centers, even if we see them forced, by political pressures of the empire, into a commonality of disaster. One of the eye-opening moments of the symposium, for me, occurred when Derek Walcott said that the old refrain, "civilization as we know it," looks wholly different, more barren, less worthy, when measured against "civilization as *they* know it." There are camps within camps, sectors unentered except by those trapped there. And over everything, the vast arrogance of the superpowers taking control, they who "know" what civilization is.

Viewed thus, what we usually call the Third World becomes simply the world, the global carpet of *de facto* colonies within contending spheres of empire. Where the superpowers will force us to go, if the bombs don't drop, I cannot know, although at least two nascent powers, the Chinese and the Islamic, might be expected to alter things as, in fact, they already have. What remains fairly constant, however, is the straight fact of political upheaval, political oppression, political intrusion to the depths of selfhood and soul. In the age of MX and "Star Wars," poetry must seem pitiful, but only for those still blinded by visions of progress or victory. For the time being, liberation is beyond us and in any case, changing the course of empire isn't poetry's concern. But whatever we do, however we decide to act, we shall need, at every point, the sanity of good cheer. Between ourselves and the world comes the word, the blessing of language rightly put.

A Lesson in Commitment

Carolyn Forché

I would like to begin with a little story about how I came to go to El Salvador in the first place, to provide a context for the statement that I would like to read. I traveled in 1977 to Spain to translate the poetry of a Salvadoran woman poet living in exile there. Her name was Claribel Alegría. I was doing translation because, following the completion of the book, *Gathering the Tribes*, I suddenly couldn't write any more poems. I suffered from what writers call a "block" and I, of course, despaired and thought that it was permanent and so I became a translator. I went to Spain because I had tried to translate the poetry of Claribel Alegría alone, in California, at my kitchen table. I was very naive. And so I appealed to Claribel's daughter, who advised me to come to Spain for the summer and if I had problems with the poetry I could ask "Mummy" and "Mummy" would tell me what I should put in her poems. "Mummy" was fond of an English which would say something like—she would say to me, "Why don't you use 'rolling hills' here?"

And I said, "Well, that's very nice but everyone else has already thought of it, also." That was the kind of problem one encountered translating the poem with the poet at one's side.

There I met a number of Latin American writers, some well-known, some not so well-known, because Claribel holds a kind of "salon" in Deya, Majorca, for any writer who has had to go into exile from any part of Latin America and has chosen to relocate in Europe. Claribel's home is a kind of way station. So, while there, I spent the summer listening to their stories of conditions in Latin America and beginning my education.

I returned to San Diego, California, in the fall and began teaching again and working for Amnesty International. I felt, however, after

a while, that writing letters for Amnesty International was, for me, not quite enough and I felt vaguely depressed and compelled to do something more—I didn't know quite what—about what I had learned in that summer. And, on into fall, the stacks of letters and literature about human rights violations in Central America grew on my table. One day, while I was grading freshman compositions, a white Hiace van pulled into my driveway. It was covered with dust and had El Salvador license plates. I went to the door, looked out and I didn't recognize the man getting out of the van, but there were two little girls with him so I relaxed. I felt, "Well, it can't be too bad. There are two little girls there." He had a very large roll of white butcher paper and a fistful of number-two pencils. And he walked up to my front door and said, "You are Carolyn Forché, and I am Leonel Gomez [Vides]." I thought for a moment and then I remembered the name. I had heard it in Spain that summer from Claribel. This was Claribel's nephew, the crazy one who slept with his motorcycle outside on the ground "like a woman," they said, which was a very odd thing, odder than the fact that he had given land away to the peasants in the countryside and was living in some kind of shack. I was worried; maybe this was him, maybe this was not, so I ran up to my room for the snapshots I had taken of the family in Spain and I said, "If you are Leonel Gomez, I want you to tell me who the people are in these pictures." I made him identify the relatives, the cousins, the babies, and he did a good job. He looked at me and said, "That was pretty good, a good test, that you find out who I am." So, I let him in and he said, "Clear this junk off the table. We have work to do." I defended my junk, my literature about human rights and my student composition papers, but I cleared it, and he told me to make some coffee; we had work to do. And then he started to cover the kitchen table with shelf paper, taping it at the corners with some tape. And he sat down and he said, "O.K., how much do you know about Central American military dictatorship?"

And I said, "Nothing."

And he said, "Good, you know that you know nothing. Now, this is a good beginning."

So he spent seventy-two hours drawing cartoons on the shelf paper— and diagrams and charts and graphs. Everything he explained to me, he drew a picture of as he spoke. And he began with a structure of the Salvadoran military and he drew the coffee plantations and the American embassy. Then he brought salt and pepper shakers over to the table, and spoons and various other household objects. And he called the salt shaker this "colonel" and he called the pepper shaker that "colonel" and this spoon was the American ambassador. And so on and so forth. And he arranged them all in a scenario, as he called it, and then he said, "All right, you are this colonel and this happens and that happens and that happens, what are you going to do?" And then he said, "Think like a colonel." So I had to answer his questions, one after the other, for seventy-two hours. He sent the little girls out in my backyard to play with the twenty-three rabbits that were the offspring of the three Easter bunnies my creative writing students had given me that spring. And so we didn't see much of them, and we put them to sleep from time to time, but he would not sleep and he would not eat. He would only talk, and he kept saying he didn't have much time. And at the end of the seventy-two hours, he said to me, "All right now, you have a Ph.D. in El Salvador studies." He said, "I have some questions for you. Do you want to do something for the rest of humanity?"

Now what would *you* say if someone asked you that? There's only one answer. So I said, "Yes."

And he said, "Would you like to do something for the people of Central America?"

A little more specific. And I said, "Yes."

And he said, "You have a Guggenheim."

And I said, "Yes."

And he said, "That means you can do pretty much anything you want, right?"

And I said, "Yes." I had received one and, of course, my friends had advised me that, since I was a poet, I should go to Paris and write poetry or, at least, New England, to become a real poet. This was my plan, but I couldn't choose, yet, where I was going to go.

And so he said, "All right, I think you should come to El Salvador. Because," he said, "you can just come and learn about the country. If you want to translate Central American poetry, you have to know more." And then he said, "Also, do you want to write poetry about yourself the rest of your life?"

And I said, "You've read my poetry?"

And he said, "Yes."

So I said, "No, well, no, I don't think so, now that you put it that way. It was something that I hadn't really thought of before."

So he said, "Listen to me, Forché. In three to five years, my country is going to be the beginning of your country's next Vietnam. Did you understand Vietnam when it was going on?"

I said, "No."

Well, Mr. Gomez had touched a nerve, because I had been married to a man who fought in Vietnam and who suffered from what they now call "Post-Vietnam Syndrome," and so for many years I had had an interest in Vietnam and read everything I could get my hands on because I thought there was some way that if I knew enough about Vietnam, I would understand what had happened to my husband. And so Mr. Gomez said, "Would you like to see it from the beginning? From inside, close?"

And I thought, "He's crazy. He must be crazy. El Salvador is the size of my small fingernail on the largest map I can find. It can't be possible."

And he said, "Look. Forty nuns have been put into exile. Two priests have been killed and the government has killed one American. There will be more American deaths." He said, "If you want to come, arrive in January, and we will take you anywhere you want to go in the country. You can sleep with various friends that we have, and stay in houses. You can work in a hospital if you want, or in an orphanage. You can do whatever you want and, as a journalist, you can interview the high-ranking officers of the military and of your own embassy."

I said, "I am not a journalist. I am a poet."

He said, "Same thing."

I said, "No, it isn't the same thing. I don't know anything about journalism."

He said, "You'll learn."

I said, "What do you want in exchange?"

And he said, "In three to five years, when the war begins, maybe you will want to be in the United States so that you can explain what is happening to the Americans."

I said, "I think you have the wrong person. I'm a poet." I said, "Americans don't listen to poets."

He said, "Well, change that." He said, "We want a poet. This is important."

So I thought about it and after he left I asked everyone if I should go or not. And everyone said, "No." They all said, "You don't know this guy. You don't know anything about El Salvador. And your Spanish is lousy. You have to go to Paris and write poetry." Everyone said that and so I went.

And when I got to the country, I was taken to Benihana of Tokyo on the first night. San Salvador. I sat there with a little dinner party that Leonel had arranged in my honor. It was three young men who were later, quite a few years later, to become guerillas, two Embassy staff members, one Peace Corps volunteer; and several other Salvadorans whom I never saw again. Men and women. And we were sitting around, having those Benihana shrimps that they fry on a hot grill, and listening to koto music. And he said, "You are in Saigon and it is 1959. Now I am going to show you everything."

Well, this was the way I was educated. I stayed two years, off and on, back and forth: Guatemala, El Salvador, the United States, and, finally, I left on March 16, 1980. I had to leave the country—I was unable to stay, even though I had wanted to stay, especially to return that summer. And so, out of that kind of feeling one has for one's friends, and loneliness, and isolation, and some kind of impulse that is not explained by personal reasons, I began to write some poems, and some of them were about El Salvador, and they were included in a book called *The Country Between Us*. I am going to read a statement now, about this issue that we are addressing: poetry and politics, now that you know how I came to be a "political poet":

I find it somewhat difficult to address the controversy concerning the issue of poetry and politics in the United States. I hadn't realized until the publication of my second book of poems in early 1982 that certain subjects were considered inappropriate for poetry in America, or beyond the grasp of American poets, who, after all, were not affected by politics, as were the poets of Eastern Europe, Latin America, Asia, Africa and the Middle East. It became clear that this objection to the political wasn't limited to explicitly polemical work, slogans, chants and the flat, predictable poetry of those who would submit art to ideology, but was extended to include the impassioned voices of witness, those whose diction departed from the acceptable mode, those who left the safety of self-contemplation to imagine and address the larger world. In my own case, the poems of *The Country Between Us* were considered political, it seems, because seven of them were written in El Salvador, a country associated, in American minds, with political turmoil, and more to the point, with a controversial American policy of support to a government deemed responsible for the systematized slaughter of its political opponents. Those who welcomed my book felt obliged to defend or celebrate its political stance, which, nevertheless, remained somewhat elusive. This is perhaps because I am most compelled by moral and ethical questions, the aesthetic nature of morality, and the moral aspect of aesthetics, but almost never was concerned, explicitly, with politics in the narrow sense of the term. This is not to disparage poets who would define themselves that way, but rather to point out the strangeness of the response to *The Country Between Us*, by both those who praised and those who condemned the book.

Before it was written, I had been unable to write for two years, a condition I attributed to the untimely death of my muse. When I left for El Salvador in early 1978, I considered that I might perhaps be leaving poetry forever, but I would take the opportunity of a Guggenheim grant to spend one year in Central America. My reasons for going there were personal, having to do indirectly with my decade-long interest in the Vietnam War, which I have explained to you. The poetry which came of my time there was written out of a private grief and a dark vision of historical repetition to which I could not reconcile myself. I approached the page, as I always have, in the wakeful reverie of impassioned remembrance, this time with more sadness than joy, but never with the intention to persuade, inspire, or define the war which could not be stopped and was to become the most significant influence upon my life and the education of my heart. The poems were written out of desperation and, for eighteen months, they were kept silent in a drawer. I had been told not to publish the manuscript for the reason that it was political, and that perhaps the work I had done was best considered a private release of emotion necessary to my recovery from the circumstances illuminated in the poems.

The poet, Margaret Atwood, discovered this reluctance and enabled the work to find a publisher. I was taken aback by the response but, fortunately, had already embarked on a four-year journey around the United States, in which I spoke continually and to whoever would listen about the tragedy of Central America and what I then perceived as the blindness of U.S. policy there. During those four years, I was generously given other opportunities to further my education in the twentieth-century human condition, so was able to travel and work in Northern Ireland, the Israeli-occupied territories of the West Bank and Gaza Strip, Guatemala and Lebanon, with pilgrimages to Yed Vashem, Hiroshima and Nagasaki. I have not been, thus far, equal to this journey, and so have lost, perhaps—and God help me, temporarily—the agility to wander within myself in that region of focused reverie which might yield another poem. I am now capable of the reverie again, but I seem no longer able to focus my imagination to the exclusion of all that haunts and distracts me. No single voice lifts pure from the cacophony of voices and each image is one of horror, with no single image burned more deeply than others and all seeming to be fragments of a vague and larger horror that has something to do with my sense that we are, as a species, now careening toward our complete destruction with ever-greater velocity and that our survival is by no means assured except by the drastic steps we have not yet begun to take. Sometimes, forgive me, but I imagine that I don't have enough time to finish another book of poems and so I am restless each time I sit before the paper thinking it might perhaps be more useful in a particular moment to do something else. I ask to be forgiven if in my current state of mind I am unfairly devaluing poetry. In preparation for this conference I questioned my Columbia University students, and those involved in the Writers' Community Workshops, regarding contemporary American poetry and the relationship between poetry and politics; they spoke of sensing a certain emptiness in American work and lamented the lack of intensity and passion so evident in the poetry of other parts of the world. One student referred to Joseph Brodsky's suggestion that each word or image used well in a poem would reveal its relation to every other in the poem and in the world. But to achieve that, countered another, one must write as if one believes in an integrated universe. Yes, he tells them, and adds to this his faith in the shapeliness of the imagination. He gives them the poetry of Zbigniew Herbert and they embrace even the palest English versions of his impassioned witness, seemingly starved for something they vaguely define as substance. During a particularly wistful classroom discussion at Columbia last week, a student praised recent efforts by American poets to confront the threat of thermonuclear war. In this, one ventured, perhaps only in this, do we share the fate of the world. The consensus on that afternoon was that perhaps it was impossible to reflect the twentieth-century human condition from a position of relative privilege and protection, except in the matter of apocalyptic annihilation. I don't know. To return to my personal case, in a sense, now, I am free of concerns about critical responses to my poems. If I continue to write about El Salvador, I am a poet of limited range, a topical poet. If I permit myself to write from experiences in other places, as for example, those in Beirut last winter, where I worked as a radio correspondent for National Public Radio, I might be considered an opportunist and a dilettante. If I abandon these subjects altogether, I would be guilty of failing to endure as the poet I was praised for having become. Or I might, lamentably, be praised for having converted to a higher aesthetic. Therefore, it doesn't matter what sort of poems I write next, and this is a happy condition. I don't have answers for many of the questions regarding the apparent self-censorship of American literary artists. I am amazed at the extent to which issues which I view as essentially moral and ethical are treated as if they are merely political in the narrowest sense: imprisonment for matters of conscience, torture, the slaughter of civilian noncombattants in time of war, the introduction of first-strike weapons under cover of defense, sexism, racism and the poisoning of common water and air supplies by private interests, are examples of these. I am hoping to learn more about the relationship between literary art and the world from my colleagues. It seems that during the four years of travel in the United States, addressing American audiences interested in poetry and peace, I have become somewhat myopic with regard to the sensibility of my countrymen—I was mistaking the sentiments of small groups for the common wisdom of the whole. After this last election (1984), it is simply no longer possible for me to nurture the same intuitive faith in the wisdom of my countrymen. It is perhaps, however, dangerous for me to believe that one writes in exile even in one's own country, and perhaps especially there.

The Novel's Grip upon Reality

Leslie Epstein

I suppose on this particular panel I'm the representative of the novel, and about the novel I hope quite briefly to speak. When I was invited some months ago to take part here today, I was reading Gogol. So I began paying attention to the words before me and jotted down, not quite at random, three sentences which I'll read you now. The first is:

> All in one moment Pavel Ivanovich rushed into his bedroom, tore off his clothes, and dropped into bed, where he at once fell to sleep, a deep sleep, a sweet sleep, a dream-free sleep, such as only those who have never suffered from hemorrhoids can know.

And here is the second:

> In this connection, it may not be amiss to inform the reader that Anton Proko-fyevich owned a pair of trousers so fantastically odd that whenever he put them on he was invariably bitten in the calves by dogs.

The third:

> Both Ivan Ivanovich and Ivan Nikiforovich hated fleas so much that they never let a Jewish trader pass without buying from him all sorts of little jars containing a flea repellent, always making certain to give the fellow a thorough scolding for being a Jew in the first place.

Now I think I have to ask what these three sentences have in common. First, no other medium, not drama or film, not even poetry, could so perfectly capture the combination of a single action, the one moment, and extend it into time, forming a kind of role for the actor. Those "nevers" and "whenevers" and "invariables" and "alwayses" make up a kind of eternity of habit, especially when repeated in this form through-out an entire work. And next, without trying to inflate these three sentences too much, I do think they possess something like a vision of the human condition, a kind of plague of sleep-destroying piles, and fanged hounds, and fleas, and infidels. Even more, beside this vision of human frailty there coexists one of courage and struggle and dignity. One hurls oneself into bed, but not without hope of relief. One can outrun fierce beasts or mend and remend one's trousers. And one can apply salves and ointments and even educate, perhaps even convert — a note of grace runs throughout Gogol — the Jews.

Finally, these three passages each provide a crucial and dynamic link to the reader. Note the tone of familiar, direct address. Note the irony. But, above all, try to sense the buried metaphor at work in each that connects the state of being of these various Ivans and Pavels to that of the reader: it's *such* a sleep, they're *such* horrid pants, there is *such* a terrible hatred of insects that, that — and a kind of scene, a silent film, made up of our own experience and memories and sufferings, the humil-iations we share with the characters, begins to unspool in our minds. The result is a full imaginative response. I don't want, quite, to leave these three sentences without making a further, more general point.

What is special about the quotations is the way they fuse event and affect, that is, the action and our feeling about the action. They engage. They pull the reader into the tale. And they demand a recognition, finally, of a common mortality. That is why they are such fine examples of imaginative writing. Let's try this another way. Reg Gibbons sent to each of us panelists an essay by Benjamin DeMott, in which he — DeMott — speaks of writing that contains a "full responsiveness to life." Now my point, and his, is, first, that there is not much of this kind of writing around anymore, and that its absence has political conse-quences. DeMott calls such paucity an "anesthetization of feeling," an "inner deadness," a "diseased response." He lays it to the impact upon a generation of writers of the war in Vietnam. But Kafka once, when asked about why World War I came about, put it the other way round. He said that war was caused by a "monstrous lack of imagination." The issue for us, I think, is what happens when the imagination becomes diseased or atrophies or loses its full assured grip — Gogol's grip — upon reality. I'll take a stab at an answer by looking first at the idea of something I mentioned earlier — the silent film.

In some way, silent movies are the last great eruption of popular art, or of the popular art that began with the Commedia dell' Arte. Chaplin, in talking about his pre-talking films, spoke of the "alphabet of gesture"

that the artist, the actors, use. The silent film is as close as we have come in the twentieth century to the popular novel, and to the Gogolian imagination, of the nineteenth: the small screen, the black-and-white image, the soundlessness, the ill-lit, jumpy figures, the stationary camera, are something like a reproduction or image of the mental process itself. Above all, for our purposes here, it requires the fullest participation on the part of the audience. In a silent film a gun points and birds suddenly rise into the sky: we flinch from the soundless report. Trees bend and the wind whistles in our ears. As Rudolph Arnheim—and these are his ideas on silent film I am shamelessly borrowing here—as Arnheim said, we "actually see something of the quality of the noise," just as we must construct the dialogue between characters and paint a world in color from shades of gray. (Compare this process, if you will, to Greek tragedy, where all violence occurred offstage, within the palace, and where we must reconstruct it, can only reconstruct it, in the mask of terror, the bleeding eyes of Oedipus as he comes back on stage—a mask, by the way, quite similar to the black-and-white image of the face on a silent screen.)

Silent films (and Greek tragedy) have vanished. Now all guns go bang. What has happened is that technology has largely replaced the imagination or the will toward full responsiveness in art. As Arnheim has pointed out, each new innovation in film, the addition of sound, of color, of wider screens, and even 3-D and Sensaround, reflects a clear craving for a more natural, more lifelike, more real image—the Faustian attempt to reproduce life completely. And because that is not possible, because the attempt will necessarily be futile, a craving is created: call it a reality fix. The more frantic the technology, the greater the gap between the inner life of feeling, affect, sympathy and the outer circumstance, the world of action. The result in a sense is the transformation of politics, the wrenching of sensibility into something which resembles, in its extreme form, plain fascism, whose hallmark in this century has been the aestheticizing of violence and the falling in love with death. A trivial example is the pretty film, which invariably follows Epstein's law: the more beautiful the movie the shallower its content. On a not-trivial level, we have Speer's use of searchlights (used both as a weapon of warfare and to advertise movie premieres) to make what, at Nazi rallies, he called "cathedrals of light." Other examples I've written about before, but can't think of better ones. Mussolini's son, leaning out of his cockpit during the Ethiopian campaign, noting how the bombs burst below him like flowers, *comme fiori*. Or the ads the Northrop Corporation likes to run—when the Mobil Corporation takes a breath from complaining about taxes—on the Op Ed page of the *Times*, the most notorious being of a beautiful, moon-like sphere, which the reader discovers upon reading the text is actually part of the guidance system for an MX missile. What is frightening here is the utter divorce, the complete lack of connection (and on the part of everyone: the corporation, the ad writers, the *Times* management, the typesetters, the type readers), between surface and content, image and meaning, act and affect.

The latest form of technology, the one that most invades our lives, is of course television, where image, surface, is so dominant that the medium comes almost to resemble Hannah Arendt's definition of evil: "Possessing neither depth nor dimension, spreading like a fungus on the surface of things." The television age has provided a new solution to the problem of the apprehension of reality. Unattainable, irreproducible, as ever, reality is simply redefined: now nothing is real *unless* it appears on the screen. And, such is our impoverishment, we cannot seem to experience it unless it is seen in replay, slowed down, and viewed from multiple angles. How exciting it was to hear that even this conference might be televised. I felt so much realer than I do right now. Perhaps, through these means, we do in a rather sad way attempt to convince ourselves from all these angles and replays and the rest that we are immortal.

Well, I've come a long way from Anton Prokofyevich and his trousers and Ivan Ivanovich and his piles. I'd like to return now, briefly, to literature, to the novel. There was a second essay in that packet Reg Gibbons sent us—by the ubiquitous Kundera, who's very fine in his essays, if not quite so fine in his novels. In the piece we were sent, he spoke of, among other things, Cervantes as the father of the novel and the founder of the modern era. And that sent me back to my Cervantes and to the end of that novel—which, its having an ending, is significant enough, because it is another mark of the dissociated sensibility, the diseased imagination, to be unable to bear conclusions. No work these days is really finished. When is the last time you read a novel that was as fully satisfying at the end as at the beginning? Where all the premises, the tensions, set up in the first half were resolved in the second? Quite some while back, no? That's because ending, finishing up, implies an acceptance of finitude, of limits, of mortality.

At the end of *Don Quixote* there's one last adventure. You remember, do you not, that the man of La Mancha, Don Quixote, has been seeking the love of Dulcinea del Toboso throughout the entire novel? Finally, after these thousands of pages, it seems he will achieve his goal—that is, that the enchantment that has prevented her from loving him will be lifted—if only Sancho Panza will agree to receive 3,300 lashes, for which the Don is willing to pay him. The scene is deep night. A clump of beech trees. A whip, "powerful and flexible," has been fashioned from a donkey's halter: and while the Don waits anxiously without, the Squire sets about administering the punishment upon his own body. After six blows, however, Sancho stops to bargain for a higher rate. To this Don Quixote agrees; then Sancho, as we are told, "let the lashes rain down":

> Rascal that he was, however, he stopped laying them on his shoulders and let them fall on the trees instead, uttering such moans every now and then that it seemed as if each one was tearing his heart out.

Soon the trees shake, the bark flies in all directions, birds take to the air, and an agonized wail rends the night. And here a strange and quite wonderful thing occurs. The Don rushes forward, seizes the cruel lash and forbids his servant to continue. "Fate, my dear, Sancho," he says, "will not have you lose your life to please me, for you need it to support your wife and children. Let Dulcinea wait for a better occasion." And he takes off his cloak and—is this not a prefiguration in comic terms of Lear doing the same upon the Heath?—puts it around Sancho's broad shoulders.

And there, ladies and gentlemen, friends, you have the precise moment at which the novel is born. For Quixote's gesture is the very paradigm of imaginative fiction. His reward, if we may call it that, occurs shortly afterward, when the Don lies upon his deathbed. It is here, really, that the wonderful event I spoke of occurs. Through grace, through a miracle—but we know it is through imagination—Quixote's diseased mind is cleared: his grip upon reality is restored. Upon his deathbed, the shroud of ignorance and obsession is swept away. "My mind is now clear, unencumbered by those misty shadows of ignorance that were cast over it . . . I am no longer Don Quixote de la Mancha but Alonso Quijano, whose mode of life won for him the name of good." And a moment later he faints, fades, vanishes altogether.

And what becomes of us, we readers? No less than the Don, our imagination has been diseased—and in good measure the source of infection was the same: reading too many books. And we too, in our lives, as in this novel, stand at midnight outside a dark and mysterious grove. As the Don's heart stirred at last for another, as he perceived that suffering more fully in imagination than Sancho did upon his shoulders; so too do our hearts launch outward toward the spectacle of the other. As the old Aristotelian emotions of pity and terror are roused in his breast, so they form in ours: and as Quixote heals himself, makes himself, frees himself from his demons through an act of imagination, so precisely do we free ourselves from ours. We are left, then, more courageous, more compassionate—saner—for having read his adventure, and other adventures in those other books that Quixote himself once called the very "light of the soul."

Session I:
Questions and Answers

BARBARA FOLEY (FROM AUDIENCE): A general question: it seems to me that what you are all saying is that discord has a context and it has consequences. I just wondered if any or all of you would like to comment on the fact that you are speaking at a campus where we have a professor in the Department of Engineering who denies that there was a Holocaust, and has written books and is editing a journal which continues to promote that lie. I just wonder how it makes you feel to have that as part of the context in which you are speaking today.

DES PRES: Yes, I've encountered this professor's work. At Colgate University I teach a course on "Literature of the Holocaust," and my students are often troubled by the revisionism of Professor Butz. I must say, and not altogether with irony, that Butz is on good ground. He is on good ground because the most advanced principles of literary criticism today tell us that words have nothing to do with reality, that no fact *is* a fact apart from the validating discourse in which it appears, and that history in the last analysis is only and purely a jumble of texts and intertexts that can be sorted out, if at all, by arbitrary agreement. From this fashionable perspective, the only way any of us can talk about the world is through tropes, and we must therefore accept that Milosz's "passionate pursuit of the real" is bunk. That, at least, is the hermeneutic position that has allowed a professor of engineering to get up his nerve and say Auschwitz never happened.

The "school" of historical nonthinking to which Professor Butz belongs calls itself "revisionist history," and the literary criticism that supports his argument is called "revisionism" or "deconstruction." This mode of hostility to truth isn't only the pride of wild folk like Jacques

Derrida. It is also, and perhaps more dangerously, the delight of the graduate schools at present, the favored discourse among great numbers of young men and women who want to get their Ph.D.'s and have nice jobs. The interesting thing about this critical method, whether in history or in literary study, is the peculiar mastery it requires; one need only know the vocabulary, the discourse itself—in short, the magic words—without burdening oneself with any real knowledge of the field to which one addresses this discourse. One can speak with entire authority about displacement, decentering and the vanishing author, without having read more than a few poems and novels. To revise history one need not know history, and to criticize literature one need not bother with anything but the text to be dissected.

That's a whole lot easier than teaching the real thing that Leslie Epstein was trying to talk about a minute ago. That he *was* talking about a minute ago. In other words, the whole question of denial, or revisionism, is a good deal bigger than Professor Butz. It's nothing less, as I see it, than being forced to concede that culture no longer supports us, but, at the same time, that culture is all we've got. And by culture I mean the whole system of symbolic *constructs*, products of imagination, or, in sum, the world of artifice that makes us human. These people, the Deconstructionists, are on true ground insofar as their target is the artificial character of all culture. The truth of *that* isn't disputed. But then they go on to insist that if fictions are only fictions then they cannot serve anything real, and must be deconstructed to reveal their creative foundation. In other words, a work of history no less than a work of literature is characterized by its *put-togetherness*, and people like Derrida and Butz want to discredit the human, perhaps all-too-human, nature of nurture. They take advantage of the fact that truth, to the extent that we feel its presence, is an artificial product, something made, an achieved truth rather than, straight from God, *the* Truth. So: we evoke our humanity through artifice. Truth always comes in mediated form. All facts are made manifest through imaginative processes. Which means that the whole business of history and the past is, to some real degree, a literary artifact. Which doesn't mean that Auschwitz didn't happen.

This is the thing that some among us seem unwilling to admit or live with—the radical dependence of truth upon art. On the other hand, Carolyn Forché's poems are a wonderful example of how this dependence vindicates itself. What we get in her Salvador sequence is an evocation of humanity through written words on a page, none of which (neither the words nor the specific humanity) existed *for us* before Carolyn wrote those poems. It was never a question of whether or not the agony of El Salvador existed, but rather of whether or not this agony would vanish in silence or find a witnessing voice. I mean to say that we shall never be rid of engineers like Professor Butz. We put up with such people and perhaps even use their meanness as occasion to renew our own passionate pursuit of the real.

EPSTEIN: Perhaps I should say: it sounds *meshuggeneh* to me [great laughter]. I mean, in all honesty, I—now that you remind me— remember that this man is here. In fact, it has no effect on me and what I think. And I wonder does it have any on you, in hearing it?

BARBARA FOLEY (FROM AUDIENCE): Yeah, it does. Because I think it is important to realize that any discourse does, in fact, organize people, and he goes and gives speeches and he talks to Klans and Nazis and I think that we can see by the grip of the country that in fact those ideas are incorporated at the end into the grip that a number of you have commented on.

EPSTEIN: But are we supposed to stop him from doing it?

AUDIENCE: Well, I think his right to do it is ultimately played off against the right of other people to live a decent life. So I think that's definitely —

EPSTEIN: Well, I am, you know, leading a decent life.

AUDIENCE: I want to say that in regards to information about a professor like that, that we were speaking about: there are numerous examples like that of negation, and omission of history, of that distortion of history, that affects people of color: Afro-Americans and, in my case, Chicano, American Indian people. We are not included in the history books. And yet, in reference to poetry today, or literature, the printing press was brought here by the Spanish some time ago. The first university was put together by the Spanish. Some of the first teaching, and scholarships. Sor Juana Inés de la Cruz in Mexico was one of the first poets. But so many people that I speak with have no idea of the contributions. Totally omitted. And then somebody says, "What's a Chicano? What's Chicano literature?" And we have a contribution. It's been here, though it's oppressed. So, the question of censorship is a real question for the Chicanos. I know for a fact, that Nephtali Deleon, our

48

San Antonio writer, was visited by Secret Service agents and told not to write poetry that was critical of the President of the United States. Stuff like that happens. But maybe because we are not endowed with NEA grants or sit on major boards and stuff, the Chicanos sometimes can be stepped on a lot easier. But our voice has been transmitted in ballads, in folk songs, in lyrics, and today is making it into the press. But I just want to say that Carolyn Forché, I think, spoke straight, spoke clear, and I do appreciate her presence here—bringing out the questions of the relationship between us and the United States and the hemisphere that we live in. Here Spanish is spoken in twenty nations at least—a language that we need to understand. Thank you.

FORCHÉ: It's good to see you. I wanted to say that that issue of censorship, I know, is going to be addressed at another panel in this conference and it's important; as you probably know, the incidence of censorship in this country increased by four hundred percent during the last four years, as monitored by a number of agencies—direct official censorship, censorship of books and censorship of classroom materials, etcetera. So, now we have another four years, perhaps it'll go up another four hundred percent or more.

AUDIENCE: I have a question for Carolyn Forché. What did you think of Duarte's election in El Salvador just a few months ago? Do you think that election was a fair election? And what did you think about the negotiations between—

FORCHÉ: I really want to answer your question, but I'm not sure that it's on this subject. So I will be very brief, please. I did not think much of it. Duarte is a very nice man, and he has always wanted to be president of El Salvador and now he is. The problem that he has is that he has no power, and that his life hangs in the balance between extremes in the military. Duarte was elected by a people who were compelled to vote, rather than be labeled as subversive, and he was elected by a people who are very fatigued and traumatized by war. I do not have very much respect for Duarte, however, because of his role in the cover-up of the investigations of the deaths of not only Salvadorans but also of American citizens.

AUDIENCE: You mentioned—Well, I'll go right into it; now that the stage is being set, has been set up, for Vietnam Part Two. I was too young when police action there took place. Now that I'm at this age and

I'm aware of what's going on, and a minute ago you just mentioned censorship—what did writers, what did literature contribute against Vietnam happening, and can what happened then be changed now? Can what we are doing here help to alter what is going to eventually happen in the next few months, in the next couple of years?

FORCHÉ: We can't know that, but we have to try, we have to do this regardless of the outcome. And, later in this conference, you have a very good chance to ask directly one of the only Vietnam-vet poets I know. And one of the only poets of my generation who writes about the war is here, and also Gloria Emerson is here and a number of people who made significant contributions during that period. I was a very young poet publishing very, very bad work on mimeographed paper at that time, and so I didn't have any effect at all. But stick around, there are people who can answer that much better than I can.

AUDIENCE: I've noticed that these three writers have all written about subjects that generally involve the United States but have their genesis outside the United States. I'm wondering why the choice was made to deal with that subject matter instead of political matter within the United States, and if that had something to do with a possible backing away from making art into ideology. Just wondering about your reaction on that.

DES PRES: How much poetry in the United States addresses the problems that Carolyn Forché listed a minute ago? Not much, and among our poets, not many. Some of the poets here do, that's why they are with us today. But how many of the four thousand or so publishing now? They simply don't. And if I ask why not, I must admit to having been perplexed for a long time with the implications of such a question. Part of the problem is our tradition: the Emersonian tradition of Self and Nature—quite literally the Self on one side and, on the other, the Universe. Recently I've been going back to look at nineteenth-century critical discourse, work by giants like Carlyle, Emerson, Whitman, and I'm astonished by the frequence and casualness with which all of them employ the word "Universe." On nearly every page, we are invited to applaud "me and the universe." That's grand, no doubt; but it surely leaves out politics. And hence, while invoking the universe, the smallness of the result.

That, then, is part of it. Another part—to what exact degree I can't say—is this thing called the poetry workshop that's all over the place just now. Poetry programs — poetry *programs!* — are often run by young poets, themselves the product of poetry programs. In the workshop, they are the masters of the craft, of the art. And as much to the point, they enjoy institutional connections and know where the new jobs will be — yet more slots for poets worked over by workshops, when, of course, everybody knows that poetry can't be taught. If the aspiring poet writes like the master, and in some way is chosen, then there might just be, if not great poetry, at least a job. This is understandable, of course. It's human, and it's sad. I think of Milton becoming a poet in order to write a great poem. And then I think of the strategy at present, which requires writing poems in order to be an employable poet. This, too, is part of the problem.

EPSTEIN: As one who runs one of those workshops, though not in poetry, I think about the Holocaust because I was not part of the Holocaust, because it was not part of my life, because I grew up in California, because it was removed from me in time and in space, and because I felt it important to understand. This whole issue of why there is not more being done in America — the night before I came up here I saw a terrific play, at Brandeis, *Woz Albert*. It's two black South Africans, a wonderful play. Interestingly enough, it is performed in South Africa. I mean it seems to me that it is not such a mystery as to why these things are happening abroad. Where there's real trouble is where there is a response in writing. I have funny feelings about this whole issue of censorship, too. While, if it were my own choice, I wouldn't even stop that man, Butz — but it is kind of a disaster for writers to be able to say whatever you want, it's kind of a disaster. I mean Art, in a way, is dealing with various kinds of censorship. And if you are able to say anything you want — there's no internal censorship at all — then, sometimes, it helps to have external censorship, pressure to get around, to disguise, to trick, to make it artistic. I mean so much good writing was done under the Czar, maybe for a reason, maybe because the equilibrium was about right. Maybe in South Africa . . . it's tough to say it, because you can say it and it comes out bitter. I don't know, it's a complicated issue.

FORCHÉ: I want to add one more thing to that. There are a number of poets here who have written extensively about questions which might be viewed as political, I suppose. I hate that word, in a way, because I think everything is political. But I also want to say that in terms of outside the United States, in my own case El Salvador, I don't want you to be too comfortable about how far outside the United States El Salvador is. The war in El Salvador could not be conducted by the Salvadoran government without the direct and extensive support of your tax dollars. And the government of El Salvador could not endure more than forty-eight hours if that was suspended. So you are intimately and directly involved in every square kilometer of that country. It's an American issue.

AUDIENCE: Mr. Epstein, you've asserted that, I think, that the imagination in America is dying or is dead, in a number of ways. At least that's what I was hearing. I wonder if our other two panelists would agree with that, and if they might provide some examples. Or would disagree.

DES PRES: I don't think it's dead at all, maybe at a crossroads, maybe selecting between roads taken and not yet taken, but far from dead and in fact the signs of life are here among us. The poetry of the poets with this symposium is real evidence to the contrary, although it seems to me that every poet that has participated in the symposium speaks for or from the experience of an "internal colony," or in any case an embattled position. One sees the same awakening in work published in our journals, *TriQuarterly* first among them. This diatribe of mine against the self-and-nature school is perhaps a little dated. The poetry of inconsequence is still, of course, with us, in great bulk but with little authority and no capacity to inspire. Our poets are turning elsewhere, and one of the new directions is to the terrible but also terribly exciting sphere of being-in-the-world.

The point I'm trying to make is part of my original statement about our current attraction to the great Russians or Milosz or the Latin Americans or whomever—to the poetry of cultures under siege. And further, that to the extent that all cultures are now being challenged by the new order of empire, the new mystique of force (the kick-ass mentality of Vice-President Bush, the say-uncle and make-my-day style of Him Who Rides Tall in the Saddle), then the feeling of embattlement, of fear and the muse standing watch by turns, is giving birth to a single global culture into which men and women of every language and tradition are being coerced. At this level, we can actually discern a human destiny taking shape, which, if we needed a story to set it forth, might be a sequel to Kafka's *The Castle*.

The issue again: I read someone like Breyten Breytenbach—and am amazed how familiar this Afrikaaner sounds to me, who am not an

Afrikaaner. His torment over having to use a language of oppression through which to get around conditions he hates is the more intense because his native tongue supports the state his art announces against. If this seems right or even *ordinary* to me, I begin to suspect a tie-in with the language and art of my own country. Some kind of tie-in there is. It's not just an easy way of aggrandizing imagination. The plain fact that we do turn to poets from elsewhere is proof, for me, that the Emersonian equation—the poetic notion of self as world—no longer holds. That's what's dead, a practice, a tradition. Not imagination, but merely one of its endorsements.

FORCHÉ: In my answer to the question, I am a little afraid because I am going on record here and if I address the issue of Failure of Imagination in this country at large in a general public sense, I might, in the aftermath of the presidential elections, say something a bit extreme, in agreement with that judgment. When I think about failure of the imagination in that regard I can only give you an example of why perhaps imagination is so important, and I hope that I'm right about this. Last winter I was in Lebanon during the War of February, the takeover of West Beirut and the shelling of the Shuf Mountains and the Druse villages by the USS *New Jersey*, which was stationed offshore. I have to tell you that I wonder whether that shelling would have been ordered, or whether the sailors on that ship would have complied with the orders, if any of them had bothered, for one moment, to imagine what it might be like to be bombarded by shells the size of Volkswagens and Chevrolets. I don't think anyone bothered to stop to think about what it might be like on the ground. I don't think the pilots who carpet-bombed Vietnam ever stopped to think, to imagine, really *imagine* what it might be like on the ground. So I have a little imagination exercise for you, and I was hoping I could work this in one way or another, and it might seem extraneous to the things we've been talking about but if it does seem so then understand that nothing having to do with this subject can ever be considered extraneous again by any of us. It's a passage by Jim Douglass, from *Lightning East to West*. So just follow along:

To understand Trident say the word "Hiroshima." Reflect on its meaning for one second. Say and understand "Hiroshima" again. And again. And again. 2,040 times. Assuming you are able to understand Hiroshima in one second, you will be able to understand Trident in thirty-four minutes. That's one Trident submarine.

To understand the destructive power of the whole Trident fleet, it would take you seventeen hours, devoting one second to each Hiroshima.*

It's sort of interesting, isn't it, what it does to you.

---

*Jim W. Douglass, *Lightning East to West; Jesus, Gandhi, and the Nuclear Age* (New York: Crossroad Publishing Co., 1984), p. 74.

II Poetry and History, Exile, Race

It Is the Man/Woman Outside Who Judges: The Minority Writer's Perspective on Literature

Michael S. Harper

> *The history of the American Negro is a most inti-*
> *mate part of American history.*
> —Ralph Ellison (*Shadow and Act*)

There's a folk saying that Black Americans developed in the nineteenth century which is one of my favorites. And I think about it often because I think it summarizes a certain attitude, a certain stance, a way of looking at the world. And one better be very careful about allowing two lines to stand up for the way in which you look at the world, but at the same time this particular little folk saying is important to me: I'm going to read it:

> Every shut-eye ain't asleep,
> Every good-bye ain't gone.

I recently read Joe Martinez's "Rehabilitation and Treatment," an astute commentary on the political process, on language and euphemism, on living, and the qualities of the real. And these are Joe Martinez's words. It's called "Rehabilitation and Treatment," which, of course, all of us need:

The convict strolled into the prison administration building to get assistance and counseling for his personal problems. Just inside the main door were several other doors, proclaiming *Parole, Counselor, Chaplain, Doctor, Teacher, Correction,* and *Therapist.*

The convict chose the door marked *Correction,* inside of which were two other doors: *Custody* and *Treatment.* He chose *Treatment,* and was confronted with two more doors, *Juvenile* and *Adult.* He chose the proper door and again was faced with two doors: *Previous Offender* and *First Offender.* Once more he walked through the proper door, and, again, two doors: *Democrat* and *Republican.* He was a Democrat; and so he hurried through the appropriate door and ran smack into two more doors; *Black* and *White.* He was black; and so he walked through that

door—and fell nine stories to the street. (From *Black Voices in Prison*, ed. by Etheridge Knight [Pathfinder Press, 1970]; reprinted in *New Black Voices*, ed. by Abraham Chapman [Mentor/New American Library, 1972], pp. 197–98.)

Now that's a kind of modern convict parable, which is in turn a kind of embellishment of Du Bois's *The Souls of Black Folk*, where he talks about double-consciousness and the bifurcated vision of trying to be black and an American simultaneously and how that created a kind of schizophrenia. And how one must aspire, through a certain kind of heroic action, to what he calls "self-conscious manhood." He calls that book *The Souls of Black Folk*, with emphasis on the "souls." And he ends the book, which was published in 1903, with a marvelous chapter on the "Sorrow Songs" or what we used to call spirituals. And this is a kind of modern updating of DuBois's insight, in just a few lines:

Blacks in America have contributed to the making of American speech and the American idiom, even before the Declaration of Independence, the Bill of Rights, and the Constitution, those series of documents which we call sacred texts in a free exchange at the level of culture, despite the institution of slavery, what used to be called "that peculiar institution." In fact, in this country, blacks are still a heady barometer in the relationship between culture and politics, the role of witnessing, at the level of new forms of speech and art-making, as participants and commentators on the local and national scene.

The cataloging of duplicity, the contradiction between what we do and what we say, shows the importance of perspective, a vantage point of comparative humanity.

Then there's a quotation from Frederick Douglass. Douglass wrote three autobiographies. The first, which was published in 1845, is perhaps his most succinct; certainly it was his smallest effort in terms of number of pages. In it he says: "My part has been to tell the story of the slave. The story of the master never wanted for narrators." Frederick Douglass introduced this parallelism in his first autobiography, *Narrative of the Life of Frederick Douglass: An American Slave, written by himself*. And this was the one cogent example of why the minority writer must tune in on the long dialogue since the country's inception.

Douglass was much aware of language as an evolutionary process. Like the great musicians and blues singers who came after him, he had the feel for the health of expression in stretching, by stylistics, rhetoric and form, that contrast between communal and individual values: values committed to paper after the spilling of blood; the burden of facts cadenced in the speech of words, some written on paper, that would work toward a fulfillment of the American experiment. The optimism of this attempt at self-determination, and I mean that as a country, none-theless had the problem of slavery (symbolized by the non-European past)—that high-pigmentation the country was unwilling to absorb and hasn't absorbed very well even to this day.

The best writers, and I mean the nineteenth-century moral writers that we're taught in good literature classes and in places like Northwestern—Melville, Twain, Whitman (and I'm adding Lincoln because we're in Illinois)—knew these contradictions could not be ignored, and with the help of events became both conscious and consci-entious. Notice: with the help of events. This was the nineteenth cen-tury; the country was largely unstructured, the Indians were not yet all dead, or penned up in what we might call "relocation centers," and some of the wilderness was still intact. During the reconstruction period—and one wonders what was being rebuilt, even now—the country forgot, in large part, how to talk about what was wrong, except under the blanket of humor which was minstrelsy created to entertain the white masses.

That's you.

Many of the artisans throughout the South were blacks, most of them dead or run out after the Civil War. And, though Whitman spoke of Africans as a source for an American grand opera, there was no con-scious attempt to include those singers in any anthology. Many minority writers made songs all alone because "nobody seemed to care." They knew about the outside position, about underdogs, sexual repression, much of it worked out upon them by this dominant group—so many bad films about the tragic mulatto, *The Birth of a Nation* imitation of a white band of angels, and hideous cartoons of popular culture. The creative, judgmental and moral forces which served as stylistics con-fronting the real world were muted in Melville's trickster, the crippled Negro *Confidence-Man*, Colonel Shaw's black Fifty-fourth Regiment (Robert Lowell), and Stephen Crane's *Red Badge of Courage*, where only one Negro, a tap dancer, appears, where there is no discussion of the central issues of the conflict when the individual discovers responsibility from the larger social reality. Twain's Huck was a truncated gloss on the necessities of humor, if there was to be any truth. Until one meets Faulkner's black characters, much of the moral force so bright in the best nineteenth-century writing had gone quietly, in conspired agree-ment, to sleep.

Now I'm going to leap to South Africa because I spent a little time in South Africa and I know some South African writers and I want you to listen to the rhetoric of some of their—let's use the word—ideology. This is a recitation by Wally Serote, who is currently living in Botswana, and who was picked up one day and put into solitary confinement and kept for nine or ten months and then one day he was taken out into a courtyard in bright sunshine, having not seen the sun in some months, and told that he could be let go. This is one of the tactics Breytenbach has written some things about—this kind of treatment. But Serote does not spend any time on his imprisonment. This is the poem he writes:

> White people are white people
> They're burning the world.
> Black people are black people
> They are the fuel.
> White people are white people
> They must learn to listen.
> Black people are black people
> They must learn to talk.

The poet Morgana Wally Serote, the South African, one might say an Azanian poet, in exile in Botswana.

More than a hundred years ago the Civil War was a preparation for the Industrial Revolution, the harrowing up of competitive agricultural systems which slavery engendered. Black politicians were shot down—the problems of inclusion would not soon be met, and each successive war has been disastrous on the theme of inclusion. The fight was *not* to die in a segregated war. The segregated war of words has been combatted by black poets in particular, from Dunbar and James Weldon Johnson, and Claude McKay and Jean Toomer, Langston Hughes and Sterling Brown to Margaret Walker—who happens to have been an undergraduate at Northwestern, the winner of the Yale Younger Poets series prize in 1942—and the judge Stephen Vincent Benét, the man who wrote "John Brown's Body." One who had, at least, a fairly good sense of history. Sterling Brown took Frost, Robinson and Sandburg to a deeper commitment to the vernacular and to folk speech, a renewed use of blank verse and dramatic portraits of Ma Rainey, Slim Greer—one of his characters—and Sister Lou, another. But the consummate historian with a modernistic clarity of tone and a religious post-modernist system of belief in the infinite was Robert Hayden, who died in 1980 and who was a Bahá'í, a remembrancer par excellence, born and raised in Detroit—Joe Louis's father referred to it as "Destroy." He would pronounce the word "Detroit" as "Destroy." A poet of the people in the thirties, a student of Auden at Michigan and a chronicler of racial division at Fisk for over twenty years, Hayden wrote the pure lyric in an adopted sonnet form in a poem for his father, "Those Winter Sundays."

It was called a "pure lyric" by Karl Shapiro, I think, in one of his essays. It ends with a rhetorical question:

Those Winter Sundays

Sundays too my father got up early
and put his clothes on in the blueblack cold,
then with cracked hands that ached
from labor in the weekday weather made
banked fires blaze. No one ever thanked him.

I'd wake and hear the cold splintering, breaking.
When the rooms were warm, he'd call,
and slowly I would rise and dress,
fearing the chronic angers of that house,

Speaking indifferently to him,
who had driven out the cold
and polished my good shoes as well.
What did I know, what did I know
of love's austere and lonely offices?

The poet James Wright, who was one of Hayden's friends, had this to say about Hayden's of the word "offices": "The word 'offices' is the great word here; 'offeece,' they say in French. It is a religious service after dark. Its formality, its combination of distance and immediacy is appropriate. In my experience, uneducated people and people who are driven by brute circumstance to work terribly hard for a living, the living of their families, are very big on formality."

Before he died, Hayden had managed to cover the distance of much of the Afro-American presence in the Americas. His poems include "Middle Passage," "Runagate Runagate," "The Ballad of Nat Turner," "Crispus Attucks," "A Letter from Phillis Wheatley" and "Paul Laurence Dunbar," and he wrote on Robeson and Bessie Smith and so on. So Hayden is by far the best chronicler and remembrancer of the Afro-American heritage in these Americas that I know of.

I want to leave you with two poems by two very different people. The first is from the ex-president of Senegal, Léopold Sédar Senghor, who is also a French Symbolist poet and was just recently elected to the French Academy. It's called "For Two Flutes":

I have spun a song soft as a murmur of doves at noon
To the shrill notes of my four-string khalam.
I have woven you a song and you did not hear me.

I have offered you wild flowers with scents as strange as a sorcerer's eyes.
I have offered you my wild flowers. Will you let them wither,
Finding distraction in the mayflies dancing?

Now Senghor is seventy-five years old or so and has been struggling for a long time to seek a certain kind of literary acceptance. At the same time, he's been running a whole country. (Some would say not very well.)

And last, something about the whole question of Central America: a poem that uses a metaphor to speak about the process of appropriation. I think Orwell spoke very knowledgeably about our capacity to use euphemisms and to stir up no real imagery so that we could get a clear and vital image for what was going on. So I wanted to read you a poem by a woman aptly named Rita Dove. "I have spun a song soft as a murmur of doves at noon"—it's the first line of the Senghor poem. Her poem is called "Parsley," and I am going to read the note first before I read the poem.

On October 2, 1957, Rafael Trujillo, 1891–1961, dictator of the Dominican Republic, ordered twenty-thousand blacks killed because they could not pronounce the letter "r" in the word for parsley in Spanish—*"perejil."*

Parsley

1. *The Cane Fields*

There is a parrot imitating spring
in the palace, its feathers parsley green.
Out of the swamp the cane appears

to haunt us, and we cut it down. El General
searches for a word; he is all the world
there is. Like a parrot imitating spring.

we lie down screaming as rain punches through
and we come up green. We cannot speak an R—
out of the swamp, the cane appears

and then the mountain we call in whispers *Katalina.*
The children gnaw their teeth to arrowheads.
There is a parrot imitating spring.

El General has found his word: *perejil.*
Who says it, lives. He laughs, teeth shining
out of the swamp. The cane appears

in our dreams, lashed by wind and streaming.
And we lie down. For every drop of blood
there is a parrot imitating spring.
Out of the swamp the cane appears.

2. *The Palace*

The word the general's chosen is parsley.
It is fall, when thoughts turn
to love and death; the general thinks
of his mother, how she died in the fall
and he planted her walking cane at the grave
and it flowered, each spring stolidly forming
four-star blossoms. The general
pulls on his boots, he stomps to
her room in the palace, the one without
curtains, the one with a parrot
in a brass ring. As he paces he wonders
Who can I kill today. And for a moment
the little knot of screams
is still. The parrot, who has traveled

all the way from Australia in an ivory
cage, is coy as a widow, practicing
spring. Ever since the morning
his mother collapsed in the kitchen
while baking skull-shaped candies
for the Day of the Dead, the general
has hated sweets. He orders pastries
brought up for the bird; they arrive

dusted with sugar on a bed of lace.
The knot in his throat starts to twitch;
he sees his boots the first day in battle
splashed with mud and urine
as a soldier falls at his feet amazed—
how stupid he looked!—at the sound
of artillery. *I never thought it would sing*
the soldier said, and died. Now

the general sees the fields of sugar
cane, lashed by rain and streaming.
He sees his mother's smile, the teeth
gnawed to arrowheads. He hears
the Haitians sing without R's
as they swing the great machetes:
Katalina, they sing, *Katalina*,

mi madle, mi amol en muelte. God knows
his mother was no stupid woman; she

64

could roll an R like a queen. Even
a parrot can roll an R! In the bare room
the bright feathers arch in a parody
of greenery, as the last pale crumbs
disappear under the blackened tongue. Someone

calls out his name in a voice
so like his mother's, a startled tear
splashes the tip of his bright boot.
My mother, my love in death.
The general remembers the tiny green sprigs
men of his village wore in their capes
to honor the birth of a son. He will
order many, this time, to be killed

for a single, beautiful word.

The Continental Drift—
An Eastern European
in America*

Stanislaw Baranczak

First, there is the optical shock. When the average Eastern European (E. E. for short) steps off a plane on his first visit to the New World, he is immediately struck by the orgy of colors. Of course, he had known something about America before; he used to contemplate postcards, listen to travelers' tales, watch American movies. But the reality is much more intensely colorful than Technicolor. E. E. never expected houses to be painted so brightly purple or blue, school buses to be so warmly yellow, street signs to be so invitingly green. The way America is painted seems to him shockingly, but pleasantly different from the drab color-lessness that envelops everything—streets, cars, housing projects, people's complexions—in his own country. The color of Eastern Europe is gray (with occasional flashes of red on national holidays). America has no single color; it is brightly multicolored, pluralistic and bold, even in the first visual impression it makes.

The very next thing E. E. is struck by is the the size of everything. Besides being gaudier, the components of American reality are also bigger. I don't mean the obvious things like skyscrapers, cars, the Grand Canyon or Kareem Abdul-Jabbar. But even the gulls at the beach seem to be somewhat oversized here, as if they had been fed all their lives with some specially nutritious gull food, sold in easy-to-open cans. Speaking of body size, Eastern Europe is no match for America either as far as its fat people are concerned. There are a lot of potbellies there, but their fat is the fat of sloppiness, bad food and lack of time for exercise. Compared to this, the typical American fatty seems rather to be a kind of competi-

---

*Originally delivered at this symposium, later published (under the title "E. E., The Extra-Territorial") in the November 26, 1984 issue of *New Republic*, from which it is reprinted here.

67

tor who has deliberately set about breaking the world record in body weight. He or she somehow blends in harmoniously with the Rockies, the Sears Tower and the Buick station wagon.

One hour on American soil is enough for E. E. to receive a cultural shock in addition to the optical one. Unlike his own country, the U.S.A. strikes him as a place where everything is in working order— well, most of the time. A bus may be late, but it finally does arrive. A book may be out of print, but you can order a copy or expect a reedition fairly soon. The toilet may not flush, but voilá, here comes a superintendent and repairs it (at least, until the next breakdown). This notion goes far beyond the mere availability of consumer goods and services. It's more than that; it's a philosophical difference between two visions of Fate. E. E. needs, typically, a few months to get rid of his Eastern European fatalism, bred in him by the countless hours he spent in his country hopelessly waiting at a bus stop, hunting for a sold-out book, begging a plumber to pay a visit. In Eastern Europe the best guess is to expect the worst. Nothing is guaranteed or even predictable; everything—from the meat supply to the course of your own career—is subject to the mysterious whims of "them," those who are at power on its various levels (even the plumber is one of "them"—his power lies in his being in constant demand). In America, "them" seems to be replaced by "me": everything—and this is truly a new experience for E. E.—can be worked out, if one tries hard enough. Or at least, so it seems to E. E. until he first gets into trouble with the IRS or is caught speeding.

True or not, the acceptance of the idea that everything in America works or can be worked out is perhaps the watershed moment for an Eastern European newcomer. Having gotten used to this, he becomes a new man. That is, to a certain extent; there are still some residues of his old mentality which simply cannot be eradicated. In spite of all his euphoria, the New World sometimes also provokes feelings of cultural alienation, incomprehension or disgust. Here is a partial list of things American with which E. E. will never come to terms:

1. Barbara Walters.
2. Supermarket bread.
3. Stand-up parties.
4. Baseball.
5. Small talk.
6. Dental bills.
7. Muzak.
8. Decaffeinated coffee.
9. Cat-food commercials.

10. Being addressed on a first-name basis by strangers.

The list could be easily extended, but I hope its point is clear. Mind you, not all of the things listed above are perceived by E. E. as alien. Though this is certainly the case of baseball, which seems to him to have brutally usurped the place of soccer, that one truly noble and intelligent game. Some other things seem illogical rather than alien: what's the point of standing at parties and wearing out your legs? Or what's the sense in drinking coffee that's not coffee at all? Still others remain alien, but on second thought E. E. has to grudgingly admit their logicality; the cost of filling a cavity is outrageous, but, after all, the operation is painless and well done, which cannot usually be said about dental care in his own country. On the other hand, Barbara Walters, for instance, provokes in E. E. some definitely bad vibrations precisely because she reminds him so much of the superficiality and pretentious blah-blah of Eastern Europe's own TV anchors; and certain TV commercials (those of the "no-more-ring-around-the-collar" or "you'll-never-go-back-to-thick" variety), while basically unknown as a genre in the Communist bloc, have too much in common with the general mindlessness and bad taste of what is a surrogate for mass culture there.

America is indeed a land of opportunity—at least in the sense that there is always the opportunity here to escape from what you hate or to counterbalance it with what you like. If you can't stand standing at parties, you can always sit down, even on the floor. If you hate Johnny Carson, you can watch Ted Koppel instead. It doesn't mean, though, that the cultural differences can be smoothed over easily. If E. E. happens to be a translator of literature, as in the case of this writer, he cannot help thinking about this dilemma as a problem of translation from one language into another. There would be no problem at all—and the translator's profession would not exist—if every word or expression in a given language had an exact equivalent in another language. But sometimes a word has several different equivalents, or a group of synonymous words has only a single equivalent. It can also happen that there is no equivalent at all, since the thing denoted by a word simply doesn't exist in another environment or culture. And finally, there are also situations—the most difficult ones for the translator—in which there *seems* to exist a pair of exact equivalents, but in fact each of them means something quite different in its respective language, or their meanings overlap only partially.

What I mean by "language" here can be broadly understood as any established cultural system, but in the particular situation of E. E. in America the problem is, naturally, most nagging within language in its narrow sense. A visitor or immigrant in a foreign country is, as a rule, sensitive to the pitfalls of semantics; the necessity of communicating in a language that is not his own makes him painfully aware of the constant danger of being misunderstood due to his linguistic imprecision or erratic usage. But sometimes it is not his poor vocabulary that is to blame—it is, rather, this or that in-built incompatibility of two languages. And such instances make him think, in turn, of all the potential and actual misunderstandings on a more universal level—in the communication that goes on between nations, cultures and political blocs.

Take the word "happy," perhaps one of the most frequent words in Basic American. It's easy to open an English-Polish or English-Russian dictionary and find an equivalent adjective. In fact, however, it will not be equivalent. The Polish word for "happy" (and I believe this also holds for other Slavic languages) has a much more restricted meaning; it is generally reserved for rare states of profound bliss or total satisfaction with serious things such as love, family, the meaning of life, etcetera. Accordingly, it is not used as often as "happy" is in American common parlance. The question one hears at (stand-up) parties—"Is everybody happy?"—if translated literally into Polish, would seem to come from a metaphysical treatise or political utopia rather than social chitchat. Incidentally, it is also interesting that Slavic languages don't have an exact equivalent for the verb "to enjoy." I don't mean to say that Americans are a nation of superficial, backslapping enjoyers and happy-makers, as opposed to our suffering Slavic souls. What I'm trying to point out is only one example of semantic incompatibilities which are so firmly ingrained in languages and cultures that they sometimes make mutual communication impossible—or, rather, they turn it into a ritual exchange of meaningless grunts and purrs. "Are you happy?" E. E. is asked by his cordial host. "Yes, I am." "Are you enjoying yourself?" "Sure I am." What else can be said? What would be the point in trying to explain that his Eastern European mind does not necessarily mean what his American vocabulary communicates?

But this is just an innocent example from the field of private emotions and the level of individual dialogue. The weight of the problem increases remarkably whenever E. E. has to resort to the vocabulary of what really matters on the nation-to-nation plane—to the vocabulary of history, politics and ideology. Take another word: "liberal." In my part of Europe this single word has several meanings at least. As a qualifying adjective added to the name of this or that political tendency, for instance, it means that someone belongs, within his own political camp, to the doves rather than to the hawks. Thus, a "liberal Communist" is the kind of Communist who would like to send only *some* of his country's dissidents to psychiatric hospitals. This is, however, a secondary and frequently ironic usage. In its primary sense, the word "liberal" denotes in Eastern Europe, just as it does traditionally in all of Europe, someone who is located rather towards the center of the political spectrum and who opposes, most of all, those ideological premises of both the left and the right which in his view threaten the principle of individual freedom. Now what is an Eastern European liberal supposed to say when he is asked by an American acquaintance about his political orientation? To answer "I'm a neo-conservative" would more or less transfer the desired meaning to the American ears, but E. E. cannot force his lips to pronounce that; for him, "conservative" sounds like the opposite of what he has always considered himself. After all, in his own country he never wanted to "conserve" the status quo—on the contrary, as a dissident, defender of human rights, or just a thinking individual, he was definitely "progressive" as opposed to the "conservative" powers-that-be. The translation from the language EE (Eastern European) into the language AA (Authentic American) is, at least in this particular case, virtually impossible; even though the word "liberal" has the same Latin root and a similar sound here and there, its actual meanings within two different political systems, societies and historical traditions are far from close.

This is precisely what I would call the continental drift of meanings. The word "liberal," to which other words, such as "democratic," "nationalistic," etcetera, could be added, is just one of the more glaring examples of that phenomenon; in fact, the most basic premises of life in Eastern Europe are so different from the American way of life (whatever that means) that every attempt at mutually communicating one's experience is bound to wind up in semantic conundrums and misinterpretations. This wouldn't be surprising if we dealt with an Eastern European apparatchik coming to America on an official visit; surely enough, in his peculiar newspeak words like "democracy" and "justice" mean something rather different than they do in the Declaration of Independence. But an Eastern European dissident usually believes that, given a chance, he would be able to communicate with the heirs of Thomas Jefferson without lapsing into semantic confusion. The reality, as a rule, thwarts his expectations—despite all the mutual sympathy on both sides of the Atlantic Ocean, the continental drift in semantics seems to be unstoppable. Nothing could be a better example of this than the American media's coverage of events in Poland over the past four years. Their attempts to "translate" the idiomatically Polish set of political and social meanings into a language understandable to the American audience ended up, for the most part, in a failure to communicate anything essential. The gulf between two social systems, two historical traditions, and two collective mentalities proved too wide to be bridged by sympathy alone.

However, just as the differences between two ethnic languages create the need for translators, so all the incompatibilities between the Eastern European and American mentalities only make every form of semantic mediation all the more desirable. Personally, I believe in culture as a possible go-between. A single novel, of, say, Milan Kundera or Tadeusz Konwicki, when translated into English, tells the American audience more about Czechoslovakia or Poland than ten years of *Newsweek*'s coverage. A single film of Andrzej Wajda's is an incomparably better source of information about Eastern Europe than a thousand interviews with General Jaruzelski by Barbara Walters. A general can lie; a work of art can't. If you want to know why ten million unarmed people in an Eastern European country risked being crushed by Soviet tanks four years ago, don't ask party secretaries; ask poets and artists.

In fact, Americans do just that more and more often, but a lot remains to be done. It's characteristic that in a country like Poland, despite all the officially-sponsored propaganda against the U.S.A., there has always been a powerful interest in American culture and, as a consequence, it is amazingly well-known there. If America wishes to understand better what's going on with today's world, it's time for her to abandon the idea of cultural self-sufficiency and to reach deeper into other nations' minds. The widening gulf between collective mentalities has more than once been crossed in the past and it still can be bridged by the kind of insight that culture provides. The continental drift can be stopped.

A Colonial's-Eye View of the Empire

Derek Walcott

I don't have any prepared text or manifesto, which doesn't make me more sincere than anyone else. It's simply that it is very difficult for me to put down on the page any summary of what I believe or any sense of direction of where I think I am heading. The few things that I think I know at my age are very simple and they become, after a while, corny in a sense. And one of the most reverberating simplicities to me is one that's known to anyone who begins to read, and that is that empires disappear and that there is an immortality of some kind, that the only immortality we have is literature or art—whether or not there is a religion, in the religious sense of immortality or something. I think one of the crucial things about empires is that they forget that and I think that that was what was meant earlier, in the earlier panel, about the idea of imagination.

All human experience, basically, can be reduced to legend. It can be emblematically reduced to legend or to fable. And to say this I do not lean back in a sort of cynical resignation—or sort of isolate myself like, say, Robinson Jeffers on the Pacific Coast, who cried out continually that this century, that this technological age, was doomed and is doomed. That is not the sort of figure I am trying to make myself—I am not trying to make myself anything whatsoever—I'm just giving the figure of the poet as being *that*. Somehow, for instance, a figure like Jeffers becomes another dark and tall and brooding and stony emblem more and more serious as someone to pay attention to.

The whole idea of empire, of course, is the idea of Faust. The whole idea of hubris is employed in what we do now. And if, for some reason, an empire were capable of that kind of imagination, of the *experience* of imagination, then it would seem pretty simple and pretty obvious that

man is bent on a path of self-destruction. *Why* is not a question that one answers. Other people give answers, but there are figures who remain and recur emblematically, with the highest kind of morality and warning—they are like deviations of Prometheus, or Faust, of course, or Ulysses—who is not content to stay home as in Dante (having made that trip as he does in Homer, he goes home and everything is fine). But in Dante what's marvelous is that he decides, "I have to leave, I have to go out and learn more, to seek experience of the world and of human vice and worth." And when he stops at the pillars of Hercules and is warned by some superior knowledge that you don't go past that, and he does, then, in Dante, the whirlpool closes over him and that marvelous shrugging way that Dante has is very Italian: he says, "As it pleased another." Right? And that's God. And saying: well, that's the way with things.

And perhaps it is because I am a colonial and outside, not feeling the concern of the day-to-day experience—perhaps because I feel that there is some distant island that I can be on, that is outside things, that is not really true—perhaps I can look a little more resignedly, fatalistically, and in a sense imaginatively, too, at the reality of the fact that what is called a civilization can no longer be called that. That the term "civilization" does not apply anymore and that what is called the center of civilization, whatever these centers are, are not necessarily living centers, however technologically they may develop. In that sense I think that both empires, both the Russian and the American Empire, are very Roman. For a flash I was thinking a while ago if I were to do a regressive thing and if I were in Rome, I would be someone, an outside barbarian of a remote province addressing—this is not Washington, but it is close enough—addressing members of an empire, trying to explain not what it is like outside my frontier or behind that territory or boundary, but the fact that one sees very simply from the experience of being a colonial what kind of situation exists politically around the world.

Again, it's all very obvious, but, again, it's forgotten. America contains in it a colony. It is an empire that contains a huge colony, and that colony, whether it is black, or Puerto Rican, or whatever it is—there *is* a colony that exists in this empire—and that colony obliquely, quietly, politely, gently, even encouragingly, is kept within its frontiers. That is a peculiar thing about this empire; and it *is* an empire. The point is also that this empire has a tremendous conscience as well about the rest of the world, but what we ourselves outside the boundaries of that empire cannot understand is the American conscience and passion for freedom which somehow is fine when it is exported—there is tremendous concern about the liberty of others—but there does not seem to me to be enough *care*, or enough imaginative concern, about the admission of the truth that this empire does contain and rule a colony within itself. And for me, as a colonial, it is very easy to see that.

It may be a little rude to say this but, for me, as I get older, coming back to America every time I do, I have to submit myself to what is secondary experience. I come from the Caribbean and I come in and I arrive and very quietly a kind of a mantle goes over me and I make a step down, one platform down, and I say, "Oh yes, all right, I am—that's right—I am black, that's right, I am X." That is not a heightening experience. It is not the idea of the barbarian leaving the frontier and crossing over to the center of civilization, feeling elevated by that experience. On the contrary, what one feels is, one is coming from outside the boundary and having to adjust to a human experience that is basically inferior, as a civilization, to the one which is not called a civilization, that I come from, in which there is no great technology, there is a great deal of poverty and song.

I think that that is exactly and very simply the situation of an empire attitude toward Latin America that may also be an attitude toward Afghanistan. It may be an attitude toward anywhere, but it still is the presumption and egotism, the Faustian egotism that says, in either one of these empires: one, that they will last forever and, two, that *their* consciences are the ones that matter, and that these consciences are the ones by which other ideas of liberty have to exist. And this seems to be an enormous violation of the very precepts of what the Constitution is supposed to be.

I have lived and I continue to live in various ironies but I am resigned to certain of them. This country has been extremely generous to me. That is a fact that I frequently and freely admit—that as a writer I could not have made a living in the Caribbean without the support, grants, generosity, for me. Someone else might say, "Well, that's just, you know, 'Nephew Tom'—right?—instead of 'Uncle Tom' or something, but the gratitude that you are expressing is being brainwashed." But I believe that there is inherent, in this country, a generosity, not because one receives rewards, but because there is a willingness to be generous in this empire, and that it creates conflict between what it has to *seem* to do, what it must *appear* to do, and what it does *not* do. For me to say that, as one who comes from the Caribbean to be here, saying this at present, again seems to be a sort of *banal* kind of gratitude. But that is what bothers me a lot—that this experience of remaining in America continually, and having to reduce one's spirit to adapt to what the social habits and social judgments of its own people are, makes you lower your view of the civilization. I think that if it were not miraculous, but if it were simply possible, that this empire would open itself, would ventilate itself, would embrace what its own gifts are more fully, even export them, even emphasize them, this could have been the greatest and perhaps most benign, for size—and empire is only a matter of size. But it's like a lyric trying to be an epic, in a sense. The lyric has to come to a point where it says: I am an epic. This is not a little thing here. And the scale—if you consider the conscience to be, say, like a lyric—then the scale of the conscience is too small for the size of the country. It should be as broad as its own size. And that seems to me to be one of the easiest observations one can make as colonial, which I prefer to remain because it helps judgment; it gives me a good sense of balance and distance not to be a member of any power, to feel, in a way, always slightly disenfranchised, as Leslie Epstein was saying, to feel there is something you don't quite earn.

When I was much younger I remember that there used to be a phrase that was supposed to terrify everybody and no longer scares me and that is: "the end of civilization as we know it." Well, if you transfer the end of civilization and you just change the personal pronoun, you'll see how much vanity is in that. All you have to say is: "the end of civilization as they knew it." And then something else happens. And I think that this is the continual reminder that Art gives, Art keeps simply stating that *this* is the truth, this is the historical truth, it's not linear.

Take, for instance, the amnesia of the slave, ironically enough, the forced amnesia of the black, or of people who have crossed into this America, of any immigrant, in this effort to look for the past—what America offers, once it crosses that meridian, is an obliteration of the old linear idea of progress. That is what *might* have happened. The "is-ness" of being in America becomes what is important. Now, that's true for any immigrant, in a sense, but it should be a philosophy, it should be *felt*. And I think that we who have crossed over from where we have come from, who have no memory of lineage, of a people who were forced, like Crusoe on an island, to have no history (all he has is memory, and his presence there can only make use of the immediate tools that he has) can feel this replenishment of the idea of the castaway, of the abandoned person, of the hermit, of the person who begins again. This I think is the idea of the pioneer spirit. Although it sounds, you know, very electioneering to say so, I think that this is what has continually been said about America—by Whitman as much as by Neruda.

Session II:
Questions and Answers

EMERSON (FROM AUDIENCE): Many outstanding novelists and poets have been denied visas to the United States, on the grounds that their political sympathies were not conducive to our serene political system. Sirs, perhaps you are not dangerous enough to give trouble to this country. Can you explain why, for example, Graham Greene has been denied a visa for so long? Or the playwright Fo? Or Gabriel García Márquez? Or half a dozen writers? Is this apt to happen to you at one time if you grow too critical of us?

WALCOTT: I think one of the points one must remember is that you could not have gotten up and said that publicly in another kind of situation. Right? I mean the fact that you have the right to get up and criticize the policy of the State Department towards Graham Greene or towards Dario Fo, or something, that's a first liberty, that you can do that. The other reason—as a matter of fact, I think that this has now been eroded—I think that now, because of dissent, because of objection, Dario Fo is now able to come in and I think García Márquez can now come in. So that process happens. I mean that thing continues all the time. If you are saying that because I am safe I am "in," I would have absolutely no respect for this country, and I wouldn't be here if I thought that, because then I would have been bought. But every government continually edges toward totalitarianism in terms of what it requires of conduct, of censorship. I was a little shocked when that happened. I never thought that happened here. I didn't think that—I wasn't aware until two years ago—that certain writers were banned from coming into this country. But I think with enough noise—I just certainly think with enough noise—that stupidity will stop, that's all.

EMERSON (FROM AUDIENCE): Well, it must be this country feels endangered by their presence, which is baffling.

WALCOTT: There are many things that are done in which the conduct of certain aspects of the American government doesn't seem very different from certain aspects of any totalitarian government, in terms of repressing, or trying to repress. There have been obvious efforts to repress expression, you know, or to harass expression. But I always have great confidence that people make enough noise to say that this has got to stop—then it does stop.

AUDIENCE: Could you just further explain why the word "civilization" is no longer appropriate?

WALCOTT: Well, civilization means culture. The highest expression of culture is a total acceptance of every human being, right? It has never happened, but that's the highest expression of it. They didn't have that with the Greeks, who had slaves, and so on. But what I am talking about, in terms of civilization, is that we are made to think that there is a sort of direct progress: one, two, three, four, five, six, seven, eight, right? To think in a linear way that this is the inevitability of history, that this is supposed to happen because it happened before, and the only hope—because there has to be a hope equal to nuclear weapons, there can't be the old hope; it has to be a hope that is equally strong—and the only hope is to change, to wish to have a change about ideas of thinking about history or of power, which is the same thing, as being inevitable. That's what I mean. I mean the boring tribal wars of Europe, the repetition! I am being super-cynical in the sense, if I am permitted to be, that Job or Jeremiah is cynical. I am just saying that that is the level of my cynicism, that it is not pessimism, it is cynicism. I used to think that every war that happened in Europe was an advancement in European history, and then I began to look at the tribes of Europe and realized that it was just different tribes fighting each other. No matter what the weapons were. That simplifies history considerably. Whatever ideology you put here, it comes down to the fact that Slavs don't like X and X doesn't like Who. How is that different from the bunch of people in New Guinea, going over there and clobbering each other? I don't see any difference.

AUDIENCE: What about the idea of "progress"?

WALCOTT: Well, the danger there is either like, you know, the Celtic revival or going back to the spinning wheel. That's not what I'm saying. I know you are not saying I'm thinking that. I'm saying that it doesn't mean that one *stops* using cars or one *stops* an organ, or something, an electrical organ—because there is another kind of romance in *that*. There's a sort of self-destructive romance in machines, right? That's the whole Faustian thing. It's romantic; it's thrilling, actually. These weapons are thrilling. There's a big thrill. And humankind has a big thrill over the loaded revolver, you know; the Russian roulette thrill is there. O.K., so that's part of the stupidity of man. That's a general thing. But what I am talking about that *this* part of the world might have meant, was that the idea of time was not linear. I am not talking about development; I am talking about something else that may be totally absurd. But it is not less absurd than the fact that nuclear technology has made war absurd. Right? So I mean this idea: we have come, I think, to a confrontation with a whole concept of what is supposed to be: culture, civilize, develop, power, meaning, the centralization of all human experience as being located in Moscow or in Washington or in Paris or in Athens; this is no longer true, cannot be true.

AUDIENCE: I'd like to ask Michael Harper a question based on something Derek Walcott said. Do you think, given what you were saying, that poetry has more of a good place "inside" or "outside," in the terms he was using? Because you said something similar; you talked about oral consciousness, which is a kind of way of saying inside/outside. Speaking of the interior colony.

HARPER: When questions like this are asked me, I immediately flash on people like James Baldwin and others who have written many essays on it. And I don't think that this country, the country of America, is by any means unaware of the way in which, to use Derek's metaphor, colonies are brutalized. I think it's just a question of a kind of interior capitalism. It's a way of using quantities of things. That's one of the reasons why I read Wally Serote's poem about black people being fuel. It's just some—not necessarily qualitative— some *quantitative* way in which the country feeds itself, all right? When one talks about poetry, one talks about states of consciousness and states of *conscientiousness*. Now, Derek and myself and numerous people out there would automatically see the link between a James Wright, for example, and a Robert Hayden. But most people don't see that link. And, for one reason or another, James Wright took it upon himself to comment about that word "offices," simply because he wanted to make everybody understand that the relationship between the talent or gift or imagination that it takes to write a beautiful poem, has a direct relationship to the way in which people live. That's unequivocal. Now, Hayden was a person who came from a very low and—what should we call it?—unlettered background. His gift, it seems to me as I look on it, was he had the access to the lives, the inner lives, of people, everyday people, that poets have. And I don't know what world you all out there are living in, but I'm living in a world where I feel that when I can speak at all, and I'm not sure that I can always, I always try to speak with eloquence for losers. I'm not really concerned with those people who can speak for themselves. I mean, they're running this country, in one way or another! I'm concerned with those particular people who have no voice. And I've spent a good deal of my life trying to understand the relationship between this internal-colony condition and the outside world, which is to say I've gotten out of this country. And getting out of this country, and getting away from the specter of the American Express and intercontinental hotels and all that is a way of just kind of clearing up the air. I talked about the long dialogue—this dialogue has been going on since before the country decided to define itself by writing its ambitions down on paper. I mean when the Declaration of Independence was written by Jefferson, God help him, you know women were not included in his fascination with this dream, and certainly blacks weren't, you know, etcetera.

So, the notion of being able to function at a level of improvisation without the lineage of history—the willingness to be able to make do with what is—is, I think, the poetic question, for everybody. I think we spend too much time worrying about what they said in libraries. Now, I'm not saying throw them away, but you got to live, and you got to live consciously. And, if there is going to be any change, there has got to be all the attention possible on the *now*, and on changing these patterns of thought. I have many, many friends who live in the Virgin Islands, who live here and there, and we are kind of like brothers and sisters. We don't spend all our time dealing with nations; I know that somebody comes from Trinidad, or Jamaica, and we like their accent, and we like their clothes, and some of them can cook and some of them can dance. But the point is that there's a greater linkage with us because of our common experience, or the lack of one. That's one of the reasons that I read that poem.

Let me just give you a political kind of quiz, all right? The first effort at republican democracy in the western world was in Haiti. It shares, geographically, with the Dominican Republic, in terms of terrain. If you had an egg and you cut it in half, part of it would be Haiti and the other would be the Dominican Republic. The kind of events which go on between a Trujillo, and he's just a metaphor, and a Papa Doc, culturally—*culturally*—is something which I think we have to wrestle with, because the Third World is not in agreement about many things, and we have to have our own dialogues, about all kinds of things. Those dialogues, it seems to me, are preliminaries to the great question.

What the Africans have said to me over and over again, in West and East and South Africa, is that finally our destiny is pretty much bookended by what the Soviet Union and the United States do. I mean we're really in the small ballpark and you guys in the big one. Everything that's going to be done is going to be defined this way. And if you've gotten in the plane and flown across the continent of Africa, and you fly for many, many hours, and then you hear this, then you have to begin to think about some things.

Why is the South African military as strong as it is? Why is the Israeli military? Those two military bastions—they run the continent, you know. And we created that. I mean we did that. Let's not put that on the Russians. So it depends on how you want to look at power. But from my point of view, blacks have been watching, witnessing. And when I say judge—let me just be clear about this—I mean judgment, I mean *recording* it, writing it down so there'll be a record about what happened. And a lot of people aren't listening, but Du Bois did write *The Souls of Black Folk*, and every time I read it I'm amazed. I am literally amazed that he had the perspicacity to do it, because it is a marvelous book eight decades later. It's marvelous. And he's basically appealing to the white folks. He's trying to say, I know you all didn't know what you were doing, so let me tell you what you been doing.

And I don't see very much change really, in terms of the call to the poet, in what that job is. That job is to continue to announce and to praise, until somebody changes their life. I don't think we've got any alternative. I'm not joining any army!

STONE (FROM AUDIENCE): I'm glad in a way to see that in the course of the afternoon we've arrived at at least one fundamental disagreement, and I would like to cleave to it because it has partly made the afternoon for me. Mr. Walcott, you began to speak about the aesthetic of violence, you began to touch on it. What you were saying was, it seems to me, in direct contradiction to what Mr. Epstein had been saying before in reference to Ben DeMott's article. DeMott and Leslie

Epstein seemed to me to be doing something that would be very nice to do but we can't do it. I think you were telling us that. And that is to read *out* of the aesthetic world all violence, the tools of violence, the instruments by which one person coerces another. I don't want to put words in your mouth, but I want almost to have that *said* at this point. But violent things are part of the world of aesthetics, they are an integral part of the world of aesthetics. They have their own aesthetics; aesthetics does not exist without them. There is no world so comfortable, so pure, that these things don't enter in. I think that's what you have been saying. A Hell's Angel with a swastika, walking down the street, done up in his tattoos and his colors, is not outside the world of aesthetics. He has an aesthetic. Not only does he have an aesthetic, but he has an aesthetic which, if we try to, we can relate to; we don't like it, but he is not outside aesthetics. The look of illumination rounds is not outside the world of aesthetics; it is part of an aesthetic experience. We deny this; the guidance system of a missile is not outside aesthetics. It seems to me that was a fact that somehow could get lost, that you didn't get to say. I don't know whether you agree with me or not. What I guess I'm asking you is if that's a position that you would take.

WALCOTT: What I decided, what I heard from Leslie, was not the separation, the worst, an ivory-towerish sort of thing, or whatever. I think he seemed to be saying that aesthetics is as corruptible as anything else, that there is not a pure aesthetic, and that there is a beauty in brutal architecture, for instance, which I detest, but there *is* something based on that; the flowers of Mussolini's son are the same thing—or the beauty of steel, for instance, is a difficult thing to grasp. Or something. And I don't think we were different in that sense.

AUDIENCE: I would like to ask E. E. if he is happy and enjoying himself.

BARANCZAK: Thank you. I am pretty much enjoying myself. Especially being here in this room and hearing such an interesting discussion, but this is a good occasion to point out one thing which maybe wasn't emphasized enough in my reading of the text—which is that the point of observation which that character E. E. represents in my brief essay is by no means identical to mine. I mean, it was deliberately made a little bit more naive than myself. And I guess such a superficial way of looking at the oddity, first from the optical point of view, then from the point of view of the fact that everything is in working order, is common to everybody who comes to America from Eastern Europe. But, of course, after a while you notice very many things which complicate the picture. And I'm glad I can return at this point to the question which was raised, which had to do with the problem of the Immigration Office and all those other idiotic restrictions they impose sometimes. This is one of the features of American reality which somehow discolors the general rosy picture a newcomer has, and they make him or her think about possible distortions of American democracy, possible ways that democracy can destroy itself, in the final analysis. And Mr. Walcott said very wisely that there are some isolated islands, so to speak, of such totalitarian instincts in democracy and the policy of any government, even the most democratic one, and I think what's absolutely beautiful and splendid about America is that every time that something like that occurs, there's an immediate response of public opinion. So there are still some people who are able to raise their voice in protest. And what's the most amazing thing, especially for someone who comes from Eastern Europe—it finally brings, more often than not, an effect, a reversal of such decisions. So this is what I wanted to add to my presentation.

Special Section: New Work and Work in Progress

Three Poems

Stanislaw Baranczak

The Morning After

The morning after another
collective suicide you go out
as always to get the morning paper,
as always the freshly fallen snow
gleams white or the tidy sun
of a summer dawn rises, as always
the milk bottles ring and
the croissants give off their scent, as always
a little girl with a satchel
runs to school and trips and falls
and skins her knee and there's much crying and in this crying
so much life

Translated by Magnus J. Krynski and Robert A. Maguire

Anyone Can Stand

*To the memory of an unknown woman
whose death on the eve of All Saints,
1979, led to the temporary closing of the
butcher's shop in Sciegiennego Street,
Warsaw, and hence to the understandable
disappointment and bitterness of the
remaining customers*

Perhaps not, actually, a scrag end of neck
but then, how much reassurance could have been gotten
from this story and this butcher's shop (scrag end of neck
is meat) by anyone who saw the elderly
woman who, half-fainting in the crowd (meat
is protein), slipped down
to her knees, but with a final effort,
clinging to other people's shopping bags and raincoats,
raised herself up (protein
is life) to a standing position and only
then,
held upright by the pressure of other (life
is a struggle) bodies,
died of a heart attack,
thus providing a living image, in point of fact, a dead one,
of the truth contained in the truism: It is better to die
on your feet
than live on your knees.

Translated by Antony Graham and Reginald Gibbons

We Drew the Proper Conclusions from the Events

We grabbed what we could,
and hastily,
of the burning records
being thrown out of windows;
little was lost:
our hearts are
slightly to the left side,
livers to the right,
our blood's arterial
and venous (half and half),
our hands persistently have
five fingers (counting thumb,
index, middle,
ring, little), our
brain has two hemispheres
just like our globe, whose
flattened poles
invariably remain on opposite
sides, our rivers flow
as usual down and seaward
and trees grow upward,
our apples fall
vertically while horizontally
clouds skim along above the earth,
our day's bright, night
is dark, our bread is
daily, our water boiled, houses
liveable, newspapers
regular, but our
pens, oh, our pens are even
more everlasting than before.

Translated by Frank Kujawinski and Reginald Gibbons

Equipment for Living

Terrence Des Pres

> *Politics today is the voice of horror.*
> —Jean-Luc Godard, 1985

At the TQ conference the notion of empire came up more than once, and in a tone suggesting, to me at least, that maybe Yeats had it right when he worried about "the growing murderousness of the world." Living in the Age of the Bomb, it's not hard to see that between them the superpowers have recolonized the globe; that they have carved the planet into spheres of influence, forcing smaller nations to toe the new alignment, and that now they proceed with the standoff they've locked themselves into. This means that most of the fighting gets done by proxy, by pitting groups or nations against each other to no end, of course, except *this* end—the demise of cities and countrysides as, over and over, populations get caught in the cross-fire. About these cross-fire situations, furthermore, there is a redundant pathos, a familiar sorrow, reminding me that life for all of us, today, depends on two empires not unlike Athens and Sparta, dividing their version of the world between them, preparing for war and surmising it must come because one seems to be gaining an edge on the other. As Thucydides puts it, "Finally the point was reached when Athenian strength attained a peak plain for all to see." And thus the Spartan vote for war; because—as Thucydides says—"because they were afraid." It's an old story, except for the nuclear angle. For Thucydides it was Hellas going down. Now it's life on earth. None of this is news, of course; but being caught in the cross-fire provokes interesting questions, in particular what we might still expect from fiction and poetry—enlightened feeling? finer sensibilities?—amid the *hysterico passio* of nuclear cold-war politics.

I've always thought of literature as a fierce vote for the future, but now that's not so certain. Recently Günter Grass has reminded us how much good writing depends on a hearing at some point forward in time.

Sometimes a new style or vision will not find its audience for decades; and often, too, writers must outlive, through their work, the censorship and silence that governments have a habit of imposing. Literature's "superior staying power" is what Grass has in mind when he says: "Sure of its aftereffect, it could count on time even if the echo to word and sentence, poem and thesis might take decades or even centuries to make itself heard. This advance payment, this provision of time, made the poorest writers rich." But now the promise of delayed reception can't be counted on, nor the hope of immortality through fame. Thinking on his own career, Grass concludes: "I know that the book I am planning to write can no longer pretend to certainty of the future. It will have to include a farewell to the damaged world, to wounded creatures, to us and our minds, which have thought of everything and of the end as well."

Writers must, it seems to me, vote to see the world keep going. Creating an idea or image is like planting a tree: its fullest foliage will be well beyond one's time. But if history has often shown us the long-term victory of truth, it also reveals the catastrophic outcome, both short-term and long, of power-politics. I mean to say that while notions of fate and historical necessity don't convince me, the sameness in political behavior, especially the way powers contend and empires fall, is hard to ignore. The past, in any case, seems most real to me as parable, the way Cavafy used Hellenic anecdote, or the way Zbigniew Herbert does now, to get a handle on chaos and better comprehend the odd way personal experience has begun to feel collective. Recasting big events as old tales restores, at least, a sense of scale. I can even suppose that in a post-nuclear era the pretensions of a civilization built from debris will include, among its inheritance of hearsay and junk, legends of the Bomb.

I'm trying not to fool myself, although lately I find myself thinking a good deal about the hereafter—not some thirty-minute shoot-out that brings on nuclear winter, but beyond that, in quick flashes forward, the shapes the maiming will finally settle into. For the first time, always having loathed science fiction, I discover substance in imaginings of the future. Maybe that's dangerous, implying as it does that the world I love is lost already. I am encouraged, however, by what Elaine Scarry says in *The Body in Pain*, especially her idea of personal language as counterforce to political injury, and also by this remark: "Beyond the expansive ground of ordinary, naturally occurring objects is the narrow extra ground of imagined objects, and beyond this ground, there is no other. Imagining is, in effect, the ground of last resort."

Why does that way of saying it seem so accurate? The ground of ordinary, naturally occurring objects now includes the Bomb, "Star Wars," feelings of doom. Beyond that lies whatever imagination can construct. And beyond that there's nothing. Between ourselves and nothing, then, nothing intervenes except the small creations we ourselves put forth for use, among them images of the world going on in some post-nuclear way, or, harder and more urgent, images of ourselves surviving intact despite current forecasts. Elaine Scarry can speak of imagination as a *last resort* and Czeslaw Milosz speaks of poetry as a *last rampart*. Scarry came to part of her conclusion from studying Amnesty International's reports on torture. Milosz came to his after surviving the German and then the Russian savaging of Poland. Are we ready to receive such notions and take them at face value? If we profess the value of creative language, are we ready to grant that poetry can be important? And if so, can't we go on from our limited experience to say when poems are most *wanted*?

I think we can, and by calling on nothing that I have not myself felt or witnessed, I recommend (quietly, always amazed) this example—the intense degree to which men and women live by and sometimes die for words, sheer words upheld by nothing but the strength in saying, wording that seems weightless until uttered in the force of deep feeling. Robert Hass, for example, writes of himself as a young man desperate to engage his destiny, walking the streets repeating Lowell's lines:

> And blue-lung'd combers lumbered to the kill.
> The Lord survives the rainbow of His will.

Or in Warsaw during the Nazi occupation, as Milosz tells us, "an entire community is struck by misfortune" and "poetry becomes as essential as bread." Or this, Akhmatova's image of Mandelstam as she saw him in Voronezh near the end:

> But in the room of the banished poet
> Fear and the Muse stand watch by turn,
> and the night comes on,
> which has no hope of dawn.

At times like these, perhaps because there's nothing else, poetry becomes the one thing needful. Or maybe it's because in moments that seem ultimate, nothing else is *good* enough, shared enough, of a precision equal to our joy or suffering. What's wanted to celebrate a marriage or a birth, what we ask to get us through pain, what we need by the side of the grave isn't solemn claims nor silence either, but rather the simple saying of right words. Literature, as Kenneth Burke puts it, is "equipment for living." I take Burke seriously when he talks this way, and his ideas about "symbolic action" and "disburdening" are worth remembering. When through language we confront the worst, or discover ourselves in ways that convince us we matter, we partake of available blessings. "As essential as bread" is what Milosz says, and I think yes, the gain in strength and nourishment is real.

Between the self and the terrible world comes poetry with its minute redemptions, its lyrical insurgencies, its willing suspension of disbelief in tomorrow. These ministrations, I take it, compose our chances. I don't mean that poems can have a say in nuclear matters, or that through poetry we may expect a general change of heart. Power listens to none but itself; and the myth of progress through enlightenment, in my view, died in 1914. What I mean to say is that right language can help us, as it always helps in hard moments, with our private struggles to keep whole, can be a stay against confusion, can start the healing fountains. And whatever helps us repossess our humanity, able again to take place and speak forth, frees us for work in the world. This is imagination's special task, as Wallace Stevens would say, because this contrary force, by pitching itself against external pressures, pushes back and makes space for liberty of spirit. Confronted by negation, imagination automatically starts asserting itself. We cannot *not* imagine, in which case the question becomes a matter of strategy. Shall imagination confront, or shall it evade? I think that it must confont—that poetry can no longer turn away from political torment, and for the following reason. Nuclear threat touches everyone everywhere, but unlike private kinds of death, collective wipeout has no mystery, no myth to temper its terror except the crudities of cold-war propaganda. The Bomb is a reality so pressing and so naked that it cannot be ignored. One day we *see* the enormity of it, and then also we see that between the self and the cold-war world there is no interceding champion, no worldly power on our side, but only, as Elaine Scarry puts it, imagination as last resort.

I've been speaking of imagination as the great good thing, but those who control our external fate, the handful of men in Washington and Moscow, are deep into war-games and nuclear scenarios, so it's clear that imaginative energies also serve destruction and are not always, by definition, on the side of care. This duality of function is summed up in a single hard remark by Octavio Paz: "Facing death the spirit is life, and facing the latter, death." Imagination, Paz is suggesting, pushes back *that* fiercely against the urgencies that threaten it. Politics, having always to face unruly life, in crisis ends up serving death. And if, finally, we wish to identify the kind of demonic imagination now on the loose in high places, it has been rendered with jolly grit by Thomas Pynchon in *Gravity's Rainbow*, a Zone, as he calls it, under the rule of rampant paranoia, automatic systems, and idolatry of global weapons.

Imagination can be dangerous, no doubt about that; and even to be firmly on the side of life is no guarantee. The problem with facing death in order to defend life is that death begins to cast its shadow everywhere. A sort of vertigo sets in, as if the hysteria of the world were infectious, which it is. Sometimes, in my own experience, the nuclear issue becomes so pressing—this is one of the Bomb's worst consequences, simply as threat—that it turns me from life, makes me blind to the needs of my neighbors. But living in the age of atrocity is no excuse for dismissing lesser claims because they are local or private. By way of correcting myself, I think of a woman I recently met, writing a book about sexual abuse as a child, about years of rape by Dad and brothers, the whole town knowing but crusted with silence, a Christian community deep in the heartland, letting some of its children be ruined. For this woman, the act of writing becomes a settlement of memory, a recovery of self by dreaming back through nightmare. These are very personal matters, but no, not altogether; for this awful story is precisely of the kind that, so long as it goes untold, sealed in silence, supports the larger cover-up of violences (for example, the way the superpowers keep the international arms market, on which small wars depend, stocked to overflowing). Power isn't only hierarchial, as Foucault reminded us. It accumulates in multitudes of small enactments, forcings of any sort, including those within the closed-up family. So yes, the world hangs by a thread, but no case counts less than another.

What makes our experience valuable to others is of course the way we word it. This is always a lonely task, and well might we wonder, inside the solitude of writing, where enpowerment comes from. That all language assumes relation to power is visible in the fact that simply to verbalize, to use words at all, is instantly to be *with* or *against*. To the extent that this is so, writers choose their base, and not all powers are alike. Some pay off in dollars and nonsense, or in safety, more handsomely than others. The structure of political-institutional powers is vast, a kingdom with many mansions. Some writers, however, will seek a different potency, poets especially; but if so, what power can there be besides the big ones that run the warring world? What power was it, exactly, that tribal bards possessed when they went about their office of blessing and cursing, of praising and casting blame? Or the Irish ratrhymers, what did they think they had that allowed them to clear infested places with chants? Wallace Stevens spoke of a "pressure within" that pushes back against the "pressures without." By external pressure he meant the political horror of World War Two, and by the inward kind he meant imagination, which he identified with "the sounds of words."

The self that cannot speak, as the man or woman being tortured cannot, or the self that cannot find words to make its own, as the Orwellian victim cannot, does not objectify itself, has not the means to join or withdraw from the world. As poets and politicians know, *right words count that much.* And language is right when its fictive status makes no claims, serves no program or outside power, but only when, by taking place, it inspires us likewise to behold and take our place. The power base of poetry is poetry itself, the one kind of discourse that stands on its own, empowered by ceaseless imaginative motion and the vigor of its own interior music. Other discourse gains authority by indenturing itself to political orders of one stripe or another. Only poetical language, I'd like to repeat, is capable of authorizing its own generation.

This freedom is poetry's special strength, and, today more than ever, chief among its benefits. For now that we are cornered by the force of cold-war politics, we must consider in the plainest ways our access to reality, our confidence in fact, our capacity to cut through information overload. Here, from an article by John Newhouse (the *New Yorker*, July 22, 1985) is the problem we get when knowledge bends to power:

> Reality in the nuclear age tends to become what people whose voices carry say it is. Competent technicians are available to shore up any side of any argument. A given point of view may be vulnerable to ridicule but not to being disproved by facts; these are obscured by unknowns and abstractions arising from the nature, the role, the destructive potential, and the reliability of nuclear weapons. (p. 41)

Is that how it is? I think most certainly yes, and not with nuclear issues only, for how we respond to matters of ultimate import circumscribes our thinking in general. It's worth noting, furthermore, that what Newhouse says is written by a journalist. The experts disagree with each other, but they won't be discrediting themselves (and their institutions, and their careers) by stating the larger predicament. So there it is: when it comes to the hard questions, smart people with impeccable credentials can certify any side of any issue. Where does that leave the rest of us? Is sensible knowledge now beyond us? Does reality depend on power's endorsement? Will wars be fought, as Lyotard suggests, over information?

Truth too near to power is very like light enduring the gravity of large bodies—both, in their passage, get bent from their course. Our situation in the Nuclear Age isn't so different from Winston Smith's in *1984*; he agrees, finally, that reality is what O'Brien and the Inner Party say it is. The distinction between ourselves and Smith is small, but in one particular, at least, we have a tool, and therefore a weapon, not available in Orwell's nightmare world. We still have poetry and fiction, the language of concrete perception, and the office of art isn't located in a government bunker but in the obligation to behold and witness, praise, denounce. Just here, it seems to me, the importance of poetry has never been greater. As the age of information spills over us, as ships of state drift and list in the nuclear night, the old anchor holds. A solidly imagined story, a fiercely felt poem, still tells us where and who we are, discovers the world and us in it, gives us a sanity the "competent technicians" don't lay claim to.

The integrity of art, and therefore its authority, is as ancient as pain and as trustable, and by way of example, here is a poem by Sharon Olds called "The Issues," which I quote entire:

> Just don't tell me about the issues.
> I can see the pale spider-belly head of the
> newborn who lies on the lawn, the web of
> veins at the surface of her scalp, her skin
> grey and gleaming, the clean line of the
> bayonet down the center of her chest.
> I see her mother's face, beaten and
> beaten into the shape of a plant,
> a cactus with grey spines and broad
> dark maroon blooms.
> I see her arm stretched out across her baby,
> wrist resting, heavily, still, across the
> tiny ribs.
>   Don't speak to me about
> politics. I've got eyes, man.

The strength of this brief poem is as old as primal cursing; and as current as the will to bear witness. Its authority comes from having taken in the horror it announces against. That the poem is political goes without saying, but its politics is the only kind that poetry can allow itself, the kind that responds to concrete images, and will not be taken in by ideology. Personal seeing is three times insisted upon, and opens into the deeper conflict between "politics" and "I've got eyes." The poem is datelined Rhodesia, 1978, a typical scene in post-colonial warfare, a local horror-show miniaturized and at the same time magnified by the larger U.S./S.U. struggle for control of Africa. It might be murder from any point of view, but it's also an incident that will *always* be justified and explained away if, no longer trusting our eyes, we listen to governments defining "the issues." Horror is always visual, and the gut instructs the heart. Here also the poet adds her animus to male dominion through the image of the battered woman and, by coming down hard on "man," suggests that this war like most is men's doing. The poem's central image, finally, is an "emblem of adversity," as Yeats or Seamus Heaney would call it, and behind it stands the traditional European figure of the *pietà*, for although the child is dead, the mother's condition isn't clear. She does not move, from beating, from paralysis of grief, but somehow I feel her death is yet to come. We are not, that is, granted a grain of relief. Were her eyes to open, as they might, we would find ourselves staring directly into a barrenness of pain so complete that, for this mother with dead child, language is no longer possible.

About this poem, furthermore, we understand that the poet must trust more than her eyes. She is looking at a photograph, one taken by a war-photographer (one of the deadlier modern professions), whose work can be, and usually is, exploited by any side of any conflict, but which, if simply *looked* at, if beheld with the political good sense that refuses to let politics intervene, gives good enough basis for judgment. Since nuclear politics fosters an endless array of local wars outside the U.S. and the S.U., the planet's torment comes to us mainly through forms of mediation, photography being only one form, but an especially useful one so long as we see through, as Sharon Olds does, the political glare. There has been, by the way, a remarkable increase lately in poetry that takes its impulse from photographs, documentary photos in particular. This suggests one solution to the link-up between private vision and global consciousness. It's a place to start, at least, and with clear images that inspire acts of witness and announcing against. Thereby we regain our independent right to political knowledge, seizing the issue apart from "the issues."

None of this will save the world. It won't be poetry that changes the nuclear order. But I want to stress that a poem like this makes something happen. It allows me to know what I fear, to understand (by standing under) the burden of my humanness. It also makes possible the essential decency of compassion, of suffering with—a symbolic action, to be sure, but one without which the spirit withers, the self shuts down. Finally this: by refusing my allotment of helplessness, I get myself back from the tyranny of the Bomb.

In his history of the Peloponnesian War, Thucydides several times begins his accounts of campaigns with this phrase: "At the time when the corn was beginning to ripen." Soon an army has "laid waste the land," and the scene begins to be familiar. In the time before trucks and planes, military units on the move could not carry sufficient supplies and therefore depended on pillage. The land they wasted and the food they stole were the soil and substance that local populations lived on, those millions of women and men and their children across the ages who would starve, or be killed outright, because they happened to be in the path of some king's dream. To live their small lives quietly, in ordinary sorrow, was denied them; politics intruded and they became as we are becoming today. The "issues" then weren't so different from the "issues" now, with the big powers calling, as usual, for final solutions. The cold-war world is where we are, unwilling residents on the nuclear grid. Meanwhile, the nuclear infrastructure proliferates. In increasing numbers, weapons are deployed at sea and in the air and underground and upon the starry heavens. The cross-fire spreads, won't stop, and, if it happens, a nuclear exchange will take out the earth. With this we live, trying not to cave in, doing what we can. I'm suggesting no cure, but only that poetry helps.

A Jew and Indians: A Discarded Excerpt from a Work Far from Done

Leslie Epstein

The inside of the Jew's slop shop always looked like the scene of a lynching party. Gabardines, full suits, silk and satinet frock coats hung from long poles in the air. Some fifteen months after the water wagons had begun to arrive at Milk River, Rowe, the first of the drivers, pushed his way past this clothing, through calicos, flannels and ginghams, and opened the door to the back room. There he paused, while the Jew himself waved his arms and the half-dozen pupils, little Indians, wearing rolled up bankers' pants and outsized cashmere vests, recited together:

> John Anderson my jo, John,
>> When we were first acquent,
> Your locks were like the raven,
>> Your bonnie brow was brent . . .

Rowe interrupted the high-pitched chorus: "Doctor Pinto. Mr. Townsend sent me."

Pinto turned about. Here was the face, the modest moustache and puckered lips, with which you are now quite familiar. Drooping, dark, liquid-filled eyes. A chin with a dimple. No need to dwell on the nose. "Frank Townsend?"

"He wants you at the mine. It's urgent. I've a buggy outside."

"But how can I go? We are having lessons. I cannot leave the children."

The speaker of these words felt a tug at the loose cloth of his checkered trousers. There stood Little John, aged thirty months. He had a large, round head, lolling sideways on a little neck, rather like an oversized daisy upon its narrow stem. His left arm was locked round the head of a short, squat creature, tiny-eyed, large-eared, more like a pig than— though family Canidae it doubtless was—a dog. The boy pulled once more on the pantsleg of Papa Pinto; then he turned and with some effort, tremblingly, raised his bony arm toward the distant hills, like a thin compass needle settling north. "Fa-fa-fa: dunder!" he said—or so, to the former Harvard College mathematician, the words, squeaks really, pennywhistle notes, must have sounded.

Next, the animal growled, lowering its neckless head, scratching the floorboard with a paw. Pinto crouched, listening—though whether to the toddler or the terrier, Rowe could not tell. Poor fellow! What could he think but that the three of them, with their growlings and gruntings, their peeping and piping, were having a conversation? Finally, the boy pointed again, up toward the mine: "Fa-dunder! Fa-dunder!" He shouted the phrase this time, piercingly. A crease, like that of a grown man's, appeared on his brow, so smooth, so clear, and a teardrop hung at the corner of his Mongolian eye.

"Fall down?" Pinto exclaimed. "Yes? Am I not correct?"

The boy, Little John, nodded, his head bounding now on his neck like a helium balloon on a string. The dog parted his lips in a horrible, tooth-filled grin. Proudly, Pinto patted his head, which, through some primitive reflex, caused the beast to blink. The Jew turned toward the white man: "He says, *Fall down!*"

"It's the Indians!" Rowe declared. "The workers! They're dropping! There's a sickness there! Come! You must come!"

"Yes! Of course! If there is sickness. But. But . . ."

Here Pinto, already moving toward the doorway, stopped and surveyed the makeshift schoolroom. Half the pupils were racing about the floor, rolling end over end under the table. The rest were playing a game: two, in their striped pants, stood over a bare-bottomed third, striking him with their notebooks, poking him with their sharp pencil points. "Dig! Dig!" they shouted. "Dumb Indian dig gold."

Suddenly there was a whistle, high and shrill, like that made by a boatswain's pipe: Little John, open-mouthed, was speaking. Immediately, the students dashed to their seats and fell silent. The Indian boy, on his twig-like legs, led the adults from the room.

Within the hour, Pinto stood at the base of the foothills, near the amalgamation ditches. He had a plug of cotton in each ear, to guard against the roar of the stamp machines, and a wisp of the same fluff hung from one nostril, which, owing to the tremendous percussion, had started to bleed. A number of Modocs were lined up before him. "Ha! Ha! Look, Mister Townsend: It is a dentist you need!" Quickly he reached up, to his patient's slack jaw, and plucked a molar from the black-spotted gum. The Indian, with the few teeth he had left, widely

100

grinned. Pinto knew the next man in line: Steamboat Frank, his body still gleaming with sweat from his shift underground. He stepped forward, spitting into the cup of his hand. Then he smilingly handed over three teeth, the roots red with blood. His gums, like those of the man before him, were soft, spongy, dark.

Townsend, with his dark hair still cut in bangs, gripped his friend's arm. "What do you make of it, Adolph? It's the same with the rest. You see?" He glanced toward the next man, older than his companions, who stood swaying a little, shifting his weight from one bare foot to the other. Slow-luck, his name was. Immediately he opened his mouth: no teeth in the purple gums.

Pinto pondered a bit. "Perhaps scurvy?" he said.

"Oh, of course I thought of that. From the first instance. But it's not possible: I've arranged with Bothworth for lemons. For limes. The peel is ground into their diet. I've stood over the bowls myself to make sure it goes down. Something has got them, but not the scurvy. It will ruin us!"

Just then, a cry—it was the familiar *Fa-dund! Fa-dunder!* rose from the edge of the nearest amalgamation trench, where a large brown horse had been slowly trodding back and forth, pulling a weighted stone over the tailings. The boy was there, holding both arms over the low wooden railing, almost clutching the mare. That beast had come to a halt. Pinto saw that its hide was covered with sores and that its head drooped so low the hairy muzzle almost grazed the crushed stone. For a moment it stood there, its muscles rippling, quivering, as if to drive off invisible bunches of flies. Then the hindquarters collapsed and the old nag fell lifeless in the ditch. At once the child burst into tears: you could see them, they came gushing downward; but there was no sound except for a high, almost inaudible peeping, as might come from a bat, or a bird.

One thin leg of the mare kicked still: before that movement had ceased a team of Modocs threw a hook and rope under the leather halter and began to drag the carcass first from the trench, then over the open ground toward a deep pit which, fearful to relate, was half filled with the bones and flesh of other horses, all in a heap. Meanwhile a second mare, this one a pony, still with its winter coat, had been led to the trench; it strained forward, dragging the weight behind. All this was done because the stamps, the retorts, were in those early days unable to capture much more than half the gold from the ore. The idea, an old one, primitive really, was to walk the horses back and forth across the tailings, a pulp of pebbles and quicksilver, then wash the residue off the fresh amalgam. The animals died one by one.

"Heavens!" Adolph Pinto cried, while his charge, Little John, waved his stick-arms at the latest steed, the plodding pony: "I thought it was the Indians who were dropping!"

"They are," Townsend replied. "Do you imagine I would call you here to examine their teeth? They don't chew the ore. Look at that fellow. Do you see how he sways?"

Impossible not to: the old Indian, the toothless Slow-luck, seemed to be doing a dance, lifting first one foot, then the other—but slowly, with effort, as if he were standing in molasses or mud.

"Now. Now. He will go down."

And go down he did—first to his knees, then on all fours. He crawled forward, halted; then he struggled to his feet, staggering, reeling.

"Too much to drink?" Pinto asked.

"Nothing to drink! He is as sober as you or I. But he'll fall again. Within the hour. Each time it becomes harder to rise. Already I've four strong men crawling like babes."

"I have a thought: Have these men also lost their teeth?"

"Yes. Every one: Just as this fellow has."

"Hmmm. Hmmm," went Pinto, a sound which, because of the cotton wadding, was even more nasal than usual. "The horses are also falling."

"No mystery in that: it's the mercury they absorb through their hooves."

"Do they, the poor beasts, also suffer the softness of gums?"

The answer was plain for both to see. At the smooth tracks in the soil, where the mare had been dragged between amalgamation trench and open pit, the mongrel was playing—alternately poking its snout, the color of pink india rubber, into the dirt, then throwing chunks of bone, of ivory, into the air: not human teeth, but the long, curved yellow incisors of a horse.

"Mister Townsend! You have an excellent medical training. Identical symptoms; ergo, the identical disease."

"You are mistaken. This can't be the mercury. I've been over it again and again. You saw how we manage: with ropes, with hooks, with probes from outside. No one is in contact with the element."

"But the horses. Here is a notion: What if the Indians, an untutored people, have eaten the meat, the flesh, of the dead beasts?"

"Impossible. They hardly eat meat in the first place—and only when they've killed the animal themselves."

"The water, then: the water in the ditches, the water you use to wash off the quartz."

"A closed system, Adolph. The reservoir empties into the boiler chambers, then down to the stamps; from the strainers it enters the ditches. Not a drop is used for drinking."

"And," Pinto persisted, no longer aware that he was—as he had been all along—shouting his words, "from here? From the ditch?"

"Pumped back, what's left of it," Townsend said, turning, pointing. Beyond the refinery, above the hoisting works and the flywheel and the steam machines, above even the crest of the mount, the air was shimmering, full of beams of light. Pinto knew that the natural gulch between the mine property and the hill behind had been transformed into a fair-sized lake. Squinting, he could almost see the molecules of water, hydrogen mostly, and oxygen, leaping upward, turning themselves into atoms of gas. Principle of Evaporation! If the liquid were not continually replaced, the whole of the reservoir would bound into the high, blue sky. Even at that moment, upon the western flatlands, one wagon of the water relay was stirring a column of dust. And suddenly, in a dizzying flash, as if some hidden foe had cuffed him smartly on the head, Adolph Pinto solved the puzzle. The vista of Milk River, from which that distant water wagon was now plying, stretched outward, in its frothy, shallow reaches across the young man's eyes: What he remembered, the very stink was in his nostrils, were the fish drying upon the rooftops, and the sight of the braves, their chopped-off hair, their potbellies, shooting arrow after arrow into the stream.

Once more Pinto craned his head backward, shielding his eyes against the darting light. On the hilltop he made out three ragged silhouettes. Men with bows. With spears. Fisherman! Fishing! In his excitement, the cotton flew from his nose. He gripped his friend's arm, pulling upon it like a bellrope. "*Ja! Merkur!* It *is* the quicksilver! The wagons are capturing the bullhead fish! Along with the river water. They live in the lake! In the mercury they multiply. The mercury from the ditches! There is no doubt this is the case! Look! Three Indianers! Red folk! They shoot their arrows! Throw their spears! It is they who eat the trout!"

Which is why, when the belt of the flywheel snapped and Adolph Pinto put his head out the window—that would be wintertime, 1856, yes, with a full moon shining—he could make out the familiar smell of the dried-out, leathery fish. These came, for the most part, from the mud-hut village, though of late some of the men had taken to riding out to Milk River and bringing the catch back to Modoc Town, where on hot days the spine-covered monsters would sizzle on the tin roofs like so many smelt in a skillet. By that winter more than half the tribe had moved to the shantytown, and each week still more arrived. Soon the only ones left at the ancient site, long venerated, prehistorical, would be old men, old women: practically ancestors themselves.

Why this migration? For that matter, why even a single Modoc at the Neptune? Fair question. Travel south, the length of the state, and peer into the candlelight of the mines: You'd see every sort of white man—Cornishmen, Welshmen, a German, a Swede, a Turk and even a handful of Celestials on occasion; but never an Indian from any tribe. It was rare enough to find one of that race aboveground, scrabbling through whatever mud flats, sandbars, the immigrants had abandoned. But Frank Townsend would have none of the men, the Yrekans, who had enjoyed the joke at Sazerak Saloon. The exception was Two-Toes Tom. He was put to work tending the fires in the charcoal fields. The rest of the town, after staking fresh claims, sinking their shafts throughout the foothills, scooping tons of earth from coyote holes, ended up in the long lines before the Neptune hiring shed. The owner was there, his arms folded on his chest. He moved his head a half-inch left, or right, a barely perceptible motion. Ben Piper saw it, however, and sent this townsman or that one—no chance that his features had been forgotten—trudging back to his porch-front, his saloon.

There were, of course, miners enough to take their place. They descended by the hundreds upon the Neptune from any site—Port Wine and Brandy City, Monte Cristo and, in Oregon, Yellowjacket, Olex, Cornucopia—where the lode was pinching out, the color fading in the pan. No ghost town Yreka! Even so, this flesh-and-blood population remained underground no more than a year. The problem was the heat, which at the lower levels, then nearing 400 feet, never dropped below 100 degrees Fahrenheit. Townsend dug a second shaft, parallel to the first, to which it was connected by drifts at every level. The fresh air flowed down the new ventilation shaft, crossed, and rose through the old one. But at 600 feet steam began to form at the mouth of the mine, especially in the evenings: the trapped air, hot and stale, was rising to meet the cool air of the surface. At 660, the white plume hung over the top of the shaft nighttime and daytime, in sunlight or shade. It was like the breath of a beast, the flame of a dragon which seared the men in its belly and expelled them pale and retching, upon the open ground.

Townsend tried another solution: an enormous sail, bulging white linen, which caught the high breeze and funneled it downward with more force than a modern compressor directly into the opening of the ventilation shaft. This allowed the miners to descend an additional 130 feet, and sent the ghost-like wraith of mist into motion, turning counterclockwise on its axis, like a perpetual top. That was the limit. The pick handles grew too hot to handle without stiff, thick gloves. No one could work more than twenty minutes out of the hour. Odd pockets of water shot through the puncture holes at temperatures up to 170 degrees. One day, before the Neptune had reached the 800 level, two men died on the job – one underground, at the furthermost stope, and the second, his skin white, dry, blistered, while in the cage, hurtling toward the surface. The survivors, panting at ground level, claimed the deep earth had never cooled from the volcanic period and that soon they would break through to molten rock. At this Townsend laughed, jollying the men, patting them on the back, tugging at the lank, matted hair of their heads. "Eight hundred feet? The planet across is eight thousand miles! The molten rock, supposing there is any at all, is at the very center."

A miner shook off his hand. "Do you think, then, to go that far?"

The crew raised their heads, to catch their employer's reply: "If the gold does."

Below, the five-stamp battery was at work, reducing the ore pile. But no further quartz was brought from the vein. At dusk the next shift gathered at the hoisting works. Not a man would step through the steam plume, onto the suspended cage. That was when Townsend, peering through the oncoming gloom, noticed a dark shape against the red glow of the charcoal fields. It was Two-Toes Tom, moving barefooted, like a fakir of India, over the embers, the smoldering coals.

Three days later, with the main shaft abandoned – "She's deep enough," said the idle miners, meaning they'd not risk descending again – the water wagon set out for Milk River, well before dawn. They had to leave early because the mule, Neptune, laden with gimcracks, with calicos, tin forks, cardboard shoes, could move no faster than a strolling man. As it was, the relay did not draw near the Modoc village until the sun had nearly set and a west wind, full of gusts of stinging sand, had sprung up behind them. Of a sudden, coming through the rock field, they saw the wide, cream-colored stream, with the dark row of huts – the twigs and tule looking like clumps of matted hair – on the far side. Three dogs were playing at the water's edge, chasing a mis-shapen ball, crudely stitched from horsehide. From the way they tore at it, snapping, jaws agape, throats bulging, it was clear they were howling; but the steady wind carried the din, along with the smoke of numerous fires, and the fumes of the decaying fish – off to the east.

The team turned about, backing down the hard-packed ruts, into the white, foaming water. They lowered their heads to drink. The riders – Rowe in front, Piper and Townsend and the Indian, Two-Toes Tom, wedged in the seat behind him—jumped down and began to wade across. Pinto, perched on top, with Little John twisting in his arms, paused to look about. Under the darkening sky the river curved off north and south, like a boulevard lined with lamps. Ahead, the village seemed deserted. There were no men fishing on the banks, no washerwomen: even the dogs, save now for one mustard-colored mongrel, worrying still his makeshift ball, had disappeared. Downstream, something, a flash of light, caught Adolph's eye. The infant saw it too, pointing, straining toward the glowing yellow patch that seemed to hover in midair, a few feet above the rush of the stream. "Hddbb, hddbb," he cried, in a language that lacked any vowels.

"Honeybee?" his foster father replied. "Genus *Apis?*"

"Hdyby!" the one-year-old repeated, thrusting the whole of his brown body away from the merchant, in the direction of the golden swarm.

Adolph peered through the dimming light. Above the bright, bobbing beams he could make out a stand of poplar—thin, leafless cottonwoods, growing out of the river. But this was not possible! Those trees had not been there before. Could they have sprung up in fifteen months? He looked again. Not poplars! People! Indians! Four of them, five of them! Standing upon the water! And the light: that was not a honeybee hive, but human hair. Out loud, the Austro-Hungarian exclaimed, "Mister Cole!"

That was the way the wind was blowing. The former Harvard man, waist deep in Milk River, threw up his hand in welcome. Pinto needed both of his own to grip the squirming child. But he managed to clamber down to the hoop of iron on the wheelrim, and from there into the stream. The mule, her head down, lips in the water, would not budge, for all his prodding. "Np! Np!" said Little John: The beast, celebrated for stubbornness, followed docilely behind.

In moments they came to mid-river. There, the mystery was solved. The Modocs—some, Shacknasty Jim and Jack, Humpy Joe, Adolph recognized; the others, Big Ike, One-Eye Mose, he'd come to know soon enough—were standing ankle-deep on a sandbar. The wind-whipped wavelets splashed against their muddy calves. They were naked except for loincloths, each made from the same bolt of gingham, a gay check, red-and-white squares, that Pinto had brought to the village the year before. These fluttered about the goose-pimpled flesh of their thighs. How the knees of the old men knocked! They hugged their own sagging breasts; they hugged, with their thin arms, each other. Their teeth chattered and their lips were blue, as if covered with war paint. The feathers in their hair rose, then dipped, in the breeze.

106

"Greetings, Matt Cole," Pinto, splashing near, began. But the minister put a finger to his lips, also discolored, and motioned for silence. He was drenched through. The flecks of spray, like cotton, clung to the cloth of his shoulders, to his curls, his sharp chin. Pinto halted. The boy, hardly more than an infant, clung round his neck, far from the cold current. Neptune stood motionless, the water lapping at the white tufts of her belly. They all looked upward, toward the little group of savages, who themselves turned toward the flat-headed Shacknasty Jim. That Modoc gazed down, at the dust cloud his foot was churning beneath the water. With difficulty he started to speak:

"Our Fadder—"

He paused. He screwed his eyes up in thought. He chewed upon the blue slab of his lip. "Our Fadder—" he said once again.

Big Ike, his brow also flattened, made a whistling sound when he spoke: "Dumb Indian! Got a empty head! Ike got to stand in the cold!"

Humpy Joe glanced slyly at the newcomers. "Maybe Jew-feller got a hot coffee!"

"Hot coffee good!" said One-Eye Mose.

Humpy Joe rubbed his belly. "Yum! Yum!"

At that, Shacknasty Jim looked up. His face was beaming, rosy, as if he had just swallowed that steaming brew. "Our Fadder in de heaven! Hello your name!"

Immediately his brother straightened, throwing back his bony shoulders. "The dumb king come!" he shouted. "The well be down in earth like in a oven!"

One-Eye Mose: "Give us bread!"

Big Ike grinned, revealing the gap in his teeth: "And give us four hours of pisses against those who piss on us!"

Everyone smiled, nodded, and turned once more to Shacknasty Jim. That Indian stared unblinking into the milky current, as if some fish, swimming by, might whisper the hidden message. For all the chill of the winds, the icy waters, the sweat of effort stood on his brow. A full moment went by. No one spoke. The level light of the sun fell full upon them, briefly flaring.

"And . . . ," said Shacknasty Jim. He started again, "And . . ."

Those below—the jackass, the child, the Jew—strained forward. Cole, ghost-pale, stood with one hand at his throat, in order, perhaps, to squeeze out the missing words. Were those tears running from his eyes? Or the river spray? His lips moved, forming the script.

"And lead us not," said Little John, through a jumble of consonants, burblings, pipings, "into temptation."

107

Jim understood him. He repeated the phrase word for word. His face beamed.

Little John never once took his eyes from Matt Cole, from the minister's lips. Then he spoke again, in his Chinaman's singsong.

This time Shacknasty Jack responded: "But deliver us from evil."

The process, the prattle of the boy, the men rejoining, repeated itself two more times. One-Eye Mose, in deep gutterals, spoke of the kingdom, of power, glory; while Big Ike, half whistling, half in a lisp, concluded with, "Forever. Amen."

For a moment the men stood grinning, shielding their eyes, squinting into the last of the sun's red rays. Then it grew perceptibly darker. Cole said, "Come. Down here."

The Modocs looked at each other. Jack put one foot deeper into the stream. "Cold!" he said.

But Big Ike plunged in. "Ain't gonna be no stinking Indian! Get washed! Get clean! Be a Christian man!" He splashed ahead, knee-deep, deeper, until the bright gingham floated like a spread tablecloth on the surface of the water. Still he towered over Cole. Suddenly he sank—he must have been kneeling— so that the river rushed under his chin. Cole cupped a handful of water; he poured it over the Indian's head. Whatever he said was drowned out by the rush of the remaining converts, who dashed, high-stepping, from the sandbar into the wide, bubbling stream. Over their bowed heads Cole poured the water, as white as milk, or as snow, or the festive feathers that each man had thrust into his coarse, cropped hair.

Pinto turned to the side, so as to address directly his non-German-speaking mule: "*Ja, das ist ein Baptismus.*"

Five Poems

Michael S. Harper

Presidential Quotes

Brown University

The job was up for grabs
until the students leaked
my candidacy—I withdrew.

The commute from Northfield
to the airport is easy;
a cornfield or two, then the strip.

The corporation's long table
is full of portraits of fundraising—
some of it in Baptist rhetoric:

We Shall Overcome Some Day

In the old days there were quotas
on Jews; your task was to become one—
show the world how dorm became administration.

To rest you soak in the pond;
though the waters are black in Connecticut
you are just an hour away from Power Street.
This isn't Narragansett Electric talking . . .

Security, on campus, are a cut away
from the military; the majority want to carry
guns, heel the protesters, cut loose on frats.

Chairs: a way of funding the Alumni's
patrons for distinction; ROTC set us back
a few decades; some redcaps refused to carry bags.

The King and Queen traveled in helicopters;
the security dogs came in for a sniff
of the manuscripts, no Coke bottles allowed
in the stacks, one click of the cameras
in the desert afloat in oil tankers,
the Defense Industry's handicraft:

We Shall Overcome Some Day

The Third World Center wants new quarters;
tired of theater, the musicians on incense
too sacred to play; coalitions adrift
in quotas, game plans, a trip to the press.

At the Lincoln exhibit the old man
straddles the fence of equal pay
for equal work; the library goes
to astroturf, increased quickness,
permanent injury: unions come and go:

We Shall Overcome Some Day

Affirmative Action: the women have it;
Defense Contracts: small meat for this corridor;
Scholarship/Aid: benefits to keep busy;
Management: a snuff of the white and she's gone.

110

The Deer

Election Day, 1984

He hangs on hind leg
in the garage;
already dead on his forelegs
he still runs the quartermile
into the neighbor's yard,
then drops in a steaming bundle—
he that has shot him
has done it illegally—
when gutted, the smell
drives the dogs into frenzy
though they wait for the meat,
fillets, the scent of the hide.

At Irving township the voters
come in for pencils, dry folds
of the ballot, the registration
form is several throngs away—
the mileage of imagery focused
on Halloween leftover candy,
a can of salted nuts, the field
across the road the best pheasant
country in a hundred miles.

He wouldn't've budged from the morning
news, but barefoot he nudged against
the rearend of his wife, home from school
this morning, and so he looks out
the picture window, newly replaced,
that needs sheetrock and paint
at the edges, and spots the deer;

the orange duds, the bent barrel
of the weekend, the mint malt scotch,
disappearing through the sight
of the sited deer, hit just behind

111

the shoulder, should've dropped
at the water's edge and bled
on the sandy beach for the kids
and dogs to smell after school;

but it ran on internecine instinct
like a poached egg on the toast
of a neighbor's untended grass.

In the high-noon brightness
the radio sings a taped message
of the candidates, a day for opera;
the deer is costumed into sausage
and steak—the boy next door
registers, ballots for the first time—
he could pass for a Latin American;
he will sign a Chippewa name
to the hart slung in the rafters.

Study Windows

The two Germans,
both in their seventies,
were Americans
only by birth;
for $2.50/hour
they put up
a fourteen-foot-
square study,
oak paneling,
four windows
3' square
to see the sun,
feel the lake,
touch the trees.

These men said
"they were worthless,"
had lost their zing
in their fifties,
chased women only
in springtime,
forgot the chase
of the bottle
save for Christmas.

The older one died
on the ladder
of another job,
laughing to putterings
of his heart muscle,
which gave out
on too much benzine,
bright colorations

of cured wood,
the handle of the womb
he touched as a boy,
as a man learned to wash
with the schnapps of semen
he said his father
brought from the old country.

You code your life
with the ability to work,
work at that
even while fishing;
only on the hunt
do you lie down,
the red gear
the antlers of the view
a square window.

Smooth ice, a dusting
of snow; for this world
tracks, the ruddered imprint,
the hammering of nails
so one can see.

Archives

Photos and clippings fade;
no one can find a real signature
of Rube Foster, who put together
the Negro Leagues; efforts
at why Josh Gibson died at thirty-
five are even vaguer,
his sleek strong body in the waves
of San Juan the vintage year:
1934. Later, 72 home runs,
the only ball over the third tier
at Yankee Stadium
for the games on off-days.

No flicks of Gibson as a Globe-
trotter, his golden gloves
astride the mound captured,
for real, with Curt Flood,
eating steaks on a grill,
in a parking lot in spring
training. Reggie is a mask,
astride a roadster, a paltry
lid on a rainday with Vida Blue.

Frank Robinson's loaded automatic
put him under arrest; the flick
of his headrag, a white mop,
only shown in Cincinnati,
eating Satchel's 45-lb. catfish,
chasing "Willmont" Liquors, Inc.
as endorsements in Brooklyn.

The clippings of the rest
of Negro America are full of glee;
no ounce of bitterness,
except for Jackie, who hit
better than they thought,
and was fast, stealing home
in public, voting Republican,
the whole Civil War
on his back and pigeon-toes.

On PBS the documentaries,
one trailer sideshow,
a whole hall of oral history
in transcriptions
of black and white.

Trujillo, who paid the best,
threatened execution if you lost;
the black World Series in Comiskey
full of chicken, zoot suits,
trainfare from everywhere
but endorsements, turnstyles.

"Let's play two."

Heat

Brown University, 1985

The gold key hangs around the neck;
he that runs the place, the president,
is haggard, fundraising is over
for, perhaps, a week,
the hell-raisers are packing up
from their books, parties,
protests, and the security dogs
have left their scents
to a paltry helicopter,
and no men at the turrets.

At cap & gown concerts
the game trumpeter
hastens through his repertoire:
fundraising for scholarships
for blacks; his own tunes
go off in signatures
to Grammy-seekers,
not all of them white.

Honorands joke and sweat
to Kansas Latin,
citations in the sun,
a few thoroughbreds,
emeriti profs,
an ageless alumni
carrying their banners
downhill to the First
Baptist Church in America:
Providence, God's country

The miracle of the term
is your running off the frats
and the police
from your frontyard:
peddling on your bike,
reading captions,
the sports foundation
works its way through archives;
your bones ache with compromise,
internal invectives
of the balancing act
at the wheel of fortune,
which isn't a Connecticut
swim in the pond
whose black surface
are the faces you learn to love,
while you watch your own
going soft on pressure,
hard on headlines, amulets,
a whole host of deeds unsung.

Turn the switch to live.

for Howard Swearer

Interview with
Michael S. Harper

David Lloyd

Recorded at Brown University, July 7, 1984

TQ: I want to begin by asking a few questions which are quite general and concern all of your work. The first is about the role history plays in your poetry.

HARPER: I think the important thing about Americans is that they're not very good historians. And Americans are really bad historians when it comes to moral ideas because they can't keep them in their heads very long. They're very topical people, and this is not to say that some of them are not sincere. But on the issue of black Americans in particular, the continuity of moral ideas gets thrown to the wind almost at every turn. Williams was the one who said that "History for us begins with murder and enslavery and not with discovery." I read Williams when I was in college many years ago, including *In the American Grain*, so one of the things you ought to realize is that my vantage point on American letters is a bit askew because the dualism I bring to it is one, I think, any ethnic who is fairly conscious brings to a reading of mainstream America, as opposed to a reading of what one inherits as a result of what one is born into.

TQ: Many of your poems, especially those in *Nightmare Begins Responsibility*, address or are connected to writers like Paul Laurence Dunbar, Robert Hayden and Sterling Brown, who have not yet received their due from mainstream American critics. At the same time you've got a lot of black American heroes like Jackie Robinson or Willie Mays. Are you rewriting American history in some way?

HARPER: I'm certainly giving my version of the history. I mean I share that vision with a lot of other people. But we're dealing with some people in the popular theater who are never seen as material for real literary recovery.

TQ: Even John Coltrane, the subject of your first book, is in that category.

HARPER: That's right. There is a tendency in this country towards topicality but not towards continuity. At the simplest level there are just people whom I have a perspective on and who mean a great deal to me. I'd like to remind readers about what their exploits were, because it's not so much that the exploits were unseen but that the context wasn't understood. There are too many Americans who want to forget the context out of which these people came. Now for example last night there was a television program on Jesse Owens and they had this aside where he talked about Mack Robinson, who was a sprinter and placed second in the 200-meter race in the Olympic games in Berlin. He was Jackie Robinson's older brother and ended up working in the sewers of Pasadena in California. Well, I was a student teacher at Pasadena City College and there were many people who knew who Jackie Robinson was. But Pasadena hadn't changed in twenty-five years. I did my student teaching there and was the first black person who had ever done student teaching at Pasadena City College. There was a big to-do about it, so one has to look at the reason why, in these various avenues of enterprise, why one has to go through this over and over again and why lessons have to be continually learned. I decided that I would not just be mad but would write this down and try as best I could to give some perspective to it, because there are some people who didn't even live through it. My own children are tremendously handicapped because in order for me to fill in the voids that I think are in their lives educationally I would have to preach to them constantly. It's almost like they can't be allowed their own lives because the amnesia level of this country is so high. You can't be a participant in the culture because you're spending so much time qualifying how the culture is presented, because the culture spends so much time reinforcing its own values, by a kind of forgetfulness leaving out the things which would frame these values.

We can talk about this in poetic terms. I'm really concerned about the nurturing and nourishment of my own ear and my own vision, and when you're in an isolated position as I am in large part—not as much as others, but certainly I'm isolated—you have to be reminded constantly that what you're doing is worthwhile. The only way you get that kind of solidarity oftentimes is a kind of interior work. It's not necessarily from going out and recruiting students because, first of all, students are not my equals, but even more than that, even among my contemporaries, an individual vision, a solitary coming to terms with one's Americanness is just an American problem. I mean that's an American problem for everybody. Even when you supposedly "make it." In fact "making it" has its own problems. All I have to do is look to Melville or any of a number of other writers to realize that the cost is enormously high, which brings us to the real reason history is important. The real reason why history is important is because life is tragic, and American life is particularly tragic because so many possibilities exist and there's been so much waste.

TQ: This brings me to something I was thinking about when you were talking about history earlier. While your poetry isn't propagandistic, there's a definite set of values and beliefs presented that one can put together and describe as "political material." I wonder to what extent you would define yourself as a political poet, a poet who is partly writing to remind Americans of historical context, the real historical context, but also writing to change a certain audience.

HARPER: I wouldn't characterize my work under a label. But I would certainly say my work has concerned politics, and has concerned *polity*. If I were to speak about purpose, and it's dangerous to do that, I would say that there are two or three things I'm trying to do: I'd like to be as eloquent as I can be because the language is so important to me. Certainly to live in America and to be awake means by definition to attend oneself and one's sensibilities to change. At one level or another that ends up being political. Now certainly I'm not a propagandist. But I think anybody who's a fairly close reader would figure out what my beliefs are, what my points of view are on various things, and I think that a good writer, and particularly a good writer in the American context, has to deal with the political at one level or another. The way the political is dealt with has to do not only with technique but with sensibility and with what you are able to master.

TQ: Could you define "sensibility" in relation to politics?

HARPER: I'll just take two or three examples. From my point of view *Invisible Man* is an extremely politically sophisticated novel. But Ellison would always insist that his novel is an American novel. Now I think I understand what he means. I also know that he doesn't want to be pigeon-holed, he doesn't want to be put off in some kind of segregated bunker. So the struggle to address a wider audience than just one's own ethnic audience is finally a question of eloquence. In my own case, I certainly would like to have as large an audience as I can, but at the same time I'm not naive enough to think that a large audience is going to be anything like what we consider popular. Finally I just have to live with the fact that I'm in a rather obscure art; my own vantage point isolates me even more, and I have a lot of problems with my own contemporaries, not all of them black, having to do with my position on a number of issues. I'm bothered by the fashionability of the way people adapt themselves to trends. Americans are very good at that. They're very good chameleons, and they're trying to figure out the market. I've spent a lot of time not reacting to whatever the market demanded, including having fairly lucrative things offered to me which I didn't want to do. The fact is that I'm not in the business where I do certain things because there's money to be made. I don't think it's only about my integrity, although that's part of it. In fact, I probably couldn't do them well because I wouldn't be able to put my heart into it.

TQ: What kind of things do you mean?

HARPER: When you're asked to write a biography, or when you're asked to write a novel. I was asked to write a biography of Coltrane, for example. I wrote the poem "Dear John, Dear Coltrane," the title poem of my first book, before he died. I've been interviewed numerous times by all kinds of people who wanted to get some insight into Coltrane's private life, so that was an issue. Apart from the fact that I didn't know very much about his private life, I didn't think it was anybody's business. The reason for me writing the poem, retrospectively, was very different from what it was people thought the poem was about. Now, they were moved by it, but they weren't able to look at writing techniques and really talk about them as ways of eliciting response. I ended up in defense making long lectures, trying to point out to people that this has been a tradition certainly among black Americans for many years now. The poem doesn't come in a vacuum, and the techniques were chosen for a reason, and there were earlier examples which made my job easier.

I had been listening to music all my life and therefore could have written a poem in a different time frame about any one of the other heroes, including Louis Armstrong. You notice Louis Armstrong figures very prominently in Ellison's novel. He's also one of the greatest innovators and maybe by analogy one could figure out something about what it is Louis Armstrong brought to playing the trumpet, which is a military instrument, and what it is Ralph Ellison did to the formulation of the American novel. I think that would be interesting to talk about. As it happens, Ellison's a trumpet player. So the chances are he knows more about trumpet playing than just the average novelist. Here's a person like me coming to graduate school, and the first article I read is an interview which Ralph Ellison gave for a journal published in Iowa. It shouldn't be lost on me, therefore, that maybe I would have the responsibility for trying to do in the poetic area what Ellison did in fiction. And I think that's one of the reasons why someone like Hayden was neglected. Hayden had obviously seen that analogy even before I had, because he was older than me. Although I didn't come to a real close scrutiny of Hayden's work until I was an adult, I certainly knew who he was. There's no way that a black American can read American poetry in an American anthology and skip over Hayden's "Middle Passage." It's too fundamental to his conception of the world in the same way that Sterling Brown's poem "Strong Men" is. Well, these were poems people knew about over the years. They were in anthologies even before the anthology scene became as overwhelming as it is now. I mean most people read poetry in anthologies.

As a matter of fact, I didn't read poetry that way. I grew up in a household where the poems of Langston Hughes were on the walls. Now some people might say, "Why is it you haven't dedicated poems to Langston Hughes?" And I think the answer is complex. First of all, Langston Hughes was not a literary model of mine. That doesn't mean I didn't appreciate him. But I can remember when a young woman said to me, "I guess you want to be a Langston Hughes." I was offended because I was the one who had pointed out to her in a literature class that W. H. Auden had come into Isherwood's class and was about to read. None of those people knew who Auden was. Here I am, the only black person in the class, knowing who Auden is. So that shows you a little about the aspiration of wanting to be a poet. I didn't even understand it then, but I was offended that she made no distinction between what I was trying to do and what my options were at the level of race. Now Langston Hughes was part of my family archive. I was not about to share his meaning, at the level of metaphor, with a fellow classmate who was making whimsical points. She couldn't recite any of Hughes's poems, and I could, and she didn't know Auden's poems either. Hughes was part of a long line of cultural connections, to Arthur Alfonso Schomburg, who was a family friend. To me Hughes and Auden were both poets; by definition, I wanted to understand them as artists.

TQ: It strikes me that what you say about the historical or cultural context of your work concerns a special relationship between you and your audience. In reading your work I've had to track down a lot of information to provide a context for John Brown or for Coltrane or for a lot of other references largely outside my experience or reading. So in a way you're educating readers who are serious enough to want that context and find out about Robert Hayden's poetry or Sterling Brown's poetry. I feel I want again to use the word "political" for this kind of author/reader relationship, but maybe that's wrong. Is it that you want to widen sympathies and educate your readers?

HARPER: I haven't written explicitly about my own politics. But I think that politics are explained in the sensibilities of individuals reacting to events. Now for example, I wrote a whole book on the Vietnam War, and I wasn't in the Vietnam War. My brother-in-law was in the Vietnam War, as were numerous others close to me, including some of my students. I came to have a visceral dislike for the war long before many other people did, in part because I had been connected with guys just my age or a little older who had fought in the Korean War. I graduated from high school in 1955, so I was watching people graduating high school and going right into the military and some of them getting killed. Although I haven't written about that explicitly, the attention I gave to the Vietnam War was set up by the Korean conflict, which was much closer to me. I never felt I was in jeopardy because by the time I graduated from high school the Korean War was settled.

This was one incident in a long series of incidents which one has to contextualize. For example, my father, during World War II, would have been drafted into the navy as a cook. When Gwendolyn Brooks writes a poem for Dorie Miller, a cook who wasn't trained to use an antiaircraft gun but who did manage to protect his fellow sailors, that resonates for me in a particular way because she's talking about a man who was my father's contemporary. Although my father didn't have the experience, it could very well have been him. He was preselected out of the process of being a patriot, and this was enormously important to people who came through World War II. "Baseball history: Jackie Robinson, first Negro to crack organized baseball, signs a Montreal contract" is the caption in a New York newspaper, under a photograph of Robinson in a lieutenant's uniform, October 1945. Those were the same people who brought verve and energy to watching Jackie Robinson break into the major leagues. I was living in Brooklyn when Jackie broke in. And you just can't imagine . . . if you don't understand the context, you really can't interpret that event. I left the context out of the poem ["Blackjack"], which is to say I did not talk about the attitudes and insights Jackie Robinson's contemporaries had for the pain of being in this duplicitous situation: wanting to defend your country but at the same time having no real option to do it in any but a segregated way. That particular attitude, having been two or three hundred years old, probably got internalized into a part of my approach to things generally. I've been accused of being very up-front, even warlike. That kind of "straight, no-chaser" approach was ingrained in me as a kid because the contradictions between what people said and people did was so enormous that you literally could not afford to live in this world and be deluded.

That's Ellison's premise. His premise is that the hero must go from ignorance to knowledge, but the kind of ignorance that the normal hero has in a context like this would destroy him, unless his ignorance, raised to a kind of mythic level, becomes something which turns back on the society from which he came. I just think it's extraordinary, the way Ellison orchestrated this. That would never be lost on me, as someone who has a narrative drive. I would not solve my problems in the same way he did, but I would be aware that there are multiple ways to tell a narrative. One of the ways I've told a narrative is to put a reader to work, and it doesn't really matter who the reader is. That's not the business about being obscure at all. But in order to get to important questions having to do with human existence, the reader has to be working well. Experience is not enough. Experience is great, but it's not enough. You have to have some resonance about what it means. You take some twenty-one-year-old kid, just come out of Vietnam, and you give him *The Iliad* to read, or *The Red Badge of Courage*. What that does is change his perspective on his experience, if he's willing to do the work.

So what do you have in the Vietnam War? You have a whole lot of people who were disillusioned and misunderstood, who didn't understand why they were being treated in the way they were. Whether they were for or against the war doesn't really matter. They fought an uncomfortable and untimely war, and they weren't treated as heroes. And they did lose. It takes maybe two decades for people to get to the point where they can even look at what happened. Then a few documentaries let you see events and your place in them from a very different perspective than the one you could have when you were eighteen or nineteen years old.

So we get to this whole business about retrospective—I mean this is the artist's ballpark, retrospective. It was Yeats who said, "Memories are old identities." What you have to do is figure out a way to keep the analogies which are most closely affiliated to you, experientially, in mind, but at the same time be able to extrapolate, to put those analogies experientially into other areas, which are study areas. As a friend of mine said to me a long time ago, "Anytime you want to get into a deep exploration of self you should change the gender." I thought to myself, that's interesting, because when you change the gender you are forced to get outside the self in a complementary way. Someone like Hayden does this beautifully in poem after poem after poem. Hayden was interested in drama, scene and character. He wanted to be a playwright. And his poems are so successful because he has a sense of narrative and a way of selecting character traits so you can get a picture. That technique is something for which he's never gotten proper due.

TQ: Was Lowell an influence on your treatment of history and culture?

HARPER: He was and he wasn't. The problem with Lowell is that for my ear he's not a musical poet. He certainly is a courageous one.

TQ: When you were talking about retrospective and finding ways of using your immediate experience to involve the reader, I thought of your poem "Grandfather," where you write about a mob attacking your grandfather, and you refer to the film *The Birth of a Nation*. The poem requires a reader to understand what that film means in terms of the black experience and your grandfather's experience, drawing the reader in through both a public and private perspective. So in a sense the poem uses a piece of family history to explore the culture on a metaphoric level. That technique made me think of Lowell, yet you deal with private history and public history very differently in a sequence like *Ruth's Blues*, where you look clinically at illness. Let's get the poem. [Reads "Blue Ruth: America":]

> I am telling you this:
> the tubes in your nose,
> in the esophagus,
> in the stomach;
> the small balloon
> attached to its end
> is your bleeding gullet;
> yellow in the canned
> sunshine of gauze,

stitching, bedsores,
each tactoe cut
sewn back
is America:
I am telling you this:
history is your own heartbeat.

Is she an American victim?

HARPER: In many ways the answer to that question is in the title. Not only *History Is Your Own Heartbeat,* but the section *Ruth's Blues:* what is *Ruth's Blues* is the question, what is her blues? Her blues, at least on one level, is strictly physical. But the blues is an art form. And the art form has to do with real things a person incorporates into his or her own life to fortify and sustain the living. In other words, the blues says "Yes" to life no matter what it is. That doesn't necessarily mean you're going to survive it. But it means you're going to say yes to it. You're going to be up to the demands of living, even if you don't survive. That's one level. Now if you think about America—if you're an American Indian and you're looking backwards—it's a very painful kind of looking backwards. There's no way of ever getting over the fact that some people had at least an implicit plan affecting your destiny, and you had no control over it. After that initial onslaught of other peoples, you had a completely different configuration. If you were not in that first line of contact and had a chance to adjust when the scale was small, any individual effort that you might make would have been lost. James Wright does this beautifully in his poem about Little Crow, "A Centenary Ode Inscribed to Little Crow," the Sioux chief who got himself involved in an impossible situation where he knew he wasn't going to win. First of all he was a literate Sioux and had been to the cities of the East Coast and had seen the truth: We can't whip them. Now they're fighting the Civil War, but after they get through they're coming this way. They're only halfway across the country. They've got the Mississippi River, but they've got thousands of more miles to go and we're in the way. We're going to adjust and accommodate; if we stay and fight we're going to lose.

But he was a Chief, so when given a choice—the braves came to him and said, "Will you lead us in battle?"—he couldn't say no. The culture did not allow him to say no, given who he was. He was a princely person, and so he led those braves to defeat and died an ignominious death. Little Crow is one of Wright's heroes, and Wright talks about that history because people don't know who Little Crow was.

Right down the road from where I live in the summertime there's a Little Crow Sporting Goods store. Unless you're asking the local historian, if you ask some people about Little Crow, they don't know what you're talking about. I live right in the center of some of the terrain over which much bloody fighting took place less than a hundred years ago. At the same time most people don't even know what happened. I've been to the local libraries and they've got lots of information on it, but is that the way to learn history? For me, for a poet generally, I think that you can't afford to learn history that way. You learn history in the way in which these events are reflected in the lives of the people who live there and utter these place-names that are named for somebody else and call up other images. Yet they're not available to the people who are living in these places.

So you've got this inherent contradiction about the whole business of naming. Here I come, an outsider, and I start naming by just calling attention to the fact that you all should be a lot more careful about the way you talk about these things, because you're not that much removed from it. Maybe subliminally there's your nightmare level, and you knew there was confrontation that came about. It also tells you about the toughness of the people who did the settling, and it tells you about the scale of the war.

When I look at Yeats, say, writing in the sonnet form about "Leda and the Swan," and when he talks about, in the series of *Annunciations*, the melding or blending of seemingly disparate things, of love and war born out of a certain kind of struggle, my job becomes a lot easier because Yeats has already done it at a larger level. It doesn't take much to figure out that he's really talking about his own backyard. He *ain't* that interested in the Greeks, at one level. But he does have a cosmology, which helped him write fine poetry. The body of the cosmology isn't nearly as important as the writing of the poems. In fact, there's been a lot of disputation about the viability of the cosmology, but there hasn't been much argument about the quality of the poetry. That tells you something about one of the things Yeats said a long time ago: that man can embody knowledge, but he cannot know it.

These kinds of analogies I think apply to the contemporary person. There's so much material or information that you can use to get to the creative process. But finally the creative process is a very magical one and you don't know what you're going to put together to make the fabric we call the poem. So much of that involves conscious living and conscious selection.

Miz Rosa Rides the Bus

Angela Jackson

That day in December I sat down
by Miss Muffet of Montgomery.
I was myriad-weary. Feets swole
from sewing seams on a filthy fabric;
tired-sore a-pedalin' the rusty Singer;

dingy cotton thread jammed in the eye.
All lifelong I'd slide through century-reams
loathsome with tears. Dreaming my own
silk-self.

It was not like they all say. Miss Liberty Muffet
she didn't
jump at the sight of me.
Not exactly.
They hauled me
away—a thousand kicking legs pinned down.

The rest of me I tell you—a cloud.
Beautiful trouble on the dead December
horizon. Come to sit in judgment.

How many miles as the Jim Crow flies?
Over oceans and some. I rumbled.
They couldn't hold me down. Long.
No.

My feets were tired. My eyes were
sore. My heart was raw from hemming
dirty edges of Miss L. Muffet's garment.
I rode again.

A thousand bloody miles after the Crow flies
that day in December long remembered when I sat down
beside Miss Muffet of Montgomery.
I said—like the joke say—What's in the bowl, Thief?
I said—That's your curse.
I said—This my way.
She slipped her frock, disembarked,
settled in the suburbs, deaf, mute, lewd and blind.
The bowl she left behind. The empty bowl mine.
The spoiled dress.

Jim Crow dies and ravens come with crumbs.
They say—Eat and be satisfied.
I fast and pray and ride.

From *Tremont Stone*

Angela Jackson

I grew up in a neighborhood, a block of time frozen like dry ice from which a heat arises. A drugstore and mailbox stood on one corner. A paperstand on the other. A cluster of churches completed the block, while down the street men and a few women wandered in and out The Butterfly Inn. We peeked through the dim windows of that place during daylight and saw night, the only constellation a neon sign saying "Hamm's. The beer refreshing." Where the big brown bear splashed into a lake of blue (it must be) beer. Hamm's. One time Junior said the drunkman on the block was one of the "children of Hamm's." Mama had to smile, but told him don't be so smart.

Everyone had a place on Arbor Avenue. Mr. Rucker who was the drunkman, Uncle Blackstrap who was the junkman, Miss Rose who was Eddie's mother and no one's wife, Miss Wilson who was the head lady, my father who was the good man you better not mess with his kids, my mother who was the sun. And a host of women, men and children.

From the drugstore Mama bought medicine on time. Everything did not come in a package. And people knew how to open things, like their hearts and conversations with strangers.

Summer nights Mama and Miss Rose brought their kitchen chairs outside to circle the stoop. Passersby could eavesdrop on parental melodies, "bring me some ice-cold water," "run upstairs and get me my crochet bag," and "y'all get off that curb before one of the cars go out of control and come up on the curve on you." Passersby could eavesdrop and ease up on the tension of walking unfamiliar streets because our block sounded like home.

In the absence of elders we children would sing aggressively to the women walkersby who interrupted our double-dutch rope tricks, who broke into our Red Rover lines, who zigzagged through our Captain May I, who wore a certain style—tight skirt, skinny heels, and bracelets. Gold-hoop gypsy earrings. We'd sing disapprovingly, gleefully, to their posteriors which were roundly outlined by the skirts fitting like stretch marks. "Shake it. Don't break it. It took the good Lord a long time to make it," we'd croon to the women who were no-one-we-knew's mothers.

"Nine months, Baby," a lady would sass back at us. This was a traditional call and response. A childish repartee. Harmless and endearing. More than likely it was a memory from the hamlets and towns of the South, something learned and transplanted to the City by the Lake. Something carried from Mimosa, Letha, Alligator, Greenwood, Leland, Indianola, Meridian, Monroe, Pine Bluff, Little Rock, Birmingham, Tuskegee and Tougaloo. In cars loaded down with children, luggage and survivals, our parents with hard hands and dreamy eyes and mouths thick and heavy with country colloquialisms followed the rivers to the booming factories, yards and tenements in the North where the dwelling places buffeted back the huge wind that took off from the lake like a plane or a giant bird. The wind called the Hawk, who tore the skin off your bones and set the bones to knocking on the street corners while you waited for the bus or a dream to come by.

They settled in the rambling houses on two wide boulevards setting off a part of the South Side, a mile or so from the lake, on the edge of a university and the surrounding posh section inhabited by well-to-do whites. The Black section small and contained for fifty years or more was called Bronzeville. Bronzeville in its earliest days was the home of the Blacks who served the wealthier whites and the factories and yards of industry (especially when the unions struck and owners opened their doors to Blacks).

Trains then were the veins and arteries of the nation, not a free-floating circulatory system of the sky; and dapper men of color with quick, quiet tread skimmed the railed ropes to the heart of the country, which was this City by the Lake where the Hawk, who did not then have a name, blew and tore the skin off people and the hordes of farm beasts routed there for dying. The Hawk tore the bowelly stink off the cows and pigs and spread the odor over the Irish section, the Jewish section, the Black, and then the Central European sections. The traveling men who came with the trains made homes in Bronzeville. Places for quick loving, good food, fast women and shuffling cards. Out of those places came music that captured the mood and pulse of a people. My daddy told me about that music, while he hummed it under the kitchen sink as water ran down his arms and the stubborn pipes moved under his hard turnings.

My daddy was always fixing things in that house he bought from the widowed white woman who moved to Florida. All the houses on our street were obtained from fleeing whites who scrambled to escape the expansion of Bronzeville when the post-World War II farmers and laborers came from the too-unchanging South to the city they had heard about from cousins and kin who came down with stories of plenty and progress. But by then the houses of the European escapees gave off peculiar odors, mice, roaches and calls for repair. And my father was always answering those calls. The absentee landlords of the tenement that took up half the block turned scarce and the building began to die while the people in it thrived and multiplied.

In our house there always seemed to be a baby and a babysitter. I wonder if my mother found her own swollen stomach friendly? When she was round with Anne, Earnestine and Shirley climbed into her high, big bed and drew a big smile and button eyes in red ink across her belly. Mama mostly slept lightly, but not this time. They stroked so softly it was like being tickled. The baby was curved, full and content inside of her. When Mama woke and discovered the drawing she laughed and laughed, until she found it would not wash off so easily. Over a stretch-mark design it stayed a face for more than a week.

I thought that red mouth and those smile-closed eyes were friendly, hilarious. When Mama brought Anne home from the bright Catholic hospital because the colored hospital, ill-staffed and broken down, had served her bologna that stuck in her chest when she lay after having given birth to Earnestine and Mama said nothing should be born there until they cared enough to make it a decent place for human beings—when Mama lifted the soft green blanket from Anne's face, exposed, it seemed to me, was the same face my two sisters had written on the round, outer ceiling of the ancient birth cave. Everybody had a laugh, thinking Ernee and Shir had seen into our mother's womb and translated who and what was hidden in nutritious water. Translated before its time. Or, their wish, perception, of such a joyous face was drawn into Anne Perpetua's humors. Anne is the funny one. They molded her into the sister-person of their desire. They founded a friend.

I began in the morning. Katherine Pearl was born around midnight. Sometime around the midnight train going by. Before or after the train whistle blew, she coughed out her birth. Which came first, the whistle or the scream?

Anne Perpetua was born laughing. When the doctor slapped her bottom she looked like a sweet clown or a saint with egg on her face. And she giggled to be here. She was given to appropriate and inappropriate laughter.

Once Earnestine dropped Anne. Anne began to laugh. Sympathy and panic were on my face, stamped in Anne's eyes reflecting me. Anne began to cry. She learned her pain from other people. Just as I did.

Honeybabe said she was retarded. Honey said that I was retarded too. Honeybabe says we all retarded. She is the oldest girl, and disdain is built into hierarchy.

Sometime in my preadolescence the double-dutchers began to sing a new song about disposable babies born with no certain sex and brutal destinies. They sang and I sang with them a song that came from out of the air:

> Fudge, fudge, fudge, boom, boom, boom
> Call the judge, boom, boom, boom,
> Mama got a newborn baby
> Not a girl, boom, not a boy, boom
> Just an ordinary baby.
> Wrap it up in toilet paper
> Kick it down the elevator.
> First floor, Mrs. Carter.
> Second floor, Mrs. Carter . . .

On and on the baby flew, thrown away, sexless, a brown mistake.

This was near the time of the birth of the ice-babies. The weather grew colder after the summery seasons of our early dreaming in the city. Expressways cut out memories that ran through the place once known as Bronzeville until even that name was forgotten. Families knocked against each other in the tall housing units thrown up by the city like dams to hold the deluge of Blacks who swelled past the limits of the town inside the city reserved for the darkest children of the American Dream. The old Southern gestures mutated and the young men learned new walks that leaned against the Hawk. These young men dipped in their knees. Boys gritted their teeth at an earlier age. Much of the game went out of the flirt, and girls no older than me or my sisters raised their skirts, babies fell out with gritted teeth and tears of ice.

Packed together in the frozen compartments of the public-housing projects that soared into the cold reaches of the Hawk's nest, children came out like clear, separated cubes of ice—hard and harder. The row of tall buildings that speared the sky, sparing no blue space, now (as if under the influence of a comic god) threw people away as used, spare parts.

There was a dog named Calypso. A terrible albino Doberman pinscher with long white teeth. Calypso chewed through wire that caged him and chased children's legs that moved like fascinating pistons just out of reach of his sharp face. One day he licked my calf and the fear made me break the sound barrier. My scream must have excited Calypso, who pursued me with greater zest. He was happy and evil; if he caught a child he would eat it. He could not catch me.

If you think of cruelty, think of albino haunches, fleet movement and white fangs. Cruelty is a colorless dance. Malice is a certain kind of motion that chews through wire and chases you and chases. It is not to be explained, and so fascinating that you must look at it. Look at it from over your shoulder, from behind a scream of terror and self-sympathy.

From our father, Sam Grace, Littleson learned to beat wood rats with shovels, then flip the earth and fold them in, furry, fat and poisoned bodies. Littleson caught roaches and stuck toothpicks up their tails and held them over the front stove burner, watching them crispen and curl while he laughed and I was appalled.

For Littleson these small acts of sadism were practical. I agreed with the intent, but hated the style and the delight that Littleson took in the pest-penalties. I refused to learn cruelty because I could refuse. Littleson efficiently grabbed the stray cats that lurked over the back stairwells to leap on the least suspecting. He took hold of the spitting, clawing beasts, and swung them by their tails, beating them against the back porch railing, then sent them sailing to the ground below. The cats hit the ground like terrified, but instinctual trapeze artists who know how to land on their feet. Centuries before cities had taught them this. Then they gunned across the ground like bullets with Littleson's special notch etched on their sides.

Littleson would dust his palms and stomp down the steps. Fearlessly. Without a swagger, more a glorified practicality. He was, in the moments after his raids on the roaches, the cats, and the rats, heroic. Larger than his still-boy self. He had mastered a degree of cruelty; he had triumphed in the hunt. He could walk in the company of men. He acquired new height.

The other boys, who were mostly the sons of renters, who had no place to protect, no territory to stalk and watch for, turned their cruelties elsewhere. They *boiled* into manhood. The liquor of them overflowed from their bodies and touched their fiery environment and their liquor smoked and steamed into a stench or a lingering musk that drove girls wild. Their aromas arrogant and chokingly alive. Promissory and profane. They could smell themselves.

The Watermelon Days belong to them. They pulled a plug out of summer and tasted their futures. They tapped and knocked a melon and heard the hollow fates. They tore their thirst from sweet, red meats and swallowed the black and brown seeds whole. They washed each other's faces in the green and pallid white rinds during the Watermelon Wars. After the battles they piled their flaccid weaponry in a garbage arsenal guarded by flies, and went back to the houses cursing each other, and wiping the wet from their faces before it syrupped in the sun.

They were the sons of men and women who owned nothing or little besides broken promises. They could grow up to be dangerously unfettered. They could grow up to be cart men who walked the streets and alleys like refugees from a war-torn landscape. They could be devil-may-care like young Uncle Blackstrap, or delirious like older Uncle Blackstrap.

They would always be happiest in summer. Every warm and shining summer day they'd drag their tow-cart lives over the divided avenues, carrying summer ice and various flavored syrups, a hunk of ice that they scraped, scooped and stuffed into triangular paper cones, then drenched with fruit tonic.

In winter they would pile rags and refuse (metal, paper; and porcelain toilet stool, face bowls and kitchen sinks) into the same wooden-wheeled stall and wheel it all to a yard to be weighed.

Money-things were plucked from garbage cans. Hands that delicately shoveled for wealth among the filthy odds and ends, in early fall touched the wet fruit remains of summer and remembered the feel of boyhood.

One summer day Littleson and I were eating watermelon. Our cheeks rimmed inside crescent watermelon moons. Littleson raised his foot and smashed what he thought was a roach. When he lifted his foot we did not see a roach-corpse or milky-white roach guts. There was nothing to despise; in the changing light it had been a trick of the eye. There was only, before us, an adult watermelon seed like a flat polished worry-stone perfect for the palm of a child's hand. Something to fondle the sensitive nerve. Something to touch.

It had been a magic trick of sunlight. Littleson had thought that the innocent seed that came with the sweet fruit was his natural enemy. A common mistake.

"Crawl, nigger. Crawl, worm. Crawl, dog. Got shit in yo' pants."

"Want me to put yo' nose in shit? Huh, fly? Roach? Worm."

"Stuff yo' mouth with it."

They beat him until they felt the texture of his muscles change. His head slick, syrupped over with his blood. His arms and legs limp as rubber tubing. His tongue a strap with no buckle, hanging out the side of his mouth. Mouth unhinged.

In a glistening, gritty pool of his own waste they left him where Uncle Blackstrap found him. Curious, casting a cursory glance in the basement window, a constant eye open for junk and refuse. The sight of the boy had made him sick. He took his gloves off. He wiped his mouth with the back of his hand. Erasing the scream before it was born there in the vacant basement. Soothing the vomit-reflex. Blackstrap was a man who had travelled in war-lands, where it rained shrapnel and stray pieces of human flesh. But World War II before atom bombs and death camps had been a kind of clean war. Hadn't it? That's what they'd said: A War Against Evil. In any case what he had seen was nothing like *this*. A boy who could have been his son. Ruined in this way.

The boy was so flaccid and still that Blackstrap was afraid to stir the rummaged organs. So he stumbled from the basement emptyhanded, called an ambulance, the police, alarmed the Grace household, and carried something terrible on his tongue to Eddie's mother, Miss Rose.

What happened to Eddie was the first true clue that I had that the worst thing that could happen to a boy or a man was *not* to be unemployed.

Such cruelty, narrowed kitchenette whippings, wars of protection, sister fights over clothes, and hunting to nothing. The hate was too large to go inside us. It lurked, touched us, licked at us. This was the first news heard of the birth of the ice-babies. No one ever knew who hurt Eddie or why. But we knew they belonged to winter, and they were subject to tricks of the eye. They could fall on you like bandits, but they were not bandits. Because they were the ones who had been stolen from. They and Eddie, who did not die in the days after the beating, although all the doctors knew that he would.

Winter yawned in our faces, licked our hands and feet. Caroline would tell us stories of foolhardy boys who went outside without ear-muffs, who'd lost their ears to the winter, as if the city winter were a war. The Hawk a guerilla that ambushed across the boulevard.

Rising before the sun, our Littleson pulled a sled loaded with newspapers in the light that the moon sent over its shoulder, the first glance of sunlight.

Eddie was in the hospital all through winter. We were too young to visit him. Only Miss Rose saw him every day. But once or twice I went, and Littleson went twenty times and stood below Eddie's window so that he could see him. Eddie would look out through the frost-frescoed windows. He appeared to us, a shrunken head on a pointed stick-body, smiling like an angel. Blessing us.

In spring, when Littleson (who insisted on being called Lazarus more and more) stalked before our eyes, we made new markings on the door-frame to measure his growth. Eddie, out of the hospital, had come back old, walking on wobbly legs. Like a sailor who had been lost at sea too long. His legs folded up unexpectedly under him. Littleson would catch him and hold him tenderly like an autumn leaf that he refused to allow to touch the ground and be gone.

Littleson, now known as Lazarus, who he had always been, would not let Eddie mark off his height on our doorframe. He hustled him away and gave him comic books and oatmeal cookies. Eddie soon forgot the notches on the wall, at least I thought he did. But I stood staring at the spot where he had been standing unsteadily. I have an eye for detail. I knew if Eddie had walked and stood against the wall, in that doorway, the top of his head would have come to the same etched line that he had made the year before. He had not grown, when everybody else was growing.

This knowledge, which Lazarus protected him from, was known to him. He glanced up from the gaudy pages of the comic book and stared at the doorframe.

It was a doorway he would never go through. I went to the kitchen and took a fresh batch of cookies from the oven. Oatmeal cookies were the only sweet thing that I could make alone. I gave Eddie a whole plateful for his private consumption. Littleson, who was Lazarus by then, did not complain.

Every two weeks Eddie went to the clinic with his mother. We'd see them walking down the street. Eddie with his pinched body and Miss Rose with her pinched eyes. Miss Rose told Mama that Eddie couldn't hold his water. Mama told us that Eddie's clinic visits made her think of her Uncle E. W. and the Writing Clinic.

Later that spring there was so much rain that the eaves were tipsy and the gutters were swollen and drunken, spilling over. Trash tightened the drainage. Yet in places gasoline and oil made murals of the gutters, and Lazarus, Eddie and I would watch our faces shifting in a rainbow when we found one. Such pools could be like the house of mirrors wherein faces would seem huge, gathering comic perspective. We laughed together for a while.

Before the announcement of new watermelon, before the beginning of summer, Eddie died.

Littleson let me hold his hand for two minutes at the funeral in Star of Bethlehem Missionary Baptist Church. This was when Miss Rose rocked from her spine, gathering momentum like a dark, black-breasted bird, stretched out her arms like great sepia wings, sent up one shout that she didn't own, that panicked her, and let grief try to fly above itself, above her body. Her sorrow was magnificent; ours was so quotidian, so humble that we were ashamed and even more afraid that she would pull some of the same overwhelming magnificence out of us. We were Roman Catholic and did not shout in church. Yet our mother and the sisters in white seemed to know exactly what to do for Miss Rose.

Lazarus wiped his eyes and gnawed his bottom lip. Fascinated, I craned my neck to stare one last time at the boy in the coffin in the immutable trance of death.

It was all a mystery to me. We never learned why the ice-babies had beaten Eddie. They were never caught, although some people said that a boy who was sent to the reform school for stealing a car bragged behind the barbed wire that he was "a killer." They said that he had shrugged. Said it had been something he had had to do. They told us who he was and we looked for him in the parade (named after an imaginary white-man benefactor) that wound its way down three miles of boulevard. He was in the St. Edmund's Drum and Bugle Corps that turned out the annual end-of-the-summer parade. He was a standout musician, in a troupe of gut-grabbing, finger-popping music boys. We all said that you had to respect a bad boy. He could blow a horn with incorrigible style, and his drumbeat was the rhythm that sent a wild freedom through the crowd. We pulsated with the beat they sent out. It was alive.

I remember feeling bouyed up in the crowd. Like someone who cannot drown. This was a mysterious feeling. Lazarus had climbed a tree and was poised like a lookout for a pirate ship. There were policemen all around. They looked displeased with us, as if we were breaking the law by being so happy. Secrets ran through the air. I eavesdropped under the music. Perhaps the boy who'd killed Eddie was *there* in the street, making powerful music that jarred our bones and our teeth. Maybe Eddie was listening. An angel now leaning attentively on a cloud.

Suddenly, I wanted to not be sure that the killer boy was blowing a horn. His sound, delicious as it was, could only carry germs. Cold is contagious, and soon we could all be frozen in the attitudes of ice, like whole generations playing "Aunt Dinah's dead." Oh how did she die? Oh she died like this. Assuming some bizarre position and freezing there for an endless time. Catching cold and giving it.

From *The American Ambassador*

Ward Just

Chapter Two

The operation was concluded. He knew that, in some accessible region of his mind. He remembered being wheeled into the operating room, a captive, already light-headed, the bright lights above, nurses here and there, the odor of electricity, and Fowler's wink. Fowler's mouth and jaw hidden behind an aqua mask, but the heavy Rolex on his wrist and the wink unmistakable. Fowler had leaned down and said a muffled few words, something about Africa and the twenty-year migration of the fragment of a hand grenade. He was lying on his stomach and Fowler had to bend his knees to get close to his ear. He said, Your misspent youth, as if Africa had been a pool hall. He looked straight at Fowler and was surprised to see contact lenses swimming on his irises. He smelled a leathery cologne, and noticed Fowler's immaculate manicure, a complement to the Rolex. Fowler turned and a nurse offered rubber gloves. Fowler winked at her, too. What could be worse than a vain surgeon? Except they were all vain. Why would a license to cut be an entitlement to egomania? What was their supposed pledge? *Do no harm.* Too modest a goal in the age of medical miracles. It would be just right for the Foreign Service, though. The chief surgeon put his hand on Bill's shoulder and said two words, We're ready. Then he nodded at the anesthetist. Someone in the room was humming Mozart. He hoped to Christ that they had the anesthetic right, that it wasn't someone's urine or meningitis virus or stale Coca-Cola. He smiled at the anesthetist, wanting her to like him. All prisoners wanted to be loved by their jailers. He said, What a swell job you have, putting people to sleep.

The anesthetist was looking at something and did not reply. He felt let down. The humming stopped. Curtly, she told him to count back from ten and at six it was lights-out.

He felt no pain, nor any sensation. By the pale look of the sunlight he reckoned it was late afternoon. In the next bed he heard the boy sigh loudly, and shift position. Someone turned the pages of a magazine, fingernails on slick paper: Elinor. He listened without moving. He wanted to stay within himself a while longer, holding himself in comfortable suspension; he did not want to admit to anything. Inside, he was safe and without fear. He wanted to do nothing to draw attention to himself, and in that way remain invisible, yet sentient. He thought that if he opened his mouth his spirit would fly away out the window, out of control, perhaps lost forever. He was tempted to do this, there were so many spirits round and about. They were out of sight beyond the open window, but beckoning him. If he said anything his words would take wing, lost to him forever. His open eyes would provide an exit for his many important and individual thoughts and these, too, released, would vanish. Better to remain still, immobile in clean white sheets, listening to the rustle of the pages of a magazine.

He closed his eyes but still he could see the window and the light outside. He saw it in his mind's eye, so clearly that he could not swear to God that his eyes were closed, as he knew them absolutely to be; he had closed them himself and now was inside himself, safe. It was like being the man, the mirror, and the image in the mirror, all at once. The sky was very bright and the window was open. He could see the crowns of trees and a brilliant milky sky, of the sort observed only in the Southern Hemisphere. It seemed to press down upon the civilized earth, like a great lid. In the Southern Hemisphere, of course, things were upside-down: the seasons, the very sky itself, and the angle of vision to the rest of the world. When you looked north, it was as if you were looking down. The Cape of Good Hope was the top of the world; that was how it seemed, and that therefore was how it was, a continental perspective, the practical reality in Africa, and no great surprise because after all he had grown up in Boston, hub of the universe.

The breeze was hot, like an animal's breath, but light on his skin. It did not burn, it consoled. It was an African breeze, aromatic, redolent of the earth and its dense vegetation, its rot and exotic fauna: whydah birds, mountain apes, lowland crocodiles. It had come a long way, from Southern Africa across the Atlantic. But it had maintained its integrity, collecting nothing from the sea; it was a pure land breeze. He was greatly comforted, for it brought with it the spirit of the continent, geologic time. All the emotions of Africa, his and the Africans', were carried with it. In Africa you were at ease with mystery, was that not so?

He knew that what he felt was miraculous, and not quite credible; but he did not let it go. He was awake and asleep at the same time, an ambiguous consciousness. He felt a sudden surge of ecstasy, as if all his African emotions were concentrated in a single place, a passionate kiss, a teardrop, an unexpected sighting, anything momentous.

He and Kleust in the overloaded boat, chased by a storm boiling up out of Zaire. Except it was not Zaire then, it was the Congo. It was Conrad's country. They had been hunting crocodiles. Kleust had a friend with a license from the government. The government permitted him to take two hundred crocodiles a year from the lake, transport the skins to the capital, and transship them to Paris and Rome, for handbags and shoes. Everyone got a cut. Kleust's friend was on the run, there were references to a wife, and a police matter. The friend lived in a tent surrounded by ammunition cases, heavy steel boxes filled with paperback books, gothic romances. On the covers of the books were English country houses, rearing stallions, women in deshabille, men in fox-hunting clothes. The steel cases were to protect the books from jungle rot. There were crocodiles everywhere. They hunted at night, shooting the crocs at will, eight, ten, in a single night. Kleust held the light, and the crocs' eyes lit up like the taillights of cars. The bay looked like a parking lot. They would bring them back to camp for the skinners to strip. They sat up late, drinking whiskey and talking. Kleust's friend said very little about the present, and nothing at all about the past. He and Kleust stayed for four days, then left; they were tired of killing. Early in the morning they departed from the camp. One of the skinners drove the boat, the sky above them wide and blue, and behind them great thunderheads, heavy with summer rain, black as hell; the bolts of lightning reminded him of the evil tendrils of a jellyfish, thick and white as milk.

We will outrace it, the skinner said.

I hope so, Kleust said. They both sat in the bow, eyes front, though every few minutes they would move their necks, bring their faces around in an arc, to observe the weather: the abrupt end of the wide blue sky and the beginning of the blackness, relentlessly gaining.

They were talking about Germany, what would happen to it; the weight of its past seemed a burden beyond imagining. And of course it did not need imagining, all you had to do was read the documents, the

143

testimony, the memoirs, the daily journalism, and look at the films. It was the most documented horror in history, nothing left to the imagination except to wonder at the thoroughness of it all, and the enthusiasm the killers brought to their work. Brahms and Rilke in the morning, Cyclon-B in the afternoon.

A crisis in the humanities, Kleust said with an icy smile.

The weight of the German past was what had driven Kleust to Africa, wondering if in this new political environment things might be—chaste. However, Africa's politicians were fascinated by Hitler's new order, busy as they were in fashioning a new order themselves. An African way, Africa for the Africans. They did not understand the Third Reich, how it began, how it continued, why it ended. How did the Führer organize the state? Inspire such devotion? How did Dr. Goebbels develop the propaganda ministry? What was the role of education? The church? If the Germans—so intelligent, so civilized—adapted so readily to a one-party state, why not Africa? And what was it about the Jews? There were no Jews in Africa, except a few tribes in Ethiopia—Stone-Age people, they said, sneering—and of course the Jews of European descent in South Africa. Kleust explained about the Jews, their role in history, their dispersion, their prominence in the cultural and commercial life in Germany, but still the Africans didn't get it. Were the Jews like colonialists, then? Clannish, mysterious, racist, rich, taking what they wanted, promulgating their own laws, cuisine, clothing, religious customs, raping the land? Insulting the majority race. Could they be compared to the Indian merchants who held every African town and village in thrall—in a Hindu stranglehold? Kleust spent many hours late at night, explaining modern German history to the Africans, tracing the years from 1920 to 1945; only twenty-five years, but it could have been—was!—a millenium. It was certainly an Era, beginning with Weimar and ending with the Thousand-Year Reich, even shorter than the American Century. He was barely forty-five himself, and had lived through them both. Before his posting in Africa—this one, the second posting—he had been a functionary in the embassy in London, a city he despised, and a first secretary in Washington, a city that amused and baffled him. On the whole, he preferred Bonn.

Americans live in a dreamworld, Kleust said.

As opposed to Germans? he asked.

Germans believe nothing, Kleust said. Germans live in a glass house, the world pressing in on all sides, everything visible.

They talked for a while about the European political climate, and the two Germanys, reunification, and what the future held. *Ostpolitik* was the symmetrical policy, though conducted with sleight-of-hand; its foundations had already been laid. Germans had long memories. Everything in Germany was approached with profound ambivalence. Germans were afraid of themselves. Many Germans wished for a pastoral life, Goethe's "naturalness." Kleust waved his hand. Perhaps the harmless commercial activity of the Buddenbrookses. On the one hand, Germans wanted to move their shoulders, gain room to live and breathe. On the other hand, Germans wanted to disappear into Europe. Kleust fell silent. They were almost in the middle of the lake. Far in the distance was a small fishing boat.

Do you love your country? he had asked.

It is the fatherland, Kleust agreed.

That is not an answer, he said.

It is the best I can do, Kleust said. It is where I am at home. It is where I can breathe easiest. At least in Germany nothing is withheld. Of course it is necessary to keep your eyes open, always alert. And it must be the same with you.

No, he said. I am at home anywhere. And I am at home here, on this lake full of crocodiles, as I am at home there. Elinor and I, wherever we are . . . But I love my country. I love the freedom of it, its impulsiveness. The buffoonery, the instability, the romance of money, the loneliness and the grab. We do not have identity cards in the United States. I do not have to be in America in order to be at home. I like the unpredictability. Suddenly out of nowhere a Lincoln emerges, and he is absolutely his own man. Who would you compare him to? No one. Our greatest president, our greatest soul: afflicted with a melancholia so deep that he was never wholly free of it. At the moment of his greatest triumph he delivered his most somber message. A country capable of criminal stupidity but properly led, of magnanimity also. What I like most about it is that it isn't Europe.

Kleust cocked an eyebrow. Perhaps you are happier in this century than I am. Your country is happier, or luckier, than mine is. Well. It is supposed to be your century, is it not? Yet 'impulsiveness' is not the word I would have used. 'Impulsiveness' is not an attractive quality, is it?

He laughed. It's a swell century, all things considered. The American part of it has been particularly benign, don't you think? In all its impulsiveness? Then, after a moment's pause: Do you think you could commit treason?

I would not supervise a concentration camp, if that is what you mean.

It isn't, he said.

That is an order I would refuse to obey, Kleust said. I would not sell secrets to the Russian pigs.

He said, I do not mean refusing an order. There are orders all of us would refuse. And neither your government nor mine has any plans to establish concentration camps. And we have no secrets to sell, you and I, even if we were interested in selling them, which we aren't. I'm not interested in the past. I'm talking about the future. Tomorrow, the day after, next week, next year. I mean engaging in a treasonous act. Being forced to choose, and choosing an act of calculated treachery against the state. In my case, choosing against Lincoln. Telling Abraham Lincoln to go fuck himself, that it was in vain after all. *The Union doesn't count.*

That's what it comes down to?

He said, Yes.

Kleust thought a moment. Kleust in deep thought, weighing his reply. When he spoke, it was to slide off the point. He said, You mean 'the government.' Our experience with governments is not so good.

If we are not faithful, who will be?

We have a duty, Kleust agreed.

And our duty to the state is profound. We took an oath. We were not coerced to swear allegiance. At the least, we are like doctors: Do no harm. The state is in our care. We have an obligation to it.

Yes, of course, Kleust said.

The government, the nation. The Constitution, yours or mine. It's all the same thing.

Not exactly the same, Kleust said.

He smiled. You are sounding like a Frenchman.

And you are sounding like someone in trouble.

I may be in trouble, Kurt. As you say, Americans live in a dream-world.

What kind of trouble?

What would you do, forced to choose between betraying your country and betraying your friend?

Kleust smiled cynically, raising his chin so that he looked down his nose. He said, I shud rathah hope I shud have the cuddage to betray my countrah.

He laughed. Kleust's imitation of an educated Englishman owed more to Heidelberg than to Cambridge. He said, Come off it. You don't believe that Forster horseshit any more than I do. What a pretty sensibility he has. We don't have that luxury.

Kleust said, Maybe I do believe it. I think I do, as a matter of fact. It is not a convenient century we live in. It is a murderous century. It is perhaps the beginning of the end of everything. So given a choice, or forced to make one, I would choose what is closest. Most precious. Most intimate. Nearest to hand. Contemporary German naturalness. What friend, Bill?

What does it matter? he asked.

It is not theoretical, Kleust said.

He said, No one you know.

Kleust said, You are talking like a patriot. But I do not think you are a scoundrel.

He did not reply, and Kleust looked away to the fishing boat a mile or so off the bow. They were almost at midpoint in their journey across the lake. The water was green and thick with algae, and the other shore a thin dark line on the horizon. He wondered how Elinor would paint it, the green of the water, the dark line, the blue of the sky and the black clouds astern. Well, she did not care for the pastoral, landscapes or seascapes; she painted people. He looked at Kleust, lapsed now into a gloomy silence. The hunt had not been a success. Kleust had been upset by the crocodiles; the second day he declined to shoot at all. He had killed two the first night, and that was enough. He would go along and watch, but he did not want to shoot. He thought the beasts had a strange powerful beauty, and it was so easy to mesmerize them with the lamp. Their eyes glowed hot and red as the morning sun. Of course they were man-eaters, but there were no men on this lake; there was only the three of them, the hunter and two diplomats. At dusk they stood on the shore drinking Scotch and watching the beasts float by. They were talking shop, personnel problems, pensions. On the third day he had taken the biggest crocodile of all, eighteen feet long. He shot him three times in the skull before he died, sinking to the bottom of the shallow lagoon. The hunter and two skinners had gone into the water to raise him, then manhandle him into the boat. One of the skinners had estimated the beast's age at ninety years old, possibly one hundred. Kleust had listened attentively, then observed that if that was true, then it had been born about the time that Stanley had found Livingstone. All those years in the same lake, eating and copulating. One of the skinners reached into the beast's scrotal sac and brought out its penis, heavy, ridged, gray as death. Kleust had turned away, muttering in German. The hunter had laughed, but he too was embarrassed. He nodded sharply, and the skinner stuffed the penis back into its sac. That's better, Kleust had said. That's much better. Let us show some respect for the hundred-year-old *Grossvater*. Let the *Grossvater* rest in peace.

He could smell land, and looked at Kleust, still lost in thought. He said, God, this is beautiful country.

Kleust turned suddenly, squinting into the sun. He said slowly, Is it?

He said, You don't think so?

Kleust shook his head, No. I think it is the edge of the precipice.

He did not reply. The sun was enormous in the sky, a furnace; its light glittered on the water, opaque with algae. The land-smell was heavy in his nostrils. The sky was empty except for the the sun; he did not look behind him. There were no birds about, nor any living thing. Yet he knew that beneath the surface of the lake there was life.

Kleust said, I am not like you.

He said, You're a good man, Kurt.

The German made a noise, a kind of scornful sigh. He unbuttoned his shirt, and flapped it against his sweaty skin. He said, I came in at the end of everything—true patriotism, faith, authority, integrity, purpose. German expressionism, yes? Even the women are not what they were. They are not worthy. Everything has gotten worse, except the domestic life of the German people. Our economy is a wonder. It is because of the conditions imposed upon us: mandatory restraint, political reparations for our excesses. We lower our voices, we have no big stick to wave. We adhere to the Americans, the last colonial power. This is good. Who can doubt it? The rest of the world should be as restrained as we Germans. In this place, not your place, you look around you and say: What a beautiful country. You are entitled to say it, it is your American privilege. But do you know how bad Africa is? Have you *seen*? Have you left your compound, gone into the streets, traveled in the region? Have you traveled in the Madness Belt? The belly of the continent. Disease, famine, murder, ignorance, corruption, megalomania. It's grotesque. It pulverizes the imagination, Amin, Mobutu. They're little Hitlers, worse than Hitler, because they're exterminating their own people.

Jews were Germans, he said.

Hitler didn't think so, Kleust replied.

Their boat angled off. In the distance was the little dory with two fishermen. He and Kleust could vaguely see their rods pointed skyward; there looked to be four rods, the fishermen were trolling. It was a consoling sight, a sight almost from the century before, a peaceful scene from a painting by Caleb Bingham or Winslow Homer. If the sky were a northern sky, and the water choppier, it could be a seascape near Gloucester. Except they were nowhere near Gloucester. They were in Africa, on the edges of the Madness Belt, on a lake so remote it did not appear on maps. At the edge of the precipice, according to Kleust.

Off the starboard bow the dory rocked to and fro, shimmering in the heat. The storm was far behind them now; the skinner had been correct. They had outrun it. They were nearing land at last, smelling its thick milky smell, as if the earth itself were lactating. The skinner suddenly shook his head and sang something incomprehensible; it sounded like a funeral dirge. He throttled back and they approached the dory slowly, circling it, staying out of range.

It was not a dory, and there were no fishermen with rods. He and Kleust leaned forward, appalled. What they believed from a distance to have been a boat was a crocodile, dead and bloated, floating on its back high in the water. It had taken sick and died; perhaps it had been crippled. Its fat legs pointed skyward, rocking gently as the croc yawed on the lake's surface. Its mouth was wide open, its teeth as long as a man's finger. The inside of its mouth was pink. They idled a moment, looking at it. It turned towards them, moved by a sudden breeze or by something under the water. The skinner said, Female. The stench was terrible, curdled milk. They could not take their eyes from it, so unexpected an apparition. The tail had been eaten, severed at the base, ragged bits of white meat spilling into the water. He imagined the crocodiles tearing at it, hitting it again and again; the female too sick and terrified to defend herself, and finally giving up. Her belly was intact, though: smooth, creamy, swollen. The skinner throttled forward and their boat heaved, leaving the crocodile astern, swirling the wake. They watched it tip and bow, stiff and buoyant as a cork, obscenely inverted. It seemed to rush toward them, as if suddenly alive and giving chase. Its dead eyes burned red in the sun. It followed a moment, then dropped back; something from below butted it, and the carcass began to turn, slow as the second hand of a clock. They accelerated, the skinner jamming the throttle all the way forward. They watched it recede, still rotating. As the thing receded, it resumed its former shape; an innocent dory, two fishermen in the dory, rods pointed skyward a consoling picture.

Bill?

He turned, closing his eyes, feeling the African breeze on his face. He could not see Kleust's face. What had Kleust meant about worthy women? They had talked about everything but women. Perhaps he thought worthy women had died along with the nineteenth century. Poor Kleust, he had never married; he had no children. Instead of a family, he had his history, the modern history of the German people. He cared for the history as other men cared for a family; he had a responsibility toward it. He'd said, *I came in at the end of everything.* But what a sight it had been, that morning on the lake, the dory and the fishermen transmogrifying into the beast, and then back again. When the beast became a dory, they never looked back. The past was past, and they kept their eyes on the approaching shore, and the deserted village with the makeshift pier. They tipped the skinner, and thanked him; he departed immediately. Then Kleust remembered that there was a bottle of scotch in the Land Rover. They sat in the Land Rover drinking scotch and debating the various routes back to the capital. It was a two-day trip, hard country roads. Kleust insisted on driving. He looked at Elinor, her eyes close to his.

Bill? How are you feeling?

Fine, he said.

Midrash on Happiness

Grace Paley

What she meant by happiness, she said, was the following: she meant having (or having had) (or continuing to have) everything. By everything, she meant, first, the children, then a dear person to live with, preferably a man (by *live with*, she meant for a long time but not necessarily). Along with and not in preferential order, she required three or four best women friends to whom she could tell every personal fact and then discuss on the widest deepest and most hopeless level, the economy, the constant, unbeatable, cruel war economy, the slavery of the American worker to the idea of that economy, the complicity of male people in the whole structure, the dumbness of men (including her preferred man) on this subject. By dumbness, she meant everything dumbness has always meant: silence and stupidity. By silence she meant refusal to speak; by stupidity she meant refusal to hear. For happiness she required women to walk with. To walk in the city arm in arm with a woman friend (as her mother had with aunts and cousins so many years ago) was just plain essential. Oh! those long walks and intimate talks, better than standing alone on the most admirable mountain or in the handsomest forest or hay-blown field (all of which were certainly splendid occupations for the wind-starved soul). More important even (though maybe less sweet because of age) than the old walks with boys she'd walked with as a girl, that nice bunch of worried left-wing boys who flew (always slightly handicapped by that idealistic wing) into a dream of paid-up mortgages with a small room for opinion and solitude in the corner of home. Oh do you remember those fellows, Ruthy?

Remember? Well, I'm married to one.

Not exactly.

O.K. So it's a union co-op.

But she had, Faith continued, democratically *tried* walking in the beloved city with a man, but the effort had failed since from about that age—twenty-seven or eight—he had felt an obligation, if a young woman passed, to turn abstractedly away, in the middle of the most personal conversation or even to say confidentially, wasn't she something?—or clasping his plaid shirt, at the heart's level, oh my god! The purpose of this: perhaps to work a nice quiet appreciation into thunderous heartbeat as he had been taught on pain of sexual death. For happiness, she also required work to do in this world and bread on the table. By work to do she included the important work of raising children righteously up. By righteously she meant that along with being useful and speaking truth to the community, they must do no harm. By harm she meant not only personal injury to the friend the lover the coworker the parent (the city the nation) but also the stranger; she meant particularly the stranger in all her or his difference, who, because we were strangers in Egypt, deserves special goodness for life or at least until the end of strangeness. By bread on the table, she meant no metaphor but truly bread as her father had ended every single meal with a hunk of bread. By hunk, she was describing one of the attributes of good bread.

Suddenly she felt she had left out a couple of things: Love. Oh yes, she said, for she was talking, talking all this time, to patient Ruth and they were walking for some reason in a neighborhood where she didn't know the children, the pizza places or the vegetable markets. It was early evening and she could see lovers walking along Riverside Park with their arms around one another, turning away from the sun which now sets among the new apartment houses of New Jersey, to kiss. Oh I forgot, she said, now that I notice, Ruthy I think I would die without love. By love she probably meant she would die without being *in* love. By *in* love she meant the acuteness of the heart at the sudden sight of a particular person or the way over a couple of years of interested friendship one is suddenly stunned by the lungs' longing for more and more breath in the presence of that friend, or nearly drowned to the knees by the salty spring that seems to beat for years on our vaginal shores. Not to omit all sorts of imaginings which assure great spiritual energy for months and when luck follows truth, years.

Oh sure, love. I think so too, sometimes, said Ruth, willing to hear Faith out since she had been watching the kissers too, but I'm really not so sure. Nowadays it seems like pride, I mean overweening pride, when you look at the children and think we don't have time to do much (by time Ruth meant both her personal time and the planet's time). When I read the papers and hear all this boom boom bellicosity, the guys out-daring each other, I see we have to change it all—the world—without killing it absolutely—without killing it, that'll be the trick the kids'll have to figure out. Until that begins, I don't understand happiness—what you mean by it.

Then Faith was ashamed to have wanted so much and so little all at the same time—to be so easily and personally satisfied in this terrible place, when everywhere vast public suffering rose in reeling waves from the round earth's nation-states—hung in the satellite-watched air and settled in no time at all into TV sets and newsrooms. It was all there. Look up and the news of halfway round the planet is falling on us all. So for all these conscientious and technical reasons, Faith was ashamed. It was clear that happiness could not be worthwhile, with so much conversation and so little revolutionary change. Of course, Faith said, I know all that. I do, but sometimes walking with a friend I forget the world.

From *Children of Light*

Robert Stone

Walker worked in the film industry, having come into it seventeen years before as an actor. He had gone through the Hagen-Berghof studios with the thought of learning the theater and becoming a playwright. A few years later he had written the book and lyrics for a very serious and ambitious musical version of *Jurgen* and been astonished to see it fail utterly within a week. There had never been a play and he had come to realize that there would never be. Walker made his living—quite a good one—chiefly as an author, adjuster or collaborator of film scripts. During the past summer, he had been acting again, on stage for the first time in years as Lear. Over the years he had advanced in station within the old black fairy tale. At different phases of his life he had played Cornwall's servant, then Cornwall, then Kent, finally the King. He was still up on Lear-ness, chock-a-block with cheerless dark and deadly mutters, little incantations from the text. They were not inappropriate to his condition: during the run of the show his wife had left him.

Drink in hand, he went up the stairway again and stood just inside the bedroom door, looking in at the young woman. Such a nice house, he thought. His jaw was tight with anger. Such a pretty girl.

He leaned in the doorway and watched her. She lay facing him, her red-blonde hair partly covering her eyes, her lips parted over long cow-girl's teeth. She slept on, or pretended to. A deep blue silk sheet was gathered about her naked body; she was sheathed in it.

Bronwen was a writer, a midwestern girl honed smooth by early success and the best of California. Observing, or rather ogling, her at rest, Walker was stirred in equal measure by lust and resentment.

Children of Light was published by Alfred A. Knopf in the spring of 1986. Used by permission.

Basically, they disliked each other. They were both, in their diverse ways, performers, comics; much of their companionable humor turned on mutual scorn.

She had written three short novels, witty, original and immensely pleasureable to read. Bronwen was nothing if not funny. Each of her novels had been received with great enthusiasm by reviewers and by the public; she had become famous enough for Walker, to his deep inward shame, to take a vulgar satisfaction in his liaison with her. She was intelligent and coldhearted, a spiky complex of defenses mined with vaults of childish venom and hastily buried fears. Kicked when she was a pup, Walker would say behind her back. The game they played, one of the games, was that she knew his number. That his stratagems to please, his manner of being amusing, the political sincerities that remained to him, were petty complaints to which she was immune. Others might take him seriously—not she, the hard case, worldly-wise.

Bronwen turned in her real or pretended sleep. She was an Indiana banker's daughter and it pleased her to play the reactionary to his frayed social democratic piety and compel his complacency toward her militant Tory bigotries, which, most wittily exaggerated, were quite genuine.

He ran his eyes over her long frame and wondered if she knew he knew about the pistol she kept in the wicker chest beneath her bed, wrapped in a scarf with her Ritalin tablets. Or whether she knew his number well enough to imagine the measure of his rage, or the murderous fantasies that assailed him—of destroying her, transforming her supple youth to offal, trashing it.

He was immediately stricken with remorse and horror. Because he liked her, really, after all. He must, he thought; there had to be more than perversity. She was funny; he enjoyed her wit and her high spirits. And she liked him—he was sure. She could speak with him as with no other friend, she respected his work, she had said so. It occurred to him suddenly how little any of this had to do with the terms of the heart as he had once understood them: love, caring, loyalty. It was just a random coupling, a highbrow jelly roll. As for the question of whether she was capable of imagining that violent fantasies beset him, with herself as their object—he assumed she probably was. She was very experienced and knowing; she had his number. And the Lord knew what fantasies she spun round him.

Back in the living room, he found his wallet on the sofa where he had been sitting. It was thick with bills, jammed in haphazard. He remembered then, having almost forgotten it in his malaise, that he had won a great deal of money at Santa Anita the day before. He had gone with

Bronwen; it had been a glorious day and they had lunched at the clubhouse. Walker had scored on the double, a perfecta and an eight-to-one winner. His take was over a thousand dollars, the largest amount he had ever won at the track. It had paid for dinner at the San Gabriel Ranch and it would pay a week's rent at the Chateau. He had been living at the Chateau Marmont since the closing of *Lear*, having rented his house in Santa Monica. He did not care to be alone there.

Walker caressed the disorderly wad between thumb and forefinger. The touch of the wrinkled bright new bills gave him a faint feeling of disgust. He took out a hundred, examining the lacy engraved illumination at its border. Then, on an impulse, he rolled the bill into a cylinder, laid out a line of his coke and blew it. Nice. He sniffed and rubbed his eyes. Confidence. A little surge for the road. Immediately it occurred to him that in the brief course of his waking day he had consumed Valium, alcohol and cocaine.

We need a plan, he thought. A plan and a dream, somewhere to go. Dreams were business to Walker, they were life. Like salt, like water. Lifeblood.

He touched the tip of his index finger to the surface of the coffee table, capturing the residue of cocaine that remained there, and rubbed it on his gum.

Go, he thought. It seemed to him that if he did not go at once, death would find him there. He stood up and packed his suitcase, leaving the small fold of cocaine on the table as a house present. He had plenty more in the case.

Stacked on the mantel above the fireplace were Bronwen's three novels; Walker found that each was engagingly inscribed to him. The drill was for him to take them and leave a note. He turned the topmost book to the back jacket and looked at Bronwen's picture. Her eyes were fixed on middle distance, her lips were slightly parted, her cheekbones high and handsome, her chin dimpled. She looked hip and sympathetic and fingerlickin' good. He placed the book back on the mantelpiece and left it there. Then he put on his sunglasses, picked up his bags and went forth into the morning.

As he drove the freeway, KQED played Couperin, the *Leçons des Ténèbres*.

Walker thought of himself as a survivor. He knew how to endure, and what it was that got you through. There was work. There were the people one loved and by whom one was loved. There were, he had always believed, a variety of inner resources that the veteran survivor might fall back on; about these he was no longer so sure. The idea of inner resources seemed fatuous mysticism that morning. He had drugged and drunk too much, watched too many smoky reels of interior montage to command any inner resources. It was difficult enough to think straight.

As for work – after weeks of living on his nerves and wasting his own cerement, it would take nearly as much time of disciplined drying out before he could begin to face a job. And love – love was fled. Gone to London. The thought of her there and himself abandoned made his blood run cold. He put it out of his mind, as he had trained himself to do since Seattle. He would deal with it later, he would do something about it. When he was straightened out. A dream, he thought. That's what we need.

He left the freeway at Sunset and parked in Marmont Lane behind the hotel. At the desk he bought the morning's *L. A. Times* and the daily *Variety*. He rode up to the sixth floor in the company of a famous German actor and two stoned young women.

The air in his apartment held a faint scent of stale alcohol and undone laundry. He opened the leaded bedroom windows to a tepid oily breeze. Below him were the swimming pool and the row of bungalows that flanked it. Dead leaves floated on the surface of the dark green water. The pool gardens smelled of car exhaust and eucalyptus.

This time it was not going to be easy to get straight. He would have to go about it very skillfully. Above all he would have to want to. There would have to be reason, and Walker knew that inquiry into his reasons for surviving would bring him into dangerous territory. The world in general, he had conceded at last, required neither him nor his works. His wife was gone – for good as far as he knew, his children grown. He was going to have to pull out for his own reasons, alone and unrequired, in a hotel in West Hollywood. The taste of death and ruin rose in his throat again.

He decided not to think about it. In order to postpone thinking about it he opened his suitcase, took out the tubular talcum container that held his cocaine and tapped out a small mound of the stuff onto the smooth dark marble of his bedside lamp table. He did it up with the hundred-dollar bill. Fine, he thought. For the moment he had obviated motivation: he was the thing itself again. The thing itself shortly came to self-awareness in the kitchen, pouring out a shot of vodka. Perplexed, Walker looked at the drink he had prepared. He sniffed, drew himself erect and emptied the glass into the sink drain. He had made a luncheon engagement with his agent and keeping the appointment was all he

157

owned of purpose. He must at least postpone the next drink until lunch. A small gesture toward renewal, nothing ambitious.

Drinkless, he went into his living room, turned the television set on, turned it off again and began to pace the length of the room.

This is where we begin, he told himself. We reinvent ourself. We put one foot in front of the other and we go on.

In a moment he went back to the bedroom and did another line. Then he leaned back on the bed and stared through the balcony windows at the still surface of the pool five stories below.

From somewhere amid the damp greenery of the garden, a mocking-bird was trilling away, sounding a little fife march. For a fraction of a second Walker was beguiled by a shard of memory, the tiniest part of an old dream. It was gone too quickly to be pinned down.

He got to his feet and went to stand at the window. The birdsong came again, under the rush of traffic, stirring recall.

He had gone away from the balcony and was sitting on the bed with the telephone in his hand when the memory surfaced. He put the receiver down and turned to the window. The bird trilled again.

He was remembering Lu Anne Bourgeois, whom the greater world called Lee Verger. She had been half on his mind all the previous spring, but Seattle, the show and the dreadful events of the summer had swept everything away.

Years before, when he and Lu Anne were young and fearless, in the days of mind-drugs and transfiguration, they had invented a game together for bad nights. In fact, it was not so much a game as a state of mind to be indulged and they had called it "Bats or Birdies."

Bats or Birdies was played in the worst hours before dawn. Winning entailed holding your own until morning, making it through the night with your head intact to the moment when birdsong announced the imminence of first light and day. That was Birdies. Losing was not making it through, losing your shit. Bats. Mockingbirds, with their untimely warbles at ungodly hours, upset the game, making you think that it was morning and you had won through when in fact you were still fast in the heart of night.

But stoned, abandoned, desolate—Walker found himself listening to birdcalls and thinking of Lu Anne. His heart beat faster. It had not been quite six years, he thought. She had kissed him casually. He imagined that he could recall her touch and when he did it was the woman he had known a decade before who presented herself to his recollection.

She was married again, to a doctor; she had children. His business now was to save himself and his own marriage, restore his equilibrium. What we need here is less craziness, he told himself, not more.

Then he thought: a dream is what I need. Fire, motion, risk. It was a delusion of the drug. The production's location office number was in his black book. He found himself with his hand on the phone.

Yours in the ranks of death.

Trapped within some vertiginous silence, he dialed the far-off number. At the first ring he hung up in terror.

A few minutes later, it seemed to him that he was perfectly well again. When he picked up the telephone it was to confirm luncheon with the agent's office.

At the agency, he got Shelley Pearce on the line. She was Al's assistant, a Smithie who had gone through the Yale Rep some years after Lu Anne. She had been a student of Walker's at an acting workshop; he had gotten her her first job, as a go-fer on a production at U. A. He had introduced her to Al.

"Hello Gordon," Shelley said. She sounded glad to hear from him and he felt grateful.

"Where were you?" he said. "Every night I searched that sea of pale immobile faces. No Shelley."

"You kidding, Gordon? *King Lear?* You think I got time for that shit?" He laughed.

"Yes Gordon," Shelley said, "yes, I was there. I saw you. You were wonderful."

"How's that?"

"Wonderful, Gordon. Wonderful, O.K.?"

"I thought so too," Walker said. "I felt underappreciated."

"Didn't you see the *L. A. Times?*"

"Acceptable," Walker said. "But faint."

"Don't be greedy," Shelley said. "Al will bring you some clippings to slaver over at lunch."

"Why don't you and I have dinner tonight?" he asked her suddenly. "Why don't we go to the San Ep Hotel?"

She was silent for a moment.

"How are you, Gordon? I mean how are you doing?"

"Not so good," he said.

"Sure," she said. "The San Ep, sure. Sunset. Know when sunset is? It's in the paper."

"I'll call the Coast Guard."

"You drinking?" she asked. "You better not stand me up."

"I'll be there," he said.

Three blocks beyond the main drag rose the San Epifanio Beach Hotel, a nine-story riot of exoticism that dominated the downtown area. It was a shameless building from another age, silent-movie Spanish. With its peeling stucco walls, its rows of slimy windows and soiled shades, it was a structure so outsized and crummy that the sight of it could taint the nicest day. Walker was fond of it because he had been happy there. He had lived in the hotel years before in a room beside an atelier where a blind masseur cohabited with Ramon Novarro's putative cousin. He had been married there, in the dingy ballroom, amid cannabis fumes.

Walker pulled over into the guest parking lot. A toughlooking little Chicana with a ponytail, a baseball cap and bib overalls handed him a claim ticket.

He went past the theater-style marquee over the main entrance and walked round to the beach side of the building. Several empty tables were arranged on a veranda overlooking a nearly deserted park. At the far end of the park four black teenagers, stripped to the waist, were playing basketball. Nearer the hotel, some Hare Krishnas from Laguna were chanting for the entertainment of two elderly couples in pastel clothes.

Walker ambled across the park to the beach. The wind was sharp, it had grown chilly with the approach of sunset. The declining sun itself was obscured in dark banks of cloud. Walker watched the waves break against the dark purple sand. Once he had seen porpoises there, seven together, playing just outside the break line of the surf. He had been standing in the same place, on the edge of the park, around sunset. His wife had been beside him. His children were digging in the sand and she had called to them, pointing out to sea, to the porpoises. It had been a good omen in a good year.

He walked along the sand until he felt cold, then climbed back to the park up a dozen cement steps that were littered with plastic carriers and beer cans and smelled of urine.

The wall of the corridor between the main entrance and the inner lobby of the San Epifanio was covered in worn striped wallpaper against which were hung ghastly seascapes at close intervals. Once past them, he strolled into the candle-lit gemütlichkeit of the Miramar Lounge, all nets and floats and steering wheels. There was not much sunset to be seen through the picture windows but the lights were low and the bar and adjoining tables fairly crowded. The customers were middle-aged, noisy and dressed for golf—a hard-liquor crowd. Walker took the only vacant stool at the bar and ordered a Bloody Mary. The drink when it came was bitter, hefty with cheap vodka. Strong drinks were a selling point of the place.

On the stool next to Walker sat a blonde woman who was drinking rather hungrily of her gin and tonic and toying with a pack of Virginia Slims. She appeared to be in her early thirties and attractive, but Walker was not certain of either impression. He was not altogether sober and it was difficult to see people clearly in the lighting of the Miramar Lounge. That was the way they liked it there.

At the entrance to the bar, adjoining the corridor through which he had passed, was a phone booth, one from the old days, decorated with sea horses and dolphins in blue-and-white tile. After a moment, Walker picked up his drink and went to the phone booth. He took out his black book with its listing of the Baja location numbers and his telephone credit card.

He took a long sip, held his breath and dialed. The resonance of submarine depths seemed to him to hum in the wires as he waited for the ring. When it came, he closed his eyes.

Walker did not try to place the call again. He picked up his drink from beside the telephone and went back to his barstool.

She might have been on the line, he thought. Perhaps it was only a thrill of fear she felt at the sound of his voice. Perhaps calm resolution and refusal. Perhaps someone else had picked up the phone.

But it was Mexico. Mexican phones. As likely as not he had spoken into a dead line, into an unheeding, untroubled past. There was so much to be said, he thought, for leaving things alone.

Beside him, the blonde woman on the neighboring stool had put a cigarette to her lips, supporting it with a bridge of fore and middle finger. It seemed somehow a quaint gesture, suggestive of film-noir intrigue. Walker's hand was on the lighter in his jacket pocket, but he checked the impulse. He did not want to pick her up. And although he was curious about her, he did not feel like forcing conversation.

He studied her in the candlelight. Not bad for the San Ep, he thought. She seemed free of principal undesirable qualities common to pickups at the Lounge in that she was neither a prostitute nor a man in drag. She seemed, in fact, a fresh-faced, confused and vaguely unhappy young woman who had no business on a San Epifanio Beach barstool. He was about to give her a light out of common politeness when, from somewhere behind him, a flame was thrust forth and she inclined her cigarette to receive it. She smiled uncertainly over Walker's shoulder and murmured her gratitude. Walker, who had not turned around, found himself listening to merry masculine laughter of an odd register. A voice boomed forth, subduing all other sounds in the place.

"I've recently had the opportunity to visit Mount Palomar," the voice declared with a dreadful earnestness, "and was devastated by the sheer beauty I encountered there."

Such a sound, Walker considered, could only be made by forcing the breath down against the diaphragm, swallowing one's voice and then forcing the breath upward, as in song. He listened in wonder as the voice blared on.

"Everywhere I travel in California," it intoned, "I'm—utterly dazzled—by the vistas."

He's raving mad, thought Walker.

"Don't you find your own experiences to be similar?" the voice demanded of the young woman at the bar. It was a truly unsettling sound, its tone so false as to seem scarcely human.

To Walker's astonishment, the woman smiled the wider and began to stammer.

"I certainly . . . yes . . . why I do. The vistas are ravishing."

"How pleasant an experience," brayed the voice, "to encounter a fellow admirer of natural wonders."

With as much discretion as possible, Walker turned toward the speaker. He saw a man of about fifty whose nose and cheekbone had been broken, wearing a hairpiece, a little theatrical base and light eyeliner. Returning to his drink, Walker cringed; he had feared to see a face to match the voice and that was what he had seen. It was a smiling face. Its smile was a rictus of clenched teeth like a ventriloquist's. The thought crossed his mind that he was hallucinating. He dismissed it.

"So few," the man enunciated, "truly see the wonders nature arrays before them."

How true, thought Walker.

The man eased himself between Walker's stool and the lady's, taking possession of her company and presenting a massive shoulder to Walker, his defeated rival. Walker moved his stool slightly so that he would still be able to see her.

"I know," the woman said, with an uneasy laugh. "The average person can be blind to beauty. Even when it's right in front of them."

Walker sipped his drink. The neighboring dialogue was beginning to make him unhappy. Abandoning his observation of the two new friends, he turned to see that Shelley had come in. She was standing in a doorway that opened to the windswept terrace; she was smiling, she had seen him. A tan polo coat was thrown over her shoulders; she was

162

wearing pants to match it and tall boots. Under the coat she wore a navy workshirt and a white turtleneck jersey. Her dark hair was close-cropped.

She waved to him and he watched her make her way through the bar crowd. When she was by his side he stood up and kissed her.

"You look pretty tonight, Shell," he said into her ear.

"You look pretty too, Gordo." She cupped her hands around her mouth and croaked at him. "Why are we whispering?"

Walker put a finger across his lips and moved his eyes toward the couple on his right. Shelley peered at them, then looked at Walker with an expression of anticipatory glee. Her black eyes were so bright he wondered if she had been doing drugs.

"Do I discern a visitor to our shores?" the big man inquired in his awful voice. "Great Britain, perhaps?"

The young woman, who spoke with the accent of southern Indiana or Illinois, hesitantly explained that she was not a visitor from abroad.

"What a surprise," the man had his voice declare, while his heavy face did surprise. "Your impeccable pronunciation convinced me you must be from across the water."

Walker looked away. Shelley was hiding behind him on the stool, resting her chin on her hands, grinning madly at the bottles behind the bar.

"Let me see," sounded the man through his morbid grin. "The eastern states, perhaps. I have it. I suspect Boston is the key to your refinement."

"No," said the woman. "Illinois is my native state." She giggled. "I hail from the central region."

Walker glanced at Shelley. She was batting her eyes, doing an impression of goofy cordiality.

"Ah," honked the big man. "How charming. The land of Lincoln."

They listened as he introduced himself as Ulrich or Dulwich or something close. "May I offer you a cocktail?" Ulrich or Dulwich asked gaily. "The night is young and we seem kindred spirits."

Shelley put a hand on Walker's arm. She had seen a free table. They got up and went over to it.

"How come you never say anything like that to me, Gordon? How about offering me a cocktail?"

He called a waitress and ordered Shelley a White Russian, which was what she claimed she wanted. Before the waitress could leave with the drink order Shelley called her back.

"Do you see that man at the bar?" she asked the girl. "The big one with the blonde lady?" The waitress followed Shelley's nod. "We'd like to buy him a drink."

"Cut it out, Shelley," Walker said.

"When you give him the drink," Shelley said, "tell him we're putting assholes to sleep tonight. And we got his number."

"Shut up," Walker said. "Forget it," he told the waitress. The waitress was tall and dark, with a long melancholy face. One side of her mouth twitched in a weird affectless smile.

"You," she said to Shelley, "you used to work here, right?"

Shelley wiggled her eyebrows, Groucho Marx-like.

"That's right," Walker said.

"So," the girl asked, "you don't want me to . . .?"

"Of course not," Walker said.

"I myself hail from Tougaloo," Shelley said to Walker. "May one inquire where you yourself hail from?"

"It's so gruesome," Walker said. "It's like a wildlife short."

"What animal is he, hey Gord?"

"I don't know why we come here anymore," Walker said.

"I bring you here to listen to dialogue," Shelley said. " 'Cause I'm your agent's gal Friday. It's my job."

"It's so fucking depressing."

"Slices of life, Gordo. That's what we want from you. Verismo."

"Do you see that guy? Does he really look like that? Is it something wrong with me?"

"No," she said. She spoke slowly, judiciously. "It's a wildlife short."

"She doesn't see him."

"She doesn't seem to, no."

"It's loneliness," Walker said. He shook his head. "That's how bad it gets."

"Oh, yeah, Gordon? Tell me about it."

"I hope," he said, "you didn't get me down here to pick on."

"No, baby, no." She patted his hand and smiled sadly. She shook her head vigorously and tossed her hair, and made mouths at him.

He watched her, wondering if she were not on speed. Of course, he thought, it was difficult to tell with Shelley. She was a clamorous presence, never at rest. Even quiet, her reverie cast a shadow and her silences had three kinds of irony. She was a workout.

"What are you doing with yourself, Shelley?"

"Well," she said, "sometimes I have assignations in crummy oceanfront hotels. Sometimes I get high and go through the car wash."

"Going to open your own shop soon?"

She was watching the man with the voice and his companion. She shrugged.

"I'm not sure I want to be an agent, Gordon."

"Sure you do," he said.

"Look," Shelley said, raising her chin toward the man, "he's gonna light a Virginia Slim. His balls will fall off."

A squat man of sixty-odd passed by their table, carrying an acoustic guitar.

"Hiya, Tex," he called to Shelley. "How you doin', kid?"

"Hi," Shelley replied brightly, parodying her own Texas accent. "Real good, hey."

The older man had stopped to talk. Shelley turned her back on him and he walked away, climbed the Miramar's tiny stage and began to set up his instrument.

"That fuck," she told Walker. "He thinks he's my buddy. When I worked here he practically called me a hooker to my face."

"I can't remember how long ago it was you worked here," Walker said.

"Can't you, Gordo? Bet that's because you don't wanna. Eight years ago. When I left Paramount." She sipped from her drink and turned toward the picture window. The last light of the day had drained from the sky but no lights were lighted in the Miramar Lounge. "Yes, sir, boy. Eight years ago this very night, as they say."

"Funny period that was."

"Oh golly," Shelley said. "Did we have good times? We sure did. And was I fucked up? I sure was."

"Remember gently."

"Clear is how I remember. I had little cutie-pie tights. Remember my cutie-pie tights?"

"Do I ever," Walker said.

"Yep," she said. "Little cutie-pie tights and I wanted to be an actress and I wanted to be your girl. High old times all right."

The elderly man with the guitar began dancing about the little stage. He struck up his guitar and went into a vigorous rendering of "Mack the Knife" in the style of Frank Sinatra.

"That rat-hearted old fucker," Shelley said. "I don't know if I can take it."

"How come he called you a hooker?"

"Well shit, I guess he thought I was one." Her eyes were fixed on the singer. "So I called him on it. So he cussed me out and fired me. Now I'm his old friend."

"And you a rabbi's daughter."

"Yeah, that's right, Gordon. You remember, huh? It amuses you."

"The rabbi's raven-haired daughter. Makes a picture."

She blew smoke at him. "My father was a social worker in a hospital. He was a clinical psychologist but he had been ordained. Or whatever it's called."

Walker nodded. "You told me that too, I guess."

"I told you it all, Gordo. The story of my life. You're forgetting me, see?"

He shook his head slowly. "No." He was aware of her eyes on him.

"Hey, you don't look too good, old buddy. You looked O.K. in Seattle."

"I been on a drunk. This is what I look like now."

"You're nuts, Gordon. You live like you were twenty-five. I'm supposed to be a hard-drivin' player and I'm not in it with you."

"It's a failure of inner resources. On my part, I mean."

"You better be taking your vitamins."

"Connie left me," Walker said.

He watched her pall-black eyes fix on his. She was always looking for the inside story, Shelley. Maybe there was more to it, he thought. Maybe she cares.

She drew herself up and studied the smoke from her cigarette. Her mouth had a bitter curl to it; for a moment she was aged and somber.

"Well," she said, "wouldn't I have liked to hear that eight years ago."

"I'm sorry you didn't get to hear it eight years ago," Walker said. "You get to hear it now."

She smiled, a thin sad smile.

"Actually," she said, "Al told me."

"Ah. So you knew."

"Yes," she said. "I knew."

"Hard-ass, aren't you?"

"Come off it, Gordon. You can't cry on my shoulder. It's a fucking ritual. She'll be back."

He turned away from her. The candlelight and the red-and-green lanterns were reflected in the seaward picture window, together with the faces of the customers. In the glass, everything looked warm and glad, a snug harbor.

"I hope you're right."

She only nodded, holding her faint smile.

"Maybe I shouldn't take it seriously," Walker said. "But I think I do."

A ripple of anger passed across Shelley's face, shattering her comedy smile. Her brow furrowed.

"Do you, Gordon? Then why the hell are you . . ." Her voice was trembling. She stopped in the middle of a word.

"What, Shell?"

"Nothing. I'm not getting into it." She was facing the bar and the gaze had fastened once more on the crooning seducer and his fair intended. Her eyes were troubled. "Look at him, Gordon. He eats shit, that guy. He's a hyena. Let's take him out." She turned to Walker and seized his sleeve. "Come on, man. You can do it. You would have once. Punch the son of a bitch."

"I'm on his side," Walker said. "He's a *bon viveur*. He's a sport like me." He picked up the drink beside his hand and finished it.

Shelley Pearce shook her head sadly and leaned her head against her palm.

"Oh, wow," she said.

"I suppose we could effect a rescue," Walker said. "We could hide her out in our room."

"Our room?" She might have been surprised. He thought her double take somewhat stylized. "We have a room?"

"Yes, we have a room. Should we require one."

"How many beds it got?"

"How many beds? I don't know. Two, I guess. What difference does it make?"

Shelley was on her feet.

"Let's go look at it. I think I want to swim in the pool."

"The pool," Walker said and laughed.

She laughed with him.

"That's right. Remember the pool? Where employees weren't allowed to swim eight years ago tonight? Got your bathing suit?" She worried him to his feet, clutching at his elbow. "Come on, come on. Last one in's a chickenshit."

He got up and followed her out, past the bar. As they went by, the crooning man gave them a languid eyes-right.

"Do you enjoy great music?" he was asking the blonde woman. "Symphonies? Concertos? Divertimenti?"

They rode the automatic elevator to the top floor and followed the soiled carpet to their door. The room behind it was large and high-ceilinged with yellow flaking walls. The furniture was old and faintly Chinese in ambiance. The air conditioner was running at full power and it was very cold inside. Walker went to the window and turned it off. Two full-length glass doors led to a narrow terrace overlooking the beach. He unlocked the bolt that held them in place and forced them open. A voluptuous ocean breeze dispelled the stale chill inside.

"This is neat," Shelley said. She examined the beds, measuring her length on each. Walker went out to the hall to fetch ice. When he returned, she was on the terrace leaning over the balustrade.

"People used to throw ice," she told Walker. "When I worked the front tables people would throw ice cubes at us from the rooms. It would make you crazy."

She came inside, took the ice from Walker and drew a bottle of warm California champagne from her carry bag. As she unwired the wine, she looked about the room with brittle enthusiasm.

"Well," she said, "they sell you the whole trip here, don't they? Everything goes with everything." Her eyes were bright.

"You on speed, Shell?"

She coaxed the cork out with a bathroom towel and poured the wine into two water glasses.

"I don't use speed anymore, Gordon. I have very little to do with drugs. I brought a joint for us, though, and I smoked a little before I went out."

"I wasn't trying to catch you out," Walker said. "I just asked out of . . . curiosity or something."

"Sure," she said, smiling sweetly. "You wondered if I was still pathological. But I'm not. I'm just fine."

"Do you have to get stoned to see me?"

She inclined her head and looked at him nymph-wise from under gathered brows. She was lighting a joint. "It definitely helps, Gordo."

Walker took the joint and smoked of it. He could watch himself exhale in a vanity-table mirror across the room. The light was soft, the face in the glass distant and indistinct.

Shelley's cassette recorder was playing Miles Davis's "In a Silent Way." She took the joint back from Walker; they sat in silence, breathing in the sad, stately music. The dope was rich and syrupy. After a while, Shelley undressed and struggled into a sleek one-piece bathing suit. He went to hold her but she put the flat of her hand against his chest, gently turning him away.

"I want to swim," she said. "I want to while I still know about it."

Walker changed into his own suit. They gathered up towels and their ice-filled champagne glasses and rode the elevator down to the pool.

The light around the San Epifanio Beach pool was everywhere besieged by darkness; black wells and shadows hid the rust, the mildew

168

and the foraging resident rats. There were tables under the royal palms, pastel cabanas, an artificial waterfall.

Walker eased himself into a reclining chair; he was very high. He could feel his own limp smile in place as he watched Shelley walk to the board, spring and descend in a pleasing arc to the glowing motionless water. Across the pool from where he sat, the candles of the lounge flickered; the goose clamor of the patrons was remote, under glass. In a nearby chair, a red-faced man in a sky-blue windbreaker and lemon-colored slacks lay snoring, mouth agape.

Shelley surfaced and turned seal-like on her shoulder, giving Walker her best Esther Williams smile. He finished his champagne and closed his eyes. It seemed to him then that there was something mellow to contemplate, a happy anticipation to savor—if he could but remember what it was. Easeful, smiley, he let his besotted fancy roam a varicolored landscape. A California that had been, the pursuit of happiness past.

What came to him was fear. Like a blow, it snapped him upright. He sat rigid, clutching the armrest, fighting off tremors, the shakes. In the pool a few feet away, Shelley Pearce was swimming lengths in an easy backstroke.

Walker got to his feet, went to the edge of the pool and sat down on the tiles with his legs dangling to the water. Shelley had left her champagne glass there. He drank it down and shivered.

In a moment, Shelley swam over to him.

"Don't you want to swim?"

He looked into the illuminated water. It seemed foul, slimy over his ankles. He thought it smelled of catpiss and ammonia. Shelley reached up and touched his knee. He shook his head.

"You O.K.?"

He tried to smile. "Sure."

In the lounge, the musical proprietor was singing "Bad, Bad Leroy Brown." Light-headed and short of breath, Walker stood up.

"I think I'm feeling cold," he called to Shelley.

She paddled to a ladder and climbed out of the pool.

"You don't look good, Gordon. You're not sick, are you?"

"No," he said. "It's just the grass. It's all in my head."

They went upstairs holding hands. Walker took another shower, wrapped a bathrobe around himself and lay down on the bed. Shelley Pearce stood naked before the terrace doors, facing the black, mist-enshrouded plane of sky and ocean, smoking. A J. J. Johnson tape was running—"No Moon at All."

When the piece ended she started the tape over again, scatting along with it under her breath. She went back and stood at the window like a dancer at rest. The back of one hand was cocked against her flexed hip, the other at a right angle from the wrist, holding her cigarette. Her head was thrown back slightly, her face, which Walker could not see, upturned toward the darkness outside.

He got off the bed and walked across the room and kissed her thighs, kneeling, fondling her, performing. His desire made him feel safe and whole. After a few minutes she touched his hair, then languidly, sadly, she went to the bed, put her cigarette out and lay down on her side facing him. He thought she wept as they made love. When she came she gave a soft mournful cry. Spent, he was jolly, he laughed, his fear was salved. But the look in her eyes troubled him; they were bright, fixed, expressionless.

"Hello," he said.

"Hello, Gordon."

"Some fun, eh kid?"

"Just like old times," Shelley said.

"Why did you ask me about the beds?"

" 'Cause I work for a living," she told him. "I need a good night's sleep. If there was only one bed I'd have to drive home."

"You treat yourself better than you used to."

"Yeah," she said. "Everybody treats themselves better now. You're supposed to." After a moment she said, "Hey, Gordon, how come you're sniffing after Lee Verger?"

"Come on," Walker said. "Don't."

"I'd like to hear you tell me how that's a good idea."

"It's my script," Walker said. "I gave it my best. I want to see her do it. In fact, I want you and Al to set it up for me."

"Al doesn't want to do it, Bubba."

"Do it on your own. Play dumb. Tell him you thought it was O.K."

"Why don't you take a rest?"

"I don't rest," Walker said.

"I knew you'd pull this," she said. "Al told me about your lunch. I wasn't surprised."

"Did you call them?"

"I called Charlie Freitag's office and I spoke with Madge Clark," Shelley said in a lifeless voice. "I guess they'll put you up for a day or two. Charlie likes you. Charlie likes everybody. They have to work it out with the location people, so it'll take a little time to fix." She stared at him with a vexed child's stare. He avoided her eyes.

"How about giving other people a rest? Like Connie, huh? Or Lee. Why don't you give her a rest?"

He only shook his head.

"She's a fucking psycho."

"That's your story, Shelley."

"Oh yes she is, Gordon. She's just as crazy as catshit and you better leave her alone."

"I want to see her," Walker said.

"You belong in a hospital," Shelley Pearce told him. He smiled.

"Your boss told me the same thing."

"Sure," Shelley said. "We're in league against you." She got up and walked to the foot of the bed and leaned against the bedboard. "You know what crazy people like most, Gordon? They like to make other people crazy."

"You have it wrong," Walker said, "you and Al."

"Her husband is with her. Her kids too. You want to walk into that?"

"I want to work," Walker said slowly. "I want to get back into it. I need a project I care about. I need to work with people I care about."

"You're so full of shit, Gordon."

"Don't be vulgar," Walker said.

"You're an assassin, man. You don't even care if you don't get laid if you can make some woman unhappy."

She stood beside the bed shielding her eyes from the harsh lamplight, then turned her back on him, folded her arms and walked toward the balcony with her head down.

"Every time I see you, we talk about your love life, don't we? We never talk about mine."

"How's your love life, Shell?"

"Thanks for asking," she said.

"Seriously."

"Seriously?" she asked, rounding on him. "Well, it does just fine without you in it. I get along without you . . ."

"Very well."

"Yeah," she said. "That's the line. 'I get along without you very well.'" She turned toward him and on her face there was a pained half-smile. "It's absolutely true. No question about it."

"Good," Walker said.

She had turned away again, toward the blackness beyond the window; she was singing:

I get along without you very well.
Of course I do.

She sang it twice over, snapping her fingers, straining for the key. He watched her come over to the bed.

"Wanna sing along with me, Gord?" She raised his chin with her palm. " 'Except when autumn rain . . .' " she sang. "Da dum de da da dum. Remember, Gord?"

"No."

"No," Shelley said. "Naw. Well that's good, Gordon. 'Cause then I don't have to worry about you. Or you about me."

"Oh, I don't know," Walker said with a shrug. "People should care."

"Is that what you think, Gordon?" she asked. "You think people should care?"

"Perhaps," Walker suggested, "you find the sentiment banal?"

"No, no," Shelley said. "No, baby, I find it moving. I find all your sentiments moving." She lay down beside him. "You want to fuck some more? Or you too drunk? Tell Mama."

Slowly Walker leaned forward, took the champagne bottle from beside the bed and drank. "Stop it," he said quietly.

"Yes," she said. "Yes, all right." She took the bottle from his hand. "Why her? Why Lee?"

Walker shook his head. "I don't know."

"You think you invented her," Shelley said. "You're going to be sorry."

"No doubt," Walker said, and shortly went to sleep.

Three Poems

Derek Walcott

A Latin Primer

for H. D. Boxill

I had nothing against which
to notch the height of my work
but the horizon; no language
but the shallows in my young walk

home, so I took all the help
that my right hand could use
from the sand-crusted kelp
of distant literatures.

The frigate-bird my phoenix,
I grew high on iodine,
I saw how the sun's murex
stained the surf's fabric wine.

I watched the blue hexameter
conclude in a white scroll,
like fallen palm-trunks with their
Corinthian capital.

And the brown cave that swims
with gladitorial nets
roared with the Colosseum's
coconut-lances, helmets.

I ploughed across the surf
with a boy's shins and kept
going, though the shelf
of sand under me slipped,

and found my deepest wish
in the swaying words of the sea,
and the skeletal fish
of a boy's bones lives in me.

I brooded under the bronze
dusk of imperial palms,
and saw them curl like questions
over Latin exams.

I hated scansion.
Those strokes across a line
like a drizzling horizon
darkened my discipline.

Small dolphins of elision
that leapt by formula,
a school of Superstition
begot by Algebra.

As bad as mathematics,
they made delight design,
they altered the thrown sticks
of stars to sine and co-sine.

Raging, I'd skip a pebble
on the flat sea, it still
scanned its own syllable:
trochee, anapest, dactyl.

Even the silvery mackerel
skittering in green satin
lagoons, moved in a school
bubbling their O's in Latin.

Miles— foot soldier. Fossa—
a trench or a grave. My hand
is hefting to toss a
last sand-bomb at fading sand.

I failed Matriculation,
in maths, passed, and with that
I taught Love basic Latin:
Amo, amas, amat.

In tweed-jacket and tie,
in the hot, wooden College,
I watched a language dry
like seaweed on its page,

and I heard the surf's voice
confirm in recitation
that all our sunlit joys
were lost now in translation,

and in between, the Market
roar with its iron shadows
as I sweated to make out
some crap of Cicero's,

and mused towards the harbor
from my desk, and turned as
heads plunged back in paper
softly as porpoises;

to practice what I preached
felt like a hypocrite,
their lithe, black bodies, beached
would die in dialect.

A silence stuffed my ears
with cotton, the clouds' noise,
through the tiered, white arenas
I climbed to find my voice,

but I remember; it was on a
Saturday, near noon, at Vigie,
that my heart rounded its corner
at Half-Moon Battery,

and stopped to watch the foundry
of midday cast in bronze
the leaves of an almond-tree
on a sea without seasons,

where, under me, Rat Island
nibbled at its white furrows,
that the frigate came sailing
cleared the tree's nets, and rose,

till whatever that great bird was
in either tongue made sense,
man-o'-war bird, sea-scissors,
fregata magnificens,

soaring till the bay's crescent
globed in its yellow eye,
and the past enclosed the present
while it moved steadily

beyond sheep-nibbled columns
or plumed Corinthian trees
and the roofless pillars once
sacred to Hercules.

The Whelk-Gatherers

Since hairy nettle, forked mandrake and malign
toadstool, frog-phlegm or bristling spiny urchin
are, by their nature, poisons, we should not question
what the moon-eyed whelk-gatherers mutter they have seen.
But who is this prince? How is he helmeted?
We watch high carrion frigates grow more common,
we see that our breath makes indecisive shapes,
but what disturbs him on the drenched ramparts,
staring at the stars like the insomniac sea?
What cloaked rumors run through the kingdom
hiding from the night watchmen's lanterns in wet streets?
Slapped by our inquisitors, the whelk-pickers only gibber:
"He is like a shell soldered to the sea-stone,
and there's no knife to prise it."

                              The subtle torturers
pretend to agree. The prelate's modern sermon
proves there is no evil but misdirected will,
but the eyes of the whelk-gatherers are as white as oysters
and his black sail slithers slowly under the mossed keel.

"It is Abaddon the usurper on whose heart the toad sticks."
"There is nothing under his helmet but your fear."
"He has drunk the sucked-out sockets of his own eyes,
and his sword-hilt is gripped by scaly talons."
"And he reappears after you have made the crucifix?"
"Yes. The sea-scorpion comes to his whistle like a dog."
"In his acid spittle the vultures unfurl their umbrellas,
and the sea shines like his chain-mail through the fog.
He fastens on the nape of the world and will not be prised."
When we give them broth, and this goes on for nights,

the youngest stares in the steam till it gets cold.
"If it is Abaddon the usurper what will he usurp?"
He shudders. "May seraphs stand against him in silver sheaves."

We explain it is mutinous moonlight on the waves,
it is primitive moonshine, that they are merely crazed
from the salt cuts in their palms, yet each one believes
it is Abaddon. If so, whose faith will free them?
How shall we confirm our doubts until we see them?
Then the youngest repeats in a voice inhuman
from hoarseness like surf wearily withdrawn
from our whelk-ulcered rocks: "If it is not him, then
why do the black-cloaked clouds claw at the moon
and smother her white scream like a mad woman?"
His gaze fixed on us over the lifted spoon.

Steam

for Leslie Epstein

Shawled women shoosh black rooks from a stubble field.
They rise like letters, they resettle in swastikas.
A red star shines on a sickle, the women fold
a seven-branched candlestick deep into a mattress.

In a copper twilight a scarfed girl peels an onion.
Almost to the heart. Brass basses drone in belief.
Gloved fists pound the door. She eases the latch open.
The head of Holofernes rots on a paring knife.

I remember bird-boned Grandma joining the squeak
of the piled axles, one note high, one low,
bicycles, barrows, waggons long as a week
in the fog at the field's edge, wishing we could flow

to the end of the earth. The star-muzzled moles
sniffing us coming would quietly withdraw,
gloving their velvet skins back into holes.
The stars themselves said nothing, but they saw.

When your own name sounds odd you're in a foreign
province. They shouted ours in columns
on somewhere Strasse in the black rook's reign.
The drizzle counted our heads. We became sums.

We believe in 10, in our hands, but 10,000,000
cramps them like crabs. All those bald zeroes
add up to a joke, like the eggs of lice milling
in a stubble haircut with its razored furrows.

But Art is immortal, our shirts were the bars
of its manuscript, our bodies flutes,
through the smudged sockets of eyes hollow as oboes
we trembled at those tremolos of Schubert's.

A window cracked can thin the temperature
of a steaming bath, the mirror's wispy hair,
the voices bubbling in bald, cobbled water,
with the tap off eventually disappear,

but the fog from potato fields, the error
that Webster christened "a general mist," condensed
not one face only in your bathroom mirror
but the zeros made by faster circling hands.

Five Poems

Bruce Weigl

The Kiss

All the goodbyes said and done
I climbed into the plane and sat down.
I was shaking from the cold and ached
to be away from the love
of those waving through the frozen window . . .

(Once as a boy I was lost in a storm,
funnel cloud twisting so near
I was pitched from my bicycle
into the ditch,
picked up by the wind and yellow sky,
my arms before me
feeling my way through the wind
I could not cry above.
Out of that black air of debris,
out of nowhere, my father bent down,
lifted me and ran
to the house of strangers.)

And again that day on the plane
he appeared to me,
my forgotten orders in his hands.
He bent down to put the envelope into my lap,
on my lips he kissed me hard

and without a word he was gone
into the cold again.
Through the jungle, through the highlands,
through all that green dying
I touched my fingers to my lips.

This Man

There's another world, in which this man
dragged his prize beagle pup
off the aqua deep-pile carpet
where it had shit and pissed in excitement
when the children had wrongly
carried it in to play.

He never broke his stride.
He grabbed the pearl-handled pistol from the closet
and he dragged that pup who whined
into the backyard of an evening
in an autumn stuck somewhere, lost
in the currents of larger, less important things.

Amigo del Corazón

In a café in barrio Las Américas
a lovely dark man has become my friend
drinking so much beer
we fall into each other's arms
in the shadows of palms
while his daughter,
the flower named Ana Ester,
sips her juice through a straw
and cannot help sway to a salsa
coming in from someone's lonely radio.
Flower of the night garden,
her eyes are on her father as he speaks,
her face open to him
because a radiance is still possible.

He pulls his pants-legs up
for me to see the scar of the wound
where shrapnel burnt a white
crescent moon into his brown skin.
We live mostly in silence, he says,
in houses smaller than the shape
he draws with his finger
in the air around the room.

We have not done well enough, he says,
not even love can pull you from certain
memories, the beer spilling at his lips
until he's quiet, and the music gone
and the heart quiet too in its time
so we can hear the night bird
sing what sounds like loss
into the dark barrio, and sing again,
but no song returns and I feel myself
lift away from the ghosts he recalls,
who crowd around us to sing
their own grind of troop trucks changing gears,

to sing the rattle of weapons
in the houses of those
who will not let the terror return.
He reaches for my hand to pull me back.
He touches his heart
and then he touches my heart too.

Breakdown

With sleep that is barely under the surface
it begins, a twisting sleep as if a wire
were inside you and tried at night
to straighten your body.
Or it's like a twitch
through the nerves as you sleep
so you tear the sheet from the bed
to try and stop the spine from pounding.
A lousy, worthless
sleep of strangers with guns,
children trapped in the alley,
the teenage soldiers glancing back
over their shoulders
the moment before
they squeeze the trigger.

I am going to stay here as long as I can.
I am going to sit in this garden as if nothing has happened
and let the bruised azaleas have their way.

In the Autumn Village

Half in the street and half
upon the sidewalk
in the Village off of Eighth
a man in the Saturday cold air
without shoes
tried to crawl across the street
through busy traffic.
I'm no better than you.
You've heard this all before
but you've got to help a man
who's trying to go some place
on his hands and knees.
I don't know what it means to crawl,
or where you would go,
in whose empty arms you could believe

but I put my books down to help.
I offered my arm
as if to a girl
stepping from her father's porch
into an evening.
I thought he'd pull himself
up on my arm
to walk away from us.
I was afraid and bent over him
as if he might leap out.

I'm no better than you.
I've got my reasons.
He couldn't move another inch
so I put my arms around him
and lifted him to the sidewalk.
The wind made some trees talk, the city
noise returned upon us
a wave I could ride out on and away.

Nine Poems

C. K. Williams

Fire

The boss, the crane-operator, one of the workers, a friend of
    somebody in the junk yard —
whoever it is who watches me when I pull up to see the fire in the
    cab of the huge derrick,
the flames in crisp, hungry, emphatic shapes scaling the suddenly
    fragile ribbed steel tower,
considers it a matter of deep, real suspicion that a stranger should
    bother to want to see this:
slouched against a stack of rusty, dismembered fenders, he regards
    me with a coolness bordering threat,
a wariness touching frank hostility, while, from a low warehouse
    building across the street,
another person, with a bulky fire extinguisher, comes, like some-
    one from the UN, running,
red-faced, panting, with a look of anxious desperation, as though
    all the fault were his.

Repression

More and more lately, as, not even minding the slippages yet, the
    aches and sad softenings,
I settle into my other years, I notice how many of what I once
    thought were evidences of repression,
sexual or otherwise, now seem, in other people anyway, to be
    varieties of dignity, withholding, tact,
and sometimes even in myself, certain patiences I would have
    once called lassitude, indifference,
now seem possibly to be if not the rewards then at least the
    unsuspected, undreamed-of conclusions
to many of the even-then preposterous self-evolved disciplines,
    rigors, almost mortifications
I inflicted on myself in my starting-out days, improvement days,
    days when the idea alone of psychic peace,
of intellectual, of emotional quiet, the merest hint, would have
    meant inconceivable capitulation.

Conscience

In how many of the miserable little life-dramas I play out in my
   mind am I unforgiveable,
despicable, with everything, love, kin, companionship, negotia-
   ble, marketable, for sale,
and yet I do forgive myself, hardly marking it, although I still
   remember those fiery,
if innocently violent fantasies of my eternal adolescence which
   could nearly knock me down
and send me howling through myself for caves of simple silence,
   blackness, oblivion.
The bubble hardens, the opacities perfected; no one in here anymore to bring accusation,
no sob of shame to catch us in its throat, no omniscient angel,
   either, poor angel, child,
tremulous, aghast, covering its eyes and ears, compulsively wash-
   ing out its mouth with soap.

Como

In the Mercedes station wagon with diplomatic plates the mother
    has gone out somewhere again.

The husband is who knows and who cares where in his silver
    Porsche nine-twenty-eight.

As they come across the dismal hotel garden from their after-
    dinner promenade along the lake,

the three noisy, bratty kids are all over the pretty German teen-
    ager who minds them.

One tugs at one hand, another at the other, the snotty baby pulls
    at her wrinkled skirt and wails,

but for all the *au pair* notices they might not be there, she might
    be on the dance floor at a ball.

It's not until the grizzled kitchen mouse-cat strolls out on the path
    that she comes to life,

kneeling, whispering, fervently coaxing the coy thing with tempt-
    ing clicks and rubbings of her hands.

The Dream

How well I have repressed the dream of death I had after the war
   when I was nine, in Newark.
It would be nineteen-forty-six; my older best friend tells me what
   the atom bomb will do,
consume me from within, with fire, and that night, as I sat, bolt
   awake, in agony, it did:
I felt my stomach flare and flame, the edges of my heart curl up
   and char like burning paper.
All there was was waiting for the end, all there was was sadness,
   for in that awful dark,
that roar that never ebbed, that frenzied inward fire, I knew that
   everyone I loved was dead,
I knew that consciousness itself was dead, the universe shucked
   clean of mind as I was of my innards.
All the earth around me heaved and pulsed and sobbed; the
   orient and immortal air was ash.

Easter

As though it were the very soul of rational human intercourse which had been violated,

I can't believe you did that, the father chokes out to his little son, kneeling beside him,

tugging at the waistband of the tiny blue jeans, peering in along the split between the buttocks,

putting down his face at last to sniff, then saying it again, with quiet indignation, outrage,

a power more moral than parental: at issue here are covenants, agreements from the dawn of time.

The child, meanwhile, his eyes a little wider than they might be, is otherwise unblinking;

all the time the father raves, he stares, scholarly, detached, at a package in his hands;

a box of foil-wrapped chocolate eggs, because it's spring, because the god has died, and risen.

The Park

In that oblivious, concentrated, fiercely fetal decontraction peculiar to the lost,
a grimy derelict is flat out on a green bench by the sandbox,
gazing blankly at the children.
"Do you want to play with me?" a small boy asks another, his fine
head tilted deferentially,
but the other has a lovely fire truck so he doesn't have to answer
and emphatically he doesn't,
he just grinds his toy, its wheels immobilized with grit, along the
low stone wall.
The first child sinks forlornly down and lays his palms against the
earth like Buddha.
The ankles of the derelict are scabbed and swollen, torn with
aching varicose and cankers.
Who will come to us now? Who will solace us? Who will take us in
their healing hands?

Racists

Vas en Afrique! Back to Africa! the butcher we used to patronize in
    the Rue Cadet market,
beside himself, shrieked at a black man in an argument the rest of
    the import of which I missed
but that made me anyway for three years walk an extra street to a
    shop of definitely lower quality
until I convinced myself that probably I'd misunderstood that
    other thing and could come back.
Today another black man stopped, asking something that again I
    didn't catch, and the butcher,
who at the moment was unloading his rotisserie, slipping the
    chickens off their heavy spit,
as he answered—how get this right?—casually but accurately *bran-
dished* the still-hot metal,
so the other, whatever he was there for, had subtly to lean away a
    little, so as not to flinch.

Bishop Tutu's Visit
to the White House

I am afraid for you a little, for your sense of shame; I feel you are
accustomed to ordinary evil.
Your assumption will be that disagreeing with your methods, he
will nevertheless grasp the problems.
You will assume that he will be involved, as all humans must be,
for what else is it to be human,
in a notion of personal identity as a progress towards a more
conscious, inclusive spiritual condition,
so that redemption in whatever terms it might occur, categorically
will have been earned.
How will you bear that for him and those around him, righteous-
ness and self are *a priori* the same,
that to have stated one's good intentions excuses in advance from
any painful sense of sin?
I fear you will be wounded by his obtuseness, humiliated by his
pride, mortified by his absurd power.

III   Writing and War

Vietnam—Fiction and Fact

Ward Just

I wish I were completely certain that there *was* a relationship between writers and the world. My impression, increasingly, is that writers are talking to each other, while the world stands by. My topic is supposed to be "Writers and War," and the first question that comes to mind is: "Why bother?" Specifically, why bother writing fiction when all a writer has to do is to go to Beirut or Salvador or Afghanistan or, in the past decade, Vietnam or the Golan Heights or Cambodia? It's in front of your eyes and if you have descriptive gifts, you have your story. According to William Broyles in a recent *Esquire*, the experience is also very sexy. So if you go to any of the above countries you can not only have a story but you become sexually excited as well. According to this man, war and sex are virtually indistinguishable. Beirut, therefore, is a kind of Club Med with PX privileges and a sniper round at the end of the day.

There are a few of us in this room who are obsessed by the Vietnam War, and have spent the better part of a writing life trying to explain it—or exorcize it, one or the other. Maybe it is the same thing. At rock bottom it is sorting out what you really feel and think, as opposed to what you are supposed to feel and think, or have been taught to feel and think. We have tried to find words to fit the images in our memory. In my case, it is a memory stuffed to overflowing, and that may be part of the trouble. But as the details recede, the truth should advance; as the memory goes blank, the consciousness becomes vivid. My own view is that the writer comes closest to the heart of the war, its infinitely still center, when he begins to invent Vietnam.

I was in Vietnam as a newspaperman, and I have wondered that if this persistence of memory is true for someone like me, what must it be like for those who were there in the line, not living in a room in the

Caravelle Hotel but in a foxhole near Danang. There has been an outpouring of Vietnam fiction lately, some of it from soldiers, some of it from newspapermen or ex-newspapermen. And, to my knowledge, one woman. Am I alone in feeling that our arrows are falling wide of the mark? The impulse of these books seems to me to be as follows: "Come into the pages of my novel, and live there awhile; and when you finish you'll be as obsessed as I am." And as unbalanced, and as unable to return to normal life—whatever that is. One recalls the memoirs and novels following World War I. Many of the books I have read lately have to do with life on the line, meaning horrors great and small. A friend killed, a child burned, a village destroyed. When I was a journalist covering the war, and would go out for two days with a unit, and nothing unusual would happen—no contact, or a routine firefight, or an empty village torched—we would call it "A Long Walk in the Hot Sun" sort of story. Inside the paper it would go. Nothing there for Page One or the Sunday Magazine or the Op Ed page. Yet there always *was* something there, some detail that lodged in the memory, paragraph eight in a forgettable story, but an indelible part of one's own personal history.

When I came home to Illinois in the summer of 1966—the trip was involuntary, having found myself on the wrong end of a hand grenade—the first thing I did was go to a friend's funeral. He had been killed in an automobile accident on Nantucket Island, an absurd accident, as absurd as anything I had witnessed or heard about in South Vietnam. The funeral was in Louisville, Kentucky, and when I showed up there—I flew out of Waukegan airport, scared to death in a Cessna because I was accustomed to helicopters and had unwavering faith in army mechanics—I felt I had somehow walked through a looking glass. It had not occurred to me that people were dying everywhere, not just in South Vietnam. They were even dying in Nantucket.

In any event, the funeral did not affect me in any particular way; I felt very much out of uniform, in my dark suit and polished shoes and my mind twelve thousand miles away. Later, I went on to Washington, where friends insisted that I and my colleagues were having a great ameliorative effect; we were being very well read. The Secretary of Defense himself had complained to my publisher about my copy. However, our effect was not so great as the effect of the reporters on television. I had not seen the war on TV, so for a fortnight, every night, I watched Cronkite and Huntley-Brinkley. And came away from that with a sort of double vision: No question that the pictures and the commentary that went with them were very powerful. The effect on the audience was palpable. At the end of a particularly violent sequence, a friend turned to me and said: "Isn't that extraordinary? The ability to bring the war into the living room? That's War Zone C right there on the tube, inside the box. Isn't it like being there?"

"Well, no," I said. "It wasn't quite like being there."

The blood on the screen doesn't come up as blood, and you can't hear the hearts beat. In case you're interested, the real thing is pulmonary. And the particular atmosphere of violence, the creepy anticipatory feeling, the feeling that you can hear a cosmic pin drop, even if you're in the jungle—or maybe especially when you're in the jungle—a thick silence and the smell that goes with it: that isn't there, either. It's a filmed reality, an edited reality—and if you think it's extraordinary on the small screen, try it up close. Nothing encouraged me to go on writing about the war more than watching it on television, and I say this now almost twenty years later. What I saw on the Sony wasn't a lie, but it wasn't quite the truth, either. It took place, it seemed to me, in a demilitarized zone of the eyeballs. Not good enough. So twenty years later we have all these novels, a full shelf by now; four or five of them are my very own. No one has done it yet, but a satisfactory grad student's thesis would be to take the books and their locales and write a literary history of the war. This would be a fiction writer's history. The Plain of Jarres, that's where old Stringer lost the balance of his mind. My Tho, that's where Nicholson got his famous interview. Binh Dinh Province, that's where Dietz was wounded. I am using some characters from my own novels and stories because I want to include myself in the general proposition that we have not done well enough. And by well enough, I mean to make the geography of Vietnam—its moral and social terrain—as vivid and unforgettable as Yoknapatawpha County or West Egg. Whatever else it may have been, the Vietnam War is consequential. In its way it is as consequential as the American Civil War, and for some of the same reasons—except the split in this war was not north to south, but rich to poor.

I always wanted to believe that art was separate from politics, Tolstoy, Dostoyevsky, Stendhal, Hemingway, Coetzee, García-Marquéz and three-quarters of the members of this panel notwithstanding. It seemed to me that we had entered a time when politics, as I thought of politics— political government, a way to manage the affairs of the state—was old hat, beside the point, irrelevant, here today, here tomorrow. I held with the—I suppose it's the denseness—of Henry James, though I was forced to raise an eyebrow when some critic complained that James and I were kin. We both chewed more than we bit off.

This war is indistinguishable from politics and the American character. Graham Greene understood this. So trying to see the war in miniature from a foxhole near Danang or a room in the Caravelle, to take a day's action and make more of it than a long walk in the hot sun, to make it a parable of life itself—this is possible to do. It hasn't been done, but it is possible: it is also, for this war, very unlikely. The truth is, the details of this war are not very different from the details of other wars. (And I think, really, it is not even necessary to have been there: the finest description of infantry tactics I have ever read comes in volume 2 of *The Remembrance of Things Past*.) In any event, it was the atmosphere surrounding this war that makes it so different: the sneaky way it began, the ambiguities with which it continued, the arrogance, the particular craziness in Washington, the frenzy of bombing at the end, and the scandalous system of conscription in which poor boys fought a rich man's war. That's a partial list. And also, not to forget, it was really an intellectual's war, since the reasons for fighting it were abstract: no part of the United States was ever threatened by the Viet Cong or the North Vietnamese.

There are no hierarchies here, but I think of five realities when I think of the war, and think about writing about the war.

The first, and most intimate, is the personal reality of the participant or observer, the soldier or journalist or engaged civilian, that can never be translated, a reality that is buried deep inside, inaccessible forever. It cannot be explained or understood fully any more than the brain can be fully explained or understood, because the brain cannot explain itself.

Next are the pictures and the false blood that come up on the small screen, and of course the effect of the camera on the action.

Next is the reality of the reporter, who carefully marshalls a set of facts leading to one version of the truth—or in search of the truth, as Mr. Pirandello's characters are in search of an author. This is noble work: real people suffered, and their stories demand to be told. Real people caused the suffering, and their stories demand to be told, too. They must all be given voice. The reporter's search is successful more often than you imagine, in part owing to the skill of the reporter, but also because the writer of nonfiction begins with the reader's trust. He may lose it, but he begins with it.

Next, verse—a stiff shot of cognac, a few lines that can stop the heart.

Finally comes the novel, in which the reader is asked to suspend disbelief—not always easy in the twentieth century. This novel, something written from deep inside the imagination—a letter from a very private place—where invention supersedes fact (and, as a general rule, a form whose success often varies inversely to its cargo of fact). The novelist tries to reconcile the chaos of memory to the shape of history and make something that will last from today to tomorrow, and in that the object is not to remember clearly but to forget selectively.

All these questions are awkward. The painter Max Beckmann, asked to describe his work, said that he had a code—and if you understood the code you understood his work and if you didn't you didn't, alas. So finally we come to the code, the narrative. Surely there must be one. But anyone who has spent any time at war knows that there is no narrative. Events reel drunkenly from day to day, out of control always. And it always seemed to me that war is a series of moments, some violent, some tedious, with no logic at all. In Vietnam there was not even the logic of getting from here to there, since no one knew where *there* was. Some live, some die, and it's the writer's duty to produce something more illuminating than: Life Is Unfair. Sure it is. But what else is new? So the writer finds a narrative, a story. The story is the logic and it is the writer's own code. Form follows function. If he or she writes it well enough, it will become the reader's story, too.

Somewhere in all of this must also be the heartbeat of history, some grasp of the time—today, and tomorrow, also. It has always seemed to me that the business of the novelist is to make order out of chaos: to shape the time. It is therefore to make something beautiful. And the object of it all—the invention, the narrative, the Why Bother—is, I think, consolation.

And in the case of the writer and the war, the consoling message: We must never do this again.

The Children in the Field

Gloria Emerson

I wish to speak about the soldier, children and war. All societies insist they love children and will protect them, which of course is a lie. And very often they love their reasons for saying they love their children and will protect them more than the children themselves. No country is more emphatic about professing to love its children than our own – the United States, which for more than a decade was eating its own children to keep the war in Vietnam going. In a foreign country, I think, the relationship between the soldier, sometimes not so far from being a child himself, and the children of the occupied country or the one in which the war must be fought, can be one of peculiar tenderness, a strange tenderness, or an astonishing cruelty. The children, unless they are starving or dying, sometimes remind the soldier of what he has so recently been. And some years ago, in the *Atlantic Monthly*, was a small piece, something of a masterpiece, written by a young man named David Rogers, called "The Children in the Field." Mr. Rogers was a conscientious objector, an older man in his family whose father wanted him to go to prison, but he chose to be a medic with an infantry platoon and never carry a weapon. He would not do the killing. He wrote a piece about the children in a village in Vietnam where his platoon often went, and the tensions and the need between the children and his platoon.

Calling himself "the medic," he wrote: "The platoon was securing the road when the enemy hit the third squad's position. A-K fire caught Wesley in the stomach, and a rocket grenade wounded two other men. The medic had to go back for them and, afterwards, blood was all over his fatigues and hands. The children were again on the road, looking where the firing had been. They also looked at him, standing there in the stink of the heat and burned powder and blood. He wanted them to

go away, but it was he who was new. Later, the Vietnamese soldiers would bring their kills out to the road. The children on the way to the market would have to pass the bodies."

There was a child David Rogers liked, about twelve years old, with, as he wrote, "a wiser, more reserved way about her than the other children living in the villages or selling sodas along the clay road. When candy was thrown from convoys, she never ran, but only watched out for her younger brother and sister. The medic always looked for her but never bought the Cokes she teased him with. He brought her presents at Tet and she gave him paper flowers when he came the next time. After the battalion moved out they never saw one another again."

And then he comes down to something that's very dark and very serious, and perhaps he doesn't even know it. He writes how the sight of Vietnamese children affected the platoon, and he says, "The children so young and constant would have the effect of confronting the soldiers with themselves. Coming back from an operation and seeing them running out to the road, the platoon was faced with something more alive than itself, against which each man would account himself. The dead in the jungle, those the platoon had lost or those it had killed, would come back for that moment. It was an anxious time, waiting for the smile or the shout to pull them through the memories."

Mr. Rogers writes about how the children would come up to the soldiers looking for food, wanting to sell a Coke, propelled by curiosity about the large foreigners with their pale eyes, whereas the Vietnamese women and the old men, all that was left, would only stare sorrowfully at the patrols. And of the children, he wrote, "It was an uneasy truce between them: the infantry sweating under their packs and still weary after coming from the jungle, and the children pulling on the men's gear begging for food, but resisting even a gentle hand wanting to touch them." So the children could resist even the gentle hand. When the children were near the soldiers, they wanted things. They did not want to be loved or caressed or always to hold hands. But the soldiers needed the children in this platoon because they needed to keep alive that very part of themselves which still had a belief in goodness or tenderness. This is almost impossible to do in such a war.

One hears over and over again the voices of Vietnam veterans—not all, a few here and there, I'm not a statistician—saying how awful the children of Vietnam were, how really bad they were. The children had grenades and would throw them at the American troops. The children were not to be trusted. Instead of being loving and docile children, successful children, which was what America wants, they were menacing, and they were as dangerous as the army the Americans fought. Some of these accounts may be true, some exaggerated. But the man who speaks of them is usually anxious to make the point that he found himself in an evil country, a bizarre landscape we know nothing about, where children are dangerous and respond in an evil way, so the choice of how he responded is no longer there. There is some truth that to be kind is to put your life in danger in a war, but all truths are open to argument. Vietnamese children were often used as messengers for the so-called Viet Cong or the National Liberation Front, but rarely given expensive weapons, such as hand grenades, which involved pulling a pin and an ability to throw. Those were usually given to older people. The children of Vietnam may have wanted to kill to honor their fathers or mothers or people they loved. Any army can recruit children. We have only to ask ourselves if the United States had ever been invaded by Nazi Germany, or was to be invaded today, what father would not expect his son over the age of seven to help in the resistance? In an occupied village, which of us would not expect our daughter to carry messages on behalf of the endangered republic?

So very often in Vietnam the children were hated, and what Americans most wish to deny, cruelty to children, cannot be denied, for a record exists of it. And it's in *The Winter Soldier Investigation*, an inquiry into American war crimes by Vietnam veterans of war, published in 1972 by Beacon Press and long out of print. It's much too dangerous a book to have been kept in print. And as the history of the Vietnam War becomes so lacquered and revised and made into a "noble cause," as our President has put it, I would oblige every teacher in America to have every twelve-year-old boy do nothing but memorize the testimony of doomed men of the great cruelties they committed in Vietnam. If we wish to change our society, we would have every child rise to their feet and say, "This is what happened," and recite one atrocity after another. In the pages of the testimony, in which the men give their full names— for they aren't cowards, they want redemption, not shelter—ranks, units, time in Vietnam, here is part of what a Spec-4 testified: "Also we threw full C-ration cans [which are quite heavy] at kids on the side of the road. Kids would line up, see, on the side of the road, and they'd yell at us, 'chop, chop, chop,' and they wanted food. They knew we carried C rations. Well, just for a joke, these guys would take a full can, as if they were riding shotgun, and throw it as hard as they could at a kid's head. I saw several kids' heads split wide open, knocked off the road, knocked into tires of vehicles behind them, and knocked under tank troops."

Last week, talking to a veteran, I said that I was going to tell to you the high level of gratuitous cruelty in Vietnam, almost playful, almost using Vietnamese children as kind of moving targets, you know, in a shooting booth. I said, "Well, but surely this was so unusual." He said, "No, no, no. I did it all the time." "Oh," I said. He said, "At first we threw underhand at them, and then it got better. We threw like we were throwing a ball, overhand." Most American men can throw very well. And they would aim for the child's ribs or head, and the weight of a C-ration can on a child under seventy pounds on the skull or in the chest will, of course, kill that child. So I said, "Well"—what is the question to ask a man with two children of his own?—"well, do you know what you felt as you did it?" And he said, "I didn't like them." I said, "They were children asking only for food." He said, "You don't understand how we felt—kill all of it."

And the testimony in *The Winter Soldier Investigation* from a marine, First Marine Division, about going into a village—this is a direct quote:

> There was a tiny little form, that of a child, lying out in the field with straw over its face. It had been clubbed to death. As later was brought out, the Marine that clubbed the child to death didn't really want to look at the child's face so he put straw over it before he clubbed it . . . The [ARVN] commanders were rather angry, put pressure on the Marine Corps, and these men were tried. However, they got very light sentences—a little slap on the wrist. I don't know exactly how much time they got nor do I know how much time they actually served, but they're on the streets again because I ran into one about two years ago in New York.

We can't save the children they killed, but we must look at ourselves and say, "How did such soldier-children come to be?" I was told that the poet Robert Bly, who was recently speaking in Minnesota, said that people who could do that were not children who were ever loved themselves, and Americans weren't nearly as good at loving their children as they thought. And it is perhaps something to think about, not to seek to punish the men who killed the children, because they will be punished in an infinite number of ways more than we can ever imagine, but to wonder what in us contaminates our own children so badly that they would throw cans of C rations at small boys and females—sex made no difference—just for the pleasure of seeing the head and the rib cage split.

I've recently read a novel which I find extraordinary, about a child at war. It's by J. G. Ballard, the book called *Empire of the Sun*. It's a novel based on his own eyewitness account, as he calls it, of life during the Second World War, during the Japanese occupation of Shanghai, and at the camp, the notorious camp, where he was interned from 1942 to 1945. The book is even more terrifying because the English child loves the camp as he starves and thinks he has never known such happiness as he has known there, and doesn't really want the war to end. And he sees cruelties that most children will never see unless they're Vietnamese or Lebanese. And in the camp for British civilians, the boy is particularly hyperactive. He has no food, but he keeps running and doing errands, and he has built up a completely artificial memento and he tries to make sense of the war, and he, Ballard, writes this: "War had nothing to do with bravery, Jamie thought. Two years ago, earlier when he was younger, it had seemed important to work out who were the bravest soldiers, part of his attempt to digest the disruptions of his life. Certainly, he thought, the Japanese came on top, the Chinese bottom, with the British wavering in between." And the boy thought of the American aircraft that had swept the sky over China, and, however brave, there was nothing the Japanese could do to stop these beautiful and effortless machines.

In a very perverse way, the child has learned to enjoy the war. Nineteen forty-three in this camp was the most wonderful year of his life. There had been a nightly program, organized by the British, of concerts and lectures, and a former district officer in Africa had enthralled the child by insisting he had discovered a lake the size of Wales and named it after himself. And as the Japanese began to lose the war, life grew harder in the camp, so of course the child wished that the Japanese would go on winning so there would be the evening program of concerts and music, and the spirits of the English prisoners would remain better. The child is numbed by all the confusions of the arbitrary price imposed on the settled and secure landscape of the war. When peace comes, it fails to fit properly, and he senses with the conclusion of the war the prisoners' real problems will begin, because he doesn't really see how these English adults will manage once the Japanese guards are gone. Because he sees that they have fared so badly in the camp, he can't imagine them managing anything at all outside it. Released British prisoners come to the camp, men in the most desperate states, who have been confined and starved and beaten for three years. They're very cruel to the child, and Ballard writes that the boy knew that one of them, Lieutenant Price, would have liked to get him alone and then beat him to death, not because the lieutenant was a barbarian, but because only the sight of the child's agony would clear away all the pain that he himself had endured.

It is what is learned and unlearned in wartime that is shattering. The best writers do not have to give you the details of weapons, or bombing, or infantry tactics, or what artillery sounds like or what the long thin guns are like. Writers often make the mistake of thinking that by describing combat, they will seize our hearts and haunt us forever. But David Rogers's piece on the children in the field never tells us what it was like fighting in the jungle, only in his words, how after the fighting, the medic, seeing the children, wanted them to go away, but they had seen it all before, and it was he who was new. I don't think it at all necessary to ever see a 105 howitzer or a rocket-propelled grenade to write about war. In Mr. Ballard's novel about the child prisoner, hunger is described best by describing how the English child will suck on his fist because even the pus in his mouth from his filthy hands is better than not having anything.

I used to think that one of the great stories about war was a story by Salinger called "For Esmé, with Love and Squalor." An American soldier is stationed in England. He's not cut out for any of it. He's in a specialized pre-invasion course directed by British intelligence in Devon, and he's lonely. And he's a little fragile for the thrust and roughness of the American army, any army. He goes to a tearoom and he meets a child that he's just seen at choir practice in a church. She is one of those extraordinary upper-class English children with noble forehead, impeccable speech and great curiosity. She talks to him, confiding that the mother is dead and the father has been "s-l-a-i-n," spelling out the word because she doesn't want her younger brother Charles in the tearoom to hear the word "killed" as spoken by her. And the soldier says that he is a writer, and Esmé—her name—asks the soldier, since he is a writer and going to war, if he'd write a story for her. And what does she want the story to be about, a thirteen-year-old little girl? She says that she would love it to be about squalor. "I'm extremely interested in squalor," Esmé says. So he makes a promise. And the next part of the story takes place at the end of World War II, in Bavaria, and the narrator is now called Sergeant X, and he and nine other Americans are quartered in a civilian house that belonged to Germans. In fact, Sergeant X, who was going to write a story about squalor for Esmé, is one of the Americans who had helped arrest one of the occupants of the house, and he has been in a hospital and is having a nervous breakdown. And he opens a book, and sees on the flyleaf in a small, hopelessly sincere writing, written by the woman he has arrested, a low-level Nazi, "Dear God, life is hell." And the sergeant keeps trying to write under "Dear God, life is hell" the following: "Fathers and teachers, I ponder 'What is hell?' I maintain it is the suffering of being unable to love." And he looks at the page and sees with fright that the handwriting is illegible and he cannot spell "Dostoevski."

Sergeant X tries to open his mail, but his hands shake too much. There is a package and a letter from Esmé, who has written him, and her brother Charles has sent ten large hellos and love and kisses, because he has learned to write. And Salinger writes, "It was a long time before X could set the note aside, let alone lift Esmé's father's wristwatch out of the box. When he did finally lift it out, he saw that its crystal had been broken in transit. He wondered if the watch was otherwise undamaged, but he hadn't the courage to wind it and find out. He just sat with it in his hand for another long period." At the end of the story the sergeant feels sleepy and addresses himself to Esmé: "You take a really sleepy man, Esmé, and he *always* stands a chance of again becoming a man with all his fac—with all his f-a-c-u-l-t-i-e-s intact." She had once said, in her English way, saying goodbye in the tearoom, "I hope that you come back with all your faculties intact."

But the story, read so many years later, now has a false hum. A man who had been hospitalized, who could not sleep or write, would not be consoled by the letter of an English child he had not seen for so long or a dead man's wristwatch. He would not so easily be restored. A pity, because if Salinger had told us that, it might have come close to being a remarkable story, and not just an exquisitely sentimental one.

Me and the Universe

Robert Stone

I'd like, I think, to speak about, or to speak to, two distinct issues that have concerned me in the course of the conference. And one of them is to say as much as I can muster about the writer and war. And the other is to continue a discussion which Leslie Epstein began yesterday concerning Benjamin DeMott's article on literature after the sixties, after the Vietnam War.

One phrase that has always haunted me, whenever I came across it, is a phrase from the Civil War that referred to what was called then—I guess what's called in all the wars now—going into the line, going into combat. In the Civil War, it was called "going to see the elephant." Civil War troops referred to it that way, and you can hear some prototypical sergeant of that era being asked, "Where are we going this morning, Sarge?" "I'm going to take you pogies up to see the elephant." Going to see the elephant. Barnum's show was playing in New Haven at the same time. The idea of seeing this curious beast completely foreign, seemingly, to experience. The idea of going to see the elephant. And what, we can speculate, is the experience of seeing the elephant? I know that it can't be described.

I know that words are words, and life is life, and that between them stands an absolutely unbreachable gulf. Language is language. It's a series of symbols. Life is something altogether different from language. They must not be confused, they are not the same. Language makes its flying leap at life, but it is not life. It is a function of life, a small part of life. Life is something altogether different. We can write our little poems. We can organize our series of words about the experiences that we undergo. But they cannot ever be brought into balance with living, because living is living. Basically, you do it alone. Basically, you do it in

silence. You cannot look to literature to live with you. You cannot try and live within literature, nor can you inform your life, even though you make your living writing, with literature. You've got to live, and there's no way around it. Literature won't pull you through, although it's there to help you. It can't get you through.

And I want to go back to my own seeing of the elephant. And I don't really know where to start. But I think it's necessary for me to describe the first that I ever saw of war in the proper sense. I was eighteen years old. I was in the Navy. I was assigned to the U.S.S. *Chilton* on a tactical air-control squadron. I was a radioman. We were at Port Said in October 1956. And we were called to general quarters because Port Said was under attack by French jets. I was supposed to know, it was my job to know, what kind of ordnance they were firing, although I didn't. I also had two general-quarters jobs—one was to set the sight on the five-inch gun on the rear of the ship. This was an old tub, an AKA, like the ship in *Mister Roberts*, except that it had boats to lower. It was an amphibious ship, and we were withdrawing civilians. I didn't know that I was supposed to be setting the sights of the five-inch. I thought I was supposed to be in the emergency communications room back aft. And I had learned Morse code. I had just learned to send it, and I was developing a fist, and I was seeing how fast I could send it. In order to do this, I would shave my own personal keyboard until it had a kind of hair trigger, so I could make it go faster and faster and faster and faster. And I could blow the other guy away, because he wouldn't be able to copy me, because I'd be so fast in this little game that we played. And I was back in emergency steering filing away at my tap board when my divisional petty officer, whose name was Schultz, arrived, looking for me.

Schultz began all his conversations with a little rhyme. The little rhyme he was using that day was "Spring has come, the grass is ris, I wonder where the birdies is." So I heard him come in and say, "Spring has come, the grass is ris, I wonder where the birdies is. Stone, how come you ain't up on the five-inch?" I said, "Well, this is my station, Schultz." He said, "You're up on the five-inch, setting the sight." And he said, "You go do it, and you're going to love it up there." So I hustled up, put my thing down, where it was stored, my own board, and I went up to set the five-inch. The five-inch sight on an AKA sits up on a little platform all by itself amidships. You climb up it on a little ladder. I didn't know how to set it. Nobody had ever taught me. I had no idea. Fortunately, it didn't matter one way or another. It was the French against the Egyptians. But when I got up on deck, the first thing I saw was that the sea was red. It was red.

And I stood there in the middle of the hatch looking at this water which was customarily more or less aqua and sometimes coral was visible through the bottom of it, and it was red. And not only was it red, it was swarming with people. It was swarming with Egyptians. Some of them were in this naval uniform thrown together, some of them were in little reed boats. Some of the people in the reed boats were trying to sell things to the boatswain's mates, who were shoving their reed boats off with marlin spikes, backed up by another level of boatswain's mates with machine guns. A French jet would go in. You'd hear it, I don't know how many minutes later. It was going along the corniche of Port Said, and it was killing every living thing. A man was sitting in a boat saying "Allah Akbar Rachman, Allah Akbar Rachman, Allah Akbar Rachman," all by himself in a reed boat, rocking back and forth, saying "Allah Akbar Rachman," completely out of his mind. And what it's always reminded me of was the pictures of cavalry combats where the horses' eyes are turned to one side in the middle of a cavalry charge. It reminds me of the eyes of the Egyptians who were all around us in their reed boats while the French shot them down, blew them up. Came right over our radarmen, as close as they could. And we were tied up to what's called Med Moor, tied up to a mole. We were secured. And so I climbed up on my little five-inch, and all around me was this red water and exploding reed boats and Egyptians floating face down and Port Said being absolutely blown apart. And I thought, "This is what I always thought it was like. This is the real thing. This is the way it is."

And it never occured to me that anybody was doing anything wrong. Not for a moment. And when I went down after my watch and I met the man who'd stood on the fifty-millimeter through that watch, we looked at each other and we smiled. And he said something like, "How about that?" And I thought to myself, "God, I'm glad I'm here. I'm so glad that I'm here." And it still didn't occur to me that anybody was doing anything wrong. And then I went up to take the five-inch again and the sun was going down, and the illumination rounds were being fired. And I had never seen illumination rounds being fired. And it seems to me that I had never seen anything more beautiful than illumination rounds. Every tenth round red, every fifth round blue, as it was in those days. Green—it varies. And the illumination rounds being fired against the sunset, I thought was the most beautiful thing I'd ever seen. And people were still being killed. And these jets were still coming in. And it took us half the night before we began to get angry, and only angry because our space was being violated.

Because some guy came up on this crazy azimuth with his Mirage, and he shot the mole out from behind us. So we were anchored basically to nothing. So we began to go to general quarters and we'd track them with our little five-inch and our fifty-millimeters every time, until more and more, every time they came over, they came over, it seemed, lower and lower; and we really really wanted to kill them, because it began to penetrate our consciousness that the harbor was filled with dead people. We lost two people accidentally and made a protest to the French.

But the overwhelming response that I had was "I always knew this was the way things were." I always thought that the world was filled with evil spirits, that people's minds teemed with depravity and craziness and weirdness and murderousness, that that basically was an implicit condition, an incurable condition of mankind. I suddenly knew what was meant when Luther said, "The world is in depravity." I thought I always knew it was like this. It took me all night long to figure something terrible was happening. But when I figured it out, I thought, "This is the way it is. There is no cure for this. There is only one thing you can do with this. You can transcend it. You can take it and you make it art."

Art doesn't nearly do it. Words are not life, they're only words. But you can transcend it. It is part of what we are. There is no way we can lose it. But we can turn it into art and if you turn it into art, it means that on some level the world's consciousness gets that tiny bit higher, and maybe somehow, in some unforeseeable distance, we can get beyond this and it will stop. But we cannot make it stop by saying, "This is not us. This is them. This is him, this is someone else." No, this is me, this is me. This is my head that's filled with murderousness. What I'm seeing out there exists as much within me as it exists within some French pilot who's now a middle-aged, or an elderly, middle-class man. He's no worse than me. I'm no better than him. I'm no better than you, you're no better than me. If we took the composite mentality within this room, if we took the fantasies, the perversities, the madnesses, the weirdness, the strangeness, the odd directions, our own crippled making-it-through-life psyches—because we are only people, we are only this imperfect play which is only so much—if we took our mentalities, or even mine, and projected it on a wall, we'd drive each other mad. If we took the psychic energy going on in this room now, it would drive us all crazy if we saw our own thoughts. We have only the responsibility, not to compete in terms of moral, in terms of moral status, but simply to get on with each other, and to extend to each other the civility that we do, and above all, if we are artists, to try and transcend this level of our lives, which is *of* us and which *is* us.

And it's this, in a way, that makes me think of Leslie's reference to Benjamin DeMott's article on how fiction became vaguely strange or weak or somehow immoral after the sixties. Which I think is, on

DeMott's part, meretricious; and in Leslie's statement, Leslie seemed to be dividing culture and the world between, you know, that which is life-affirming and that which is death-affirming, that which is positive, and—I don't think we can do that. I mean, if we could do that, what magicians, what wonderful magicians, we'd be! We'd make an end of this inferior condition of humanity, and we'd transcend it one step up, and we'd be the next thing up, whatever that is. But we aren't that. We can't make that separation between what's negative and what's life-affirming. We cannot. We are only who we are.

The other thing that struck me from the discussion was the idea of me and the universe, that great, that old American idea, which provoked laughter from people in the audience, as though it were some kind of absurd, pretentious position to take. Me and the universe. If I am not concerned with me and the universe, what am I concerned with? If I don't honor myself within the universe, whom do I honor? If I'm not concerned with myself in the universe first, why am I concerned with what's happening in Central America? Am I in favor of the cause of small, brown people because they are groovy? Because as an American, I like to see the little guy beat the big guy? Because some kind of received, pseudo-moral wisdom has rubbed off me from some institutional walls? Because I'm some kind of sentimental asshole? What is it to me, the condition of black people in South Africa, what do they care about me? Why should I care about them, when people of my blood, which is very political, and my language, which is very political, are in danger? Why do I care about them? They don't care about me. If I don't care about my position in the universe, if I don't care about me in the universe, what do I care about anyone? If it isn't me in the universe, what is it? There is nothing that motivates the nuns, the activists in Central America, except their position in the universe. That's all there is. That is the only morality there is, you and the universe. That is what makes it go, that we conceive of ourselves within the universe. If someone stands up and says, "I have decided to devote myself to political activities because I believe that history's decrees demand that the working class ultimately control the social system, and until that's achieved, things aren't going to work right," then as far as I'm concerned, I'm talking to a poison toad. That is not what draws me into politics, which I cannot stay away from. I don't know the dialectic from a Guernsey. But I've been drawn into politics only because what concerns me is me and the universe, and if me and the universe is not the bottom line, then is my preaching vain, then is your faith vain.

Session III:
Questions and Answers

AUDIENCE: Mr. Stone, you say you can't separate life-affirming and life-denying, that these things are together. And yet how can you say life and language or words are altogether different, if by art we can transcend the evil? In fact, aren't these two always connected, also?

STONE: No, they are *only connected*. They are not the same. No, I hold to it that life and language are not the same, that language cannot ever be up to life. We know that. There's hardly anything you can read that's going to give you the rush of adrenalin that plenty of things in life are going to give you. I put it on that coarse evidence. You can't get the same rush out of language, out of a description, that you can get out of the real event. I mean, that's coarse common sense, but it's true. Nevertheless, stories, the writing of stories—it's like dreaming. We require this as our psyches require dreams, to purge themselves, and as we require the sense of order, so that we can proceed day by day through life, this is our way. Art, not only language, not only the art of language, but all the arts, are our way of making it through life—of making a kind of sense, a kind of transcending, of the experience itself. Our words have only the relationship that the antelope in the Lascaux caves have to the real antelope. But nevertheless that's a lot of antelope in that cave. That is really essence of antelope. It really gives you a sense that if there is nothing else in the world, there are antelopes, and that's what language can do.

EMERSON: I don't know, I cannot disagree with Robert Stone, he's too intelligent to disagree with, but I'm so different.

STONE: I can't tell how relieved I am to hear that. That I'm so intelligent, that Gloria is not going to disagree with me.

EMERSON: I don't feel proud to disagree with him, I disagree with him profoundly. I just want to say one thing. I'm sure I lead a peculiar life, but the great consolation and the great compass of life has been literature, and all through the war in Vietnam (having helped a woman who undoubtedly was a Viet Cong—but *we* had not declared war, the *New York Times* had not declared war, I would have helped a GI, I would have helped anyone!) a line kept going through my head, after I'd helped her, "Never, never through me, never, never through me." And that helping her as I did escape certain death or punishment, "Never, never through me." By God, so shallow is my cultural life that I was watching television the other night, and there were Peter, Paul and Mary from the sixties getting up, and there was Mary Travers singing, "Never through me shall you be overcome," and it was Edna St. Vincent Millay's poem called "Conscientious Objector." I can't say that I was unhappy to see Peter, Paul and Mary. I didn't think Mary did well by the poem, but "never, never through me" ran, hammered, ran through my mind. And once, on a separate occasion, seeking to reach a group of Vietnam veterans, we were so separate that I said, "Look, there was a guy, who was an officer in the Great War, who in 1918 before he died, wrote a poem. Here's the poem, 1918, 'My friend, you would not tell with such high zest / [And they got that.] To children ardent for some desperate glory, / The old Lie: Dulce et decorum est / Pro patria mori,' which means, 'It is sweet and fitting to die for your country.'" And they said, "Wow, 1918, say it again," and I said it again, and they memorized it. What could I have said in a thousand, ten thousand, twelve thousand words, what could a psychologist have said to them, other than "You children, ardent for some desperate glory, you have been lied to and tricked"? And it was said in 1918, and more than anything, more than psychiatry, more than tranquilizers, they could link to that and say, "So we are not alone. Someone on the western front knew they were the surplus, too." And I find almost anything on the printed page comparable to almost any experience I've ever had. What rush is he talking about?

PALEY (FROM AUDIENCE): In talking about why we can't get the whole story, in a sense, maybe it's because the Vietnamese part is missing. And I wonder if you maybe know more than I know about it. I'd like to know to what degree, in what way, we can get the Vietnamese part, the Vietnamese story. I know, for instance, that one of the things we talk a lot about, a very simple thing, is Agent Orange, and we have lots of older, younger, men now suing the government, and so forth. And I hope they win every penny. But I haven't seen anywhere, really, a description or many articles on what happened to the Vietnamese with Agent Orange, which is still in the soil of their country and in the body and blood of their children.

JUST: That's inaccessible, so far as I know. It might not be, if some people would go over there and make a major effort. To my knowledge, nobody has.

EMERSON: Yes, a group of Vietnam veterans went in 1982, but they're not writers and poets. But, Grace, as you well know, what American magazine wishes to devote pages to the suffering of the Vietnamese people?

STONE: The *Nation*.

EMERSON: Name the magazine that wishes to write—

STONE: The *Progressive*.

EMERSON: The *Progressive*. And The *Nation*.

STONE: *Mother Jones*.

EMERSON: Maybe.

AUDIENCE: Who was the Australian journalist who wrote about the Viet Cong during the war?

EMERSON: Wilfred Burchett.

JUST: Wilfred Burchett is dead.

BARBARA FOLEY (FROM AUDIENCE): I'd like to make a brief comment about what Mr. Stone said and then ask a question of Miss Emerson, if I could. Mr. Stone is a very eloquent speaker, but I find myself really repelled by some of the implications of what he said, and he's certainly welcome to respond, if he wishes. I think the notion that war is somehow a consequence of innate depravity is just a rewarmed medieval notion of original sin. And if that is in fact the case, then there is in fact nothing we can do to prevent war. Now you may say the notion that war derives from class society is a poison toad to you, but frankly I find your view much more of a poison toad, because at least when you have the view that war comes from something in the social organization, then in fact there is something that can be done about it. I think that, secondly, therefore, the task of art is not just in some sense to transcend this depravity, but to be sure to give us a sense of the rough frame of that depravity, to represent it. But in trying to reveal its cause, all that you reveal is essence—if you are not in some sort of specious way simply dispelling its ugliness by somehow rising above it. I find the implications of what you have to say very reactionary in this sense. I'm sure that you'd like to respond, but the question I want to ask Miss Emerson—

STONE: First I respond, and then you ask—but I will respond only briefly. I think that you're the prisoner of a verbal machine.

PALEY (FROM AUDIENCE): Honest to God, Bob, cut that out.

STONE: That's what I'm here for.

JUST: Stop that. No violence.

EMERSON: All right. No violence.

AUDIENCE: Words *do* refer to reality—

STONE: Sure, they refer to reality. Reality is, well—

BARBARA FOLEY (FROM AUDIENCE): I think that is not a direct answer. My question to Miss Emerson is simply whether you think it would be useful, in talking about what it is that produces this whole syndrome of inhumanity that you described very eloquently, to stress more the question of racism. I was interested that you talked about very inhuman relations between the GI's and the Vietnamese children, and it seems to me that racism would have an awful lot to do with their ability to mistreat those children.

EMERSON: Yes. Do you suppose that American soldiers would have thrown full ration cans at small white children with long curls? I thought —

STONE: Sure, they would have —

JUST: Sure, they would have —

EMERSON: I don't know.

STONE: Oh, they do in Ireland.

AUDIENCE: Here in this country they did the same. How about in the sixties, when the kids got their heads knocked in on the streets of Chicago? What makes that different?

EMERSON: No, no, I was thinking of children under seven. Sure. All right. It's an interesting point.

AUDIENCE: Some of them were pretty damn young.

EMERSON: You're probably right. I don't know.

AUDIENCE: I wanted to ask the panel something about perception of reality. Maybe people who were involved with enormous acts of violence during World War II noticed that the inexperienced soldiers, who were, as Gloria says, little more than children themselves, seemed to relate what had happened to them through their previous experience, which in those days was only with the movies — we didn't have television before the World War. When there was a bombing or a shelling or a disaster somewhere in the English Channel, they would say, "Holy gee, holy gee, it's so real, just like the movies." In other words, their perception of reality was entirely shaped by the fact that they had no experience themselves except what had been presented to them by media in those days.

EMERSON: Well, what I'm talking about *is* the contamination of a culture, and of our very definition of masculinity, which seems personified in all its evil and fatuousness by President Reagan. And it is the greatest danger to every male child the world has ever known. And is what I'm calling for so preposterous? I'm calling for a redefinition of masculinity in our society, and a new way of raising male children—and punishment to those who persist in the old definition of masculinity, which mutilates the spirit of men so that they remain defective and injured and haunted in many cases.

STONE: Will it hurt, the punishment?

EMERSON: Yes.

STONE: I knew it would.

EMERSON: There is a moral equivalent to war, and it is not castrati. Instead of promising them the desperate glory, we send them out in our own country to do the hardest, most dangerous jobs. A man wants to join the Marines, the Marines say they are looking for a few good men. Give him to me and we'll send him to Detroit and he'll have thirty of the toughest kids in Detroit, and he can teach them basketball and arithmetic. And that's how we'll do it. I'm not suggesting that they lead lives that are pacified and predictable, but within our own country there are wars of ignorance and bigotry that they can enter into, and it is not the police I'm thinking of. And I'm calling for a completely new definition of masculinity which will make men happier. I don't want to take any more questions. Mr. Just will answer for me.

JUST: No, no.

EMERSON: We've agreed on this beforehand.

CORNELIA SPELMAN (FROM AUDIENCE): I'm upset, physically upset, as I'm sure that many of us are, by the true stories that we need to hear about the war, particularly about the cruelty to children. But my comment is really to witness to a war that is going on in our own country that no one has been a correspondent to, that no one sitting on panels is talking about; and that is the war on children in our own country—not just the children who are hit, the young people who were hit. I'm talking about infants' and children's physical and sexual child abuse in our country which affects—and I'm not a statistician either—about one in every five, and children who are murdered by their parents every year. The abused, well over five hundred thousand children. Not that it is worse than the war, but I think I would like to make a call on writers and on people of conscience to pay attention to the importance of this war in our own society. Of course, it's just "me and the universe," and the people who were killed overseas we must care about also. But it's shocking to me that more of us aren't aware of what's happening to children here, when we could be changing laws, working specifically with our neighbors when we see a child being hurt. But we don't because we still have the idea that the child is the property of his parents and that however parents want to treat their children is all right, and we don't have the right to interfere. We must stand up for these children the same way that we stand up for others. There are thousands of veterans of another kind in this country for whom no one is speaking, and I'm speaking for them now.

EMERSON: And I'm grateful.

AUDIENCE: As a combat veteran with many mixed feelings about what happened to me, one of the feelings that I did have when I came back was that I was grateful that our nation appeared to not want the war, and the war was not being honored by a segment of the population. And the concept that ours was a noble cause is repulsive to me —

EMERSON: Hear, hear.

AUDIENCE: — and yet, on the other hand, as a human being who experienced the event, I find it difficult to hold my head up high at times. I respect myself, or I try to, and I was curious as to you people, who have an understanding of it, how you would combat that concept that it was a noble cause, when in reality it wasn't, yet the people and the men who were there, in the majority, were good men.

JUST: The noble-cause question, it seems to me, should have no bearing, and does have no bearing on the people who were sent over there to fight. The two don't connect, because the various horrors that went on — principally in Washington, but also I suppose at My Lai — do not, it seems to me, stain the effort of the infantryman who was in Vietnam. It's not easy, and I feel awkward talking about this, because anybody who was actually there and fought has got the right to say anything he wants to say, and have it believed. That really comes with the territory. For my own part, I think if I were an infantryman over there, I would take all Washington rhetoric, or my rhetoric, or the rhetoric of anybody on this panel for that matter, and just push it aside. You've got your own story, and it doesn't have to be validated by me or by Gloria or by Bob or by Westmoreland or Ronald Reagan or anybody else. It's yours, and it needn't in that context — I do believe this — it need *not* be a dishonorable story. The personal story of somebody over there is not a dishonorable thing, I think.

EMERSON: And console yourself with the thought that, indeed, many of you were certainly better men than those who sent you. Of that there is no question.

JUST: Amen.

EMERSON: And I often think of revenge, and I wish to share with you my obsession with revenge, which I'm told repeatedly is unhealthy. I would have the war criminals chained to the great Vietnam monument done by Maya Ying Lin at twenty-three and have them read each of the 59,614 names, chained to the memorial, one by one, so we could see William Colby, Walt Rostow, General Westmoreland, all the colonels, read each name once aloud, and then set them free and watch their madness. That's nastiness.

SETTLE (FROM AUDIENCE): I want to defend Mr. Stone on the story that he told. And I want to defend him for a certain reason, and also the man back there who just spoke. There is an almost unbridgeable gulf between the person who has joined the forces and cannot get out, who is expected to obey orders, who is expected to stay within a system which is a wartime system, and anyone, anyone, watching it for any reason. This is a gulf so profound that it's almost, as I say, impossible to talk about. You had one man stand up there and tell you what was true about a war experience. It was not judged, there was no right in it, no wrong in it. The sea was red, and there were boats. He tried to tell you something of what it is really like to be at war, really like to have joined up, and really like to have faced it, personally, in the night, yourself, and realize that you are a responsible part of it. And I honor you, Bob, for saying it. It was not easy, and I know it.

AUDIENCE: Mr. Stone, aren't there different levels of moral corruption? We may all have some corruption in our souls, but I would not put myself, nor you, in the same league as an Augusto Pinochet or a Roberto D'Aubisson.

STONE: I don't think there's a generic difference. It depends on what the sources of your conception of morality are. It gets back to an old

Marxian question. Having a long association with Marxism, believe it or not, trying and turning it back and forth, I always get back to Marx's idea that reality is not conditioned by perception, perception is conditioned by reality. Well, what is the difference between me and Pinochet, and what is the difference between me and D'Aubisson? What's the difference between you, sir, who I don't know, as you don't know me, and D'Aubisson and Pinochet? That's a tough one. My conditioning is quite different from Pinochet's. On the other hand, sometimes I think that if I didn't have the mode of language and my art, that I would fall apart as a result of my own fear and anger. And sometimes it occurs to me that there's hardly anything to me except fear and anger, and yet sometimes it occurs to me that I have fear and anger licked, that my fear and anger are no threat to me at all. You want to know if some people are better than others, is that what you're asking? I don't think I tried to reduce everyone to the same moral level, but I think that morality in terms of violence is more complex. I think we should not hurry to make assumptions. I think we should live in a state of some tension about our own behavior. This is part of the medievalism which I'm going around, centuries after the fact, attempting to reestablish, because my plan is to start western civilization all over again.

AUDIENCE: I would like to have Bob Stone's comment on the figure that they're going to dedicate tomorrow at the memorial in Washington. Why has it taken it so long, and why does it have to be not the gift of the nation, but the funds of the veterans themselves?

EMERSON: Oh, you know the answer. You know the answer already.

STONE: I'm kind of torn about that. The wall, as anyone who's seen it knows, is so moving and so overpowering. I really think it's being spoiled by what looks like something that should be in the main square of Irkutsk. But on the other hand, I get the feeling that a lot of the combat soldiers want that monument, and I'm kind of torn between—if that's what they want, that's what they ought to have, because they are the people who had to do it, despite the fact that I think it really is rather a reactionary piece of sculpture, and it's really meretricious. I think it's meretricious art, I think it spoils the wall. I have certain reservations, because I think if that is what the majority of combat troups want, they ought to get what they want. So I have mixed feelings about it. I think that was a very wise thing, that wall, it was a very wise kind of monument, and I don't like to see it cluttered. But I have mixed feelings.

IV The Writer's Work— The Solitary and the Social

Of Poetry and Women and the World

Grace Paley

Our panel has a kind of an odd definition, and I think the three of us have taken it to mean whatever we want to talk about. And since what I want to talk about really partly follows the last panel, it may be a very good way of working our way into other subjects.

I have to begin by saying that as far as I know, and even listening to all of the people talking earlier, I have to say that war is man-made. It's made by men. It's their thing, it's their world, and they're terribly injured in it. They suffer terribly in it, but it's made by men. How do they come to live this way? It took me years to understand this. Because when I was a little girl, I was a boy—like a lot of little girls who like to get into things and want to be where the action is, which is up the corner someplace, where the boys are. And I understand this very well, because that was what really interested me a lot. I could hardly wait to continue being a boy so that I could go to war and do all the other exciting boys' things. And it took my own life, really, for me to begin to change my mind somehow—after a number of years of actually living during the Second World War. I lived a lot in army camps. And I liked living in those army camps; I liked them because it was very exciting, and it seemed to be where it was all at, and there were a lot of boys there, one of which, one of the boys, was my husband. The other boys were just gravy, so to speak.

But as time went on in my own life, and as I began to read and think and live inside of my own life, and began to work as a writer, I somehow stopped being a boy. At some certain point, I stopped being one, I stopped liking being one, I stopped wanting to be one. I began to think that I couldn't think of anything worse in this world than being one. I thought it was a terrible life, a hard life, and a life which would ask of me

behavior, feelings, passions and excitements that I didn't want and that I didn't care about at all. But, meanwhile, at the same time, what had happened was that I had begun to really live among women. Well, of course, I had always lived among women. All people, all girls, live among women, all girls of my time and culture live among mothers, sisters and aunts—and lots of them too. So I had always lived among them, but I hadn't really thought about it that much. Instead, I had said, "Well, there they are and their boring lives, sitting around the table there, while the men are playing cards in the other room. That's pretty exciting, right?" And it wasn't really until I began to live among women, which wasn't until I had children, that I began to look at that life, and began to be curious about it.

Now that brings us to writing, how we come to writing, and how we come to think about it. When I came to really thinking as a writer, it was because I began to live among women. Now the great thing is that I didn't know them, I didn't know who they were. Which I should have known, since I had all these aunts, right? But I didn't know them, and that, I think, is really where lots of literature, in a sense, comes from. It really comes, not from knowing so much, but from not knowing. It comes from what you're curious about. It comes from what obsesses you. It comes from what you want to know. (A lot of war literature comes from that, too, you know—the feeling that Bob Stone had, that "this is it." The reason that he felt like this is that it *hadn't been it* at all. So he wondered about that; but more of that later.) So I wondered about these lives, and these are the lives that interested me.

And when I began to write about them, I saw immediately, since my thinking in my early thirties really followed a period of very masculine literature, that I was writing stuff that was trivial, stupid, boring, domestic and not interesting. However, it began to appear that that was all I could do, and I said, "O.K., this is my limitation, this is my profound interest, this life of women, and this is what I really have to do. I can't help myself. It's going to be crummy. Everybody's going to say that it's trivial, it isn't worth anything, it's boring, there isn't a bullet in it, you know. Nobody's hitting anybody very much [but later on, I had a few people hitting each other]. And what else can I do?"

I tell that story only for other writers who are writing about things and thinking about things. To tell them that, no matter what you feel about what you're doing, if that is really what you're looking for, if that is really what you're trying to understand, if that is really what you're stupid about, if that's what you're dumb about and you're trying to understand it, stay with it, no matter what, and you'll at least live your own truth.

233

We've talked about whether art is about morality or—I don't even understand some of those words, anyway. But I do understand words like "justice," which are simpler. And one of the things that art is about, for me, is justice. Now, that isn't a matter of opinion, really. That isn't to say "I'm going to show these people right or wrong," or whatever. But what art does—and this is what justice, to me, is about—although you'll have your own interpretations—is the illumination of what isn't known, the lighting up of what is under a rock, of what has been hidden. And I think people feel like that who are beginning to write. I was just speaking to somebody who's a native American, who was saying that what he's doing is picking up this rock at the mouth of a cave, or whatever it is, just out there in the desert, picking it up and saying, "I've got to light this up, and add it to the weight and life of human experience." I'm saying that's what justice is about, and that's what art is about, that kind of justice and that kind of experience.

As for me, I didn't say, "Well, I'm going to pick up this rock and see if there are any women under it." I didn't think about it that way. But what I thought to myself is "Gee, am I tired of some of these books that I'm reading! Some of them are nice, and some of them are exciting, but, really, I've read about this stuff already. And who's this guy, Henry Miller? You know, big deal. He's not talking to me. My life's not going to get a lot sexier on account of him. His is, no question about it."

So, luckily, I sort of understood it. It was just luck or pride or something like that. Or just not being able to accept slurs at myself or my people, women, Jews or whatever. Even in Shakespeare, it always hurt my feelings. So I didn't really know that that's what I was going to do, but that's really what I set out to do, and I did it, and I said, yes, that's really what I want to add to the balance of human experience.

We were accused of having been doomstruck the other day. And in a way we should be, why shouldn't we be? Things are rotten. I mean things really—I'm sixty-one and three-quarters years old, and I've seen terrible times during the Depression, and I think the life of the people was worse during the McCarthy period. I just want to say that, throw that in extra. That is to say, the everyday life, the fearful life, of Americans was harder in that time than this. But the objective facts of world events right now are worse than at any time. And we all know that and we can't deny it, and it's true that it's very hard to look in the faces of our children, and it's terrifying to look in the faces of our grandchildren. And I cannot look at my granddaughter's face, really, without sort of shading my eyes a little bit, and saying, "Well, listen, Grandma's not going to let that happen." But we have to face it, and they have to face it, just as we had to face certain things much less frightening.

If I talk about going to the life of women, and being interested in that, and pursuing it, and writing about it all the time and not thinking about whether it was interesting or not, and finding by luck—I like to say by luck, you know, it's polite somehow—finding by luck that it was interesting and useful to people, I also need to talk a little bit about what the imagination is. The word "imagination," as we're given it from childhood on, is really about imagining fantasy. We say, "Oh, that kid has some imagination, you know. Some smart kid, that kid imagined all these devils and goblins, and so forth and so on, and hills and falling down and another world, and so forth." But the truth is that—"the truth," you know what I mean: when I say the truth, I mean *some* of the truth—the fact is, the possibility is, that what we need right now is to imagine the real. That is where our leaders are falling down and where we ourselves have to be able to imagine the lives of other people. So that men—who get very pissed at me sometimes, even though I really like some of them a lot—men have got to imagine the lives of women, of all kinds of women. Of their daughters, of their own daughters, and of the lives that their daughters lead. White people have to imagine the reality, not the invention, but the reality of the lives of people of color. Imagine it, imagine that reality, and understand it. We have to imagine what is happening in Central America today, in Lebanon and South Africa. We have to really think about it and imagine it and call it to mind, not simply refer to it all the time. What happens is that when you keep referring to things, you really lose them entirely. But if you think in terms of the life of the people, you really have to keep imagining. You have to think of the reality of what is happening down there, and you have to imagine it. When somebody said, "Isn't there a difference between the life of Pinochet and of you, sir?" [to Robert Stone], you have to imagine that life, and if you begin to imagine it, you know that there's a damn lot of difference between those two lives. There's a lot of difference between my life, there's a lot of difference between my ideas, between my feelings, between what thrills, what excites me, what nauseates me, what disgusts me, what repels me, and what many, many male children and men grownups have been taught to be excited and thrilled and adrenalined by. And it begins in the very beginning. It begins in the sandbox, if you want to put it that way. It begins right down there, at the very beginning of childhood. And I'm happy, for my part, to see among my children and their children changes beginning to happen, and among a lot of young men—that's one of the things that's a most encouraging thing to me: to think that some of these young guys have been listening, and imagining the lives of their daughters in a new way, and thinking about it, and wanting something different for them. That to me is what some of imagining is about.

I don't think that all human beings from the beginning of time have dreamt about war, have thought about war. It's possible they have, but I don't swear to that—because I wanted to say earlier that I don't think it's "me and the universe."* I think in the western world it's "I and the universe," because that's the western world. We're individualists! And we say "I and the universe," we say "I and the tree, I and the mountains," I and almost anything. Whatever it is, it's "it and I." But there are cultures, after all, which said "we." They said "we." And the fact that we can't imagine the word "we" as sometimes a word meaning all of humanity, sometimes "we" meaning all of nature, is also a failure of imagination, as far as I can see.

So those are the things that I've been thinking about a lot as a writer, both solitary in the world and at my desk, and I just want to read you one little thing and that's how I'll conclude. I probably left something out, but you can't say everything. We're really talking about society and artists, and this was in relation to the question of what was the responsibility of the writer, if there was any. And I thought, "Every human being has lots of responsibility, and therefore the poet and the artist also has responsibility, why not?" But this is the responsibility of society:

It is the responsibility of society to let the poet be a poet
It is the responsibility of the poet to be a woman
It is the responsibility of the poets to stand on street corners
    giving out poems and beautifully written leaflets
    also leaflets they can hardly bear to look at
    because of the screaming rhetoric
It is the responsibility of the poet to be lazy, to hang out
    and prophesy
It is the responsibility of the poet not to pay war taxes
It is the responsibility of the poet to go in and out of ivory
    towers and two-room apartments on Avenue C
    and buckwheat fields and army camps
It is the responsibility of the male poet to be a woman
It is the responsibility of the female poet to be a woman
It is the poet's responsibility to speak truth to power, as the
    Quakers say
It is the poet's responsibility to learn the truth from the powerless

---

*See Stone, p. 213.

It is the responsibility of the poet to say many times: there is no
freedom without justice and this means economic
justice and love justice
It is the responsibility of the poet to sing this in all the original
and traditional tunes of singing and telling poems
It is the responsibility of the poet to listen to gossip and pass it
on in the way storytellers decant the story of life
There is no freedom without fear and bravery. There is no freedom unless
earth and air and water continue and children
also continue
It is the responsibility of the poet to be a woman, to keep an eye on
this world and cry out like Cassandra, but be
listened to this time.*

---

*First spoken in almost exactly these words at the *American Poetry Review* Conference on Poetry and
the Writer's Responsibility to Society, spring 1984.

Of Poetry and Justice

C. K. Williams

In Euripides' tragedy, *The Bacchae*, there's a curious moment. One of the focuses of the play is the band of women, the Bacchae, or Maenads, whom the god Dionysus has driven to ecstacy and madness and who have fled to the mountain Cithaeron. The episode I'm referring to concerns some men who tend cattle on the mountain, who come across the women and behold various miraculous, clearly supernatural happenings. The women weave snakes into their hair, suckle deer and wolves, and cause milk and honey to spurt from the earth. The men are awed, realize that they are surely in the presence of divinity, and yet when one of them suggests that they capture the women and bring them to the young king Pentheus, so as to gain honor from him, they readily agree. There's no doubt that they know what they're doing is injudicious, that they are meddling with things beyond them, but they do it anyway: they attack the women and of course are put to flight, their cattle are destroyed and the women run amok, destroying a nearby village.

I have come to be fascinated by the speech, the quality of speech, of that one among the men who persuades them to act against their own best interests, for a reward of, at best, dubious promise. The messenger who relates the events—one of the cattlemen—refers to this other person as a wanderer, reports that he had lived in towns, where he'd learned, as I translate it, to "talk fast," and thus he was able to convince the others to undertake their rash action.

There's a similar episode near the beginning of *The Iliad*, when Agamemnon, inspired by a dream, means to stir his armies to greater ardor. The dream he reports to them is not the one which promised so much, but one he makes up, which seems to indicate that there is no hope for the Argives to conquer Troy, that they should, as he himself interprets it, cut their losses and go home. His soldiers are only too glad to comply: there's a general roar of relief and everyone heads for the ships. Agamemnon, though, has already plotted with the other generals, and Odysseus, in a surprisingly brief exhortation, cons the warriors into staying, convincing them that they are more than dishonoring themselves by thinking of their own mere mortality when there is triumph and glory to be gained, even though, as one of the common soldiers points out, the booty and riches of that triumph will actually go to Agamemnon and the other kings.

One last short example:

In his confessions, when St. Augustine is ruefully recounting the more than wild-oats days of his youth, at one point he says: "I fell in with a set of sensualists, men with glib tongues who ranted and had the snares of the devil in their mouths."

"The snares of the devil in their mouths." What is Augustine saying here? What is Agamemnon counting on in his duplicitous scheming? What is this "fast-talking" that Euripides recounts? In all these instances, there seems to be implied a special mode of speech, which is available to certain people. What that mode precisely is, is difficult to specify. Augustine gives no example of the persuasive power of his tempters. Neither the speech of Euripides' character nor that of Odysseus seems particularly eloquent. But it's clear that, in all these instances, the one who does have access to this way of speaking has an almost magical power of persuading others, of changing their minds, of convincing people to act against their own clear best interests.

We have seen, of course, a recent, and to many of us a particularly disturbing, instance of this phenomenon in the recent campaign and election. I don't think it is necessary to be radically partisan (although I fiercely am) to find the Reagan phenomenon at the very least mysterious, at the slightly less than very least, potentially sinister. The "Teflon presidency," yes, but the issues go much deeper, and our sense of disquiet, or of despair, should be much more acute.

What informs that despair, what we can find terribly upsetting, is the sheer power of Reagan's presence before the electorate. There *is* something magical in his speech, in just the terms I have meant to emblemize with my stories of the ancients. He is neither particularly eloquent, nor does he, according to surveys, really offer a program which for most voters is actually inspiring. Rather, there is something in the way he speaks himself, in the way he interprets reality for his listeners, which seems to nourish a hunger in the spirits of those who believe in him.

Historically, we know this isn't a rare circumstance. Perhaps the latest and certainly one of the most effective of this line of inspiring persuaders was the utterly banal, undersized, contemptible Hitler, who proposed a master race of creatures who were as unlike him in as many ways as possible, but who was received with the same sort of adoration and acceptance, and who maintained his eerie power over the German nation until it was in utter ruin.

It is the business of philosophers and psychologists, I suppose, to make deep investigations of this uncannily delusive and effective language, to analyze its efficacies and its victims' susceptibilities. As a poet, though, a poet with an extreme interest in the conflicts and paradoxes of our common life, I feel a deep and intimate sense of both menace and impotence when I consider all of this. For the poet, too, clearly has a special relationship to language. Traditionally, our mode of speaking has also been conceived of as approaching the magical or the mythical. When Plato banished the poets from his ideal state, he obviously had in mind our capacity for speaking in just such a potentially disruptive and compelling way to the youth of his Republic.

But it is unfortunately one of the continuing quandaries and struggles of the poet's life that although we know poetry is our most rigorous and most compelling mode of speech, as well as of action, for the most part it is as what we call "private citizens" that we find we actually can and do enter the public realm, as advocates, as organizers or as participants in movements and pressure groups.

I'd like, for a moment, to disregard all of this, though. Just for the time of this talk, I'd like to try to postulate a poetry which would actually fulfill Plato's prophecy about its potential effectiveness. Perhaps I, too, am being utopian, but I want to imagine a poetry which would indeed incorporate all the persuasive powers Plato envisaged for it, while not ceasing to be poetry in a way that the poet can feel *is* poetry. I mean even to imagine a purely lyric poetry which would have this power of moral persuasiveness and social effectiveness. The reason I feel comfortable in making such an audacious program for poetry, even for the most innocuous lyric, is because I believe that many—most—poets, *do*, in reality, have in mind just such ends when they are composing their poems, and I believe it is really *all* poetry which can be defined this way. You'll notice I am in some, but not really very much, disagreement with some of our speakers yesterday. I believe it is poetry itself which must be reaffirmed, not any particular sort of poetry. The very act of writing poetry is profoundly social, and beyond this, the consciousness which composing poetry presupposes in our age I believe also presupposes an awareness of the democratic vision which has been our opportunity and our responsibility since the French and American revolutions.

I do not believe there is or can be such a thing as an "innocuous" lyric, because the most delicate and apparently fragmentary poetic meditation must, sooner or later, come to consider its own basis, the soil, as it were, which nourishes it, in the self of the writer and in the wider social situation of that self. Poetry is, in its most profound definition, just exactly that relation between the most intimate self and the most public. The way we define the interaction has to do with how we define our poetry. The way we conceive of the private self as being in relation to the broader issues will determine for us the very music with which we speak, the image-world which we will evoke for our readers, and the symbolic intensities by which we'll affect that reader. How directly or obliquely a poem deals with social or political issues is a large question, too unwieldy to be dealt with here, but the question is always rooted deep within the poet, in our most personal hope and love and terror; otherwise, what we are writing simply isn't poetry. The soul is not a creature living in a creature, isolated by walls of space from other creatures, but neither is it a kind of commandant of public reality, exclusively obsessed by larger issues, greater ideals, to which other individuals might be called upon to sacrifice their own precious individuality.

There's a term for the condition I am so awkwardly groping towards here, a condition in which the individual's passions and commitments, sense of intimate need and desire for spiritual and social progress are in an active relation. That term is "justice," and it is in our consciousness of justice, that astonishing concept, that poetry can become the affective and essential agent that poets intuitively understand it to be.

We have come, since the American revolution, to misunderstand and even unwittingly to belittle the concept of justice. We have tended to equate it with liberty and the pursuit of happiness, as a part of that apparatus which represents for us freedom *from* various oppressive potentials in government, and in our fellow citizens. But justice is *not* a recitation of the Bill of Rights. As the Greeks conceived it, as the founding fathers of America envisaged it, as the great so-called romantic poets dreamed it, justice is the human absolute, it is that which subsumes all the lesser categories. It is the active state of awareness of the individual participating in and bringing about the highest possibilities of human life in common, and of the human life in the individual, because these are inseparable. Justice is not, in this visionary sense, a public state of affairs, but a personal condition: it offers the human spirit its most passionate participation in common life, in common hope, in a contemplation of a society which is a process towards the moral perfection of every individual in that society.

I would offer, further, the notion that there is a positive and an active hunger within the soul for justice. I believe that once we are offered a vision of justice which includes the individual as the active and effective agent of his participation in that vision, there is no going back: we will henceforth, however inarticulately, suffer from that hunger.

It is my sense that the great historical paradox of our epoch, the age of revolution, the age of justice, is that those who manipulate us against our best interests and our best intentions, those who enact their malevolent magics on us, work through just this hunger, and this need. I believe that the efficacy of the diabolical Hitler and the incompetent Reagan is in their offering us simulacra of a vision which the spirit craves and needs, not for economic well-being, not for our securities and our fear of neighbors, but for that inward sense we have that human life, the human adventure, offers more than is being delivered, offers just this promise — justice — which is so demanding and so elusive.

Poetry cannot offer such false gods. Because poetry must arise from and be received in the most intimate places of the soul, it cannot lie in its speaking, nor can it speak at all without a general vision of that flow between the public and the private which is our spiritual adventure. The reason Plato banished the poets wasn't because he didn't like our singing, it was for these reasons: because we cannot not tell the truth in what we see, because the way we speak is truth, and because expediency and a petrified vision of soul, however apparently benign, cannot withstand the dialectic of the poem: that dialectic is the dialectic of the self and the soul, both of the individual and the community.

I do not know exactly what we will offer America and the world in its coming crises. I do know, though, that our poetry must offer, or rather continue to offer, a positive vision of that larger conception of justice which is our grandest political heritage. We must not despair for the susceptibility of the human to be deceived and deluded, but we must rededicate, redefine and rearticulate our basic ideals.

That is clearly not *all* we can do, as poets and as citizens, in this terrible time, but it is the very least.

Facets of Censorship

Mary Lee Settle

I had a sense, at the beginning of this, that it was going to be as hard for our quiet subject to follow the dramatic one of war as it is for peace to follow war. I begin to think that this is not so, even though Tolstoy, when he wrote *War and Peace*, if you remember, wrote about the peace part first, and then he got busy on the war. I hope, and I think that the others already have made peace much more presentable than I thought it was going to be at the beginning of this session.

The word "justice" has come up, and has been beautifully defined. The last time I read the word "justice" in this context, it was by Joseph Conrad, who talked about art as the highest kind of justice—and who, by the way, I chose as my grandfather, because I think that once you're an adult you should be able to choose your psychic family. (Your born family is an accident, your psychic family is a choice.) Therefore, my grandfather, Joseph Conrad, said that the task of the writer was, "above all, to make you see, that and no more, it is everything." This is what we all have in common in the room, even though in your terms and in Auden's terms poetry makes nothing happen. It exists as itself, and when I say the word "poetry," I'm talking about the kind of writing which tries for this justice and for this vision that is transmitted to you to make you see. It is poetry when Nikolai, at his baptism of fire, feels the bullet wing past his ear and says, "Why are they shooting at me, everybody likes me?" This has gone beyond words into communal experience of the past.

Now, we all feel nice, and we're all isolated in our workroom, we're all writing rather beautifully. The room is wonderful. You're neither man nor woman, neither old nor young. As Tolstoy again, you're Natasha, seventeen years old, dancing in front of the mirror, just as much as you are Nikolai. In my isolated room, I have been a soldier in the English wars. I have written a five-volume book that starts in mid-seventeenth century, and when people ask me if any of this is autobiographical, I say, "Yes, indeed." The first volume, in which I was Johnny Church, a twenty-year-old Revolutionary soldier in the English Civil Wars, came as near to my soul as I've ever written about. Now we have to come out of the room. Outside and in the modern world, here we are together, and I want to talk about something about which we all have a ruminant and pleasant certainty.

So I'm going to talk about censorship. Now we all agree about censorship. Censorship is something that happens in another country. It's political. It has to do with diabolic people, either on the right or on the left, who won't let you print what you want to. It has to do with the freedom to write. Of course it has to do with all of that. But now I'm going to talk about three kinds of especially American censorship, which are just as dangerous to the written word as any political censorship ever was, and far more possible for us to do something about in our daily life.

We have lost our arrogance. When you sit in a room by yourself and you say, "Oh, I can't write that. It won't sell. They won't like it," that is self-censorship. We're very good at it. Grace mentioned the McCarthy period. More people were thrown out of their jobs by private companies before Joseph McCarthy ever heard tell of them than were ever stopped by McCarthy himself. The whole blacklist in Hollywood, the blacklist in the newspaper business—all of those blacklists were made by private Americans getting there first. This kind of censorship, this personal censorship, has to do with politics in that way. "I can't say that, the CIA wouldn't like it. I can't say that, the publisher wouldn't like it. [That be-all and end-all.] It won't be printed in *TriQuarterly* if I say that." This is all personal censorship, and it is a thing to be watched in that room like the devil.

The second kind of censorship, and now we can all stop feeling guilty about what we did this morning and start agreeing again, is commercial censorship. The *New York Times* serves me well quite often, usually with the crossword puzzle. This morning it did it well with the line, "Altering a bestseller for trip across the Atlantic." This has to do with the decision by two publishers and an agent that someone should alter totally the ending of a book so that some amorphous American called—are you ready?—"the housewife in Kansas City" would be pleased.

Well, I've got news for them. The housewife in Kansas City might be a Ph.D. in English with three young children, who can't afford to buy a hardcover book and is getting her books from the library. I've got more news for them. To make decisions about what this housewife in Kansas City wants is an insult to her. It's an insult to the public for the most parochial industry in the center of the most parochial city in this country—I'm talking about the publishing industry in New York, some of whom are afraid to cross the river; they think that they fall off in New Jersey—to make decisions for the rest of this country.

We're sitting almost in the geographical center of this country. How dare they speak for us? But that commercial censorship can be ominous, not because they're deciding what you can read, but because they are literally keeping you from reading, keeping you from finding what you want. Here are a few facts about the way the conglomerate industry works, now:

Sometimes the conglomerates have been very good at paying more. Often the conglomerates have scared the editors to death so that they're looking over their shoulders all of the time and saying, "I can't take that book, I've got to produce a million-five for the company, and that book isn't going to do it." Sheer fear, self-censorship plus commercial censorship. (I'm talking about the hardcover book; I'm not talking about getting over the barrier into paperback, which is when we can all afford the book.)

I'll speak about the novel now because I know more about that. Its censorship, its commercial censorship, starts with the signing of the contract. Innocently, here comes Bugs Bunny with his book, all about how to be a bunny, and a publisher talks to him and says, "I'll give you five thousand, and even ten thousand, dollars for the rights to publish this book." Whee, he's going to be published! The book goes into the publishing machine. A book with an advance like that, unless the editor of it is willing personally to fight it through the company, is already put in an economic slot about publicity. That economic slot says, "Well now, look, we've only spent five to ten thousand dollars on this book, we don't need to spend any more. Let it go on its own." Eighty percent of the novels published are sold five months at least before any review comes out, that's eighty percent of them, before even the trade reviews come out. They're sold on—I love that phrase—the bottom line. Every time I hear "the bottom line," it scares the hell out of me, because it's never going to be good, the bottom line. The two bottom lines, you will find in *Publishers Weekly*, and in the catalog that the publisher puts out: bottom line one—twenty-five thousand copies in print. This is based often, and certainly in the conglomerate publishers, on the size of the advance. They want their money back. They're in business. An advance of five to ten thousand dollars is going to get five thousand books printed. O.K., Baker and Taylor, Ingram—those are the big wholesale houses that almost all bookstores buy through—and Dalton's and Waldenbooks buy eighty percent of the hardcover books that come out. They buy them predicated on line one, twenty-five thousand copies in print; line two, paid promotion. Paid promotion means we get sent around the country to hustle. It also means that they're going to have big enough ads so that some poor bookseller who is trying to make a living is going to have people come in and ask for the book, because they're going to foment interest in this book.

Well, this is all fine if it happens to you, but what happens to the first novel? What happens to the five thousand copies? That's where you come in. That's where you read reviews you can trust. Now I'm talking about getting over the great walls of commercial censorship. You want a book? Insist that your bookseller order it. You want a book? Insist that your library order it. You know, we don't write entirely for money. We write to be read. We want to see these books. It's like throwing things over the wall, like the women in Ireland used to go to London and pack up contraceptives and throw them over the wall of the police as they came into Dublin airport. This was the first woman's movement in Ireland. Throw them way over the heads of the customs and the police so your sister Nelly can catch them. We're trying to throw these books over a great huge wall, and this is the way you can help it.

Now the third form of censorship, which we should all hang our heads in shame about, is aesthetic censorship. Frankly, who the hell are we to decide that somebody across the street can't read Judith Krantz if they want to? We suffer from being forced to push our books out in commercial censorship, why should we answer it with a kind of aesthetic censorship? We don't know. Somebody said, "Oh, it's terrible the number of detective novels that sell." Well, frankly, about half of them sell to me. When I'm working on a serious and solid book that I expect you all to read, I read about a detective novel a day. It's the best legal dope in the world. It makes you feel good until the next morning you can work again. This is the kind of thing that we can do. We can have as much respect for other people's tastes as we expect and demand that they have for ours.

There may be in a town, in a library down on the corner, only eight people that ask for Mary Lee Settle's book. They ought to get it. I don't think that it should be bought instead of Judith Krantz's book. I've never read Judith Krantz, and here I am up here, defending her. But the principle is the same.

We have been talking a lot about an election. And a lot of this has to do with the kind of aesthetic censorship I'm talking about. I come from the South, where people are very—"embarrassed" is not the word— "paranoid," I think, is the word I'm searching for, about intellectualism. The phrases are there. "So-and-so's as smart as a Philadelphia lawyer." That means "watch out." That means "Smart, they're just full of a lot of big ideas. Smart, forget it." Watching national television and listening to national radio, you would have thought a solid phalanx of rich, vicious good old boys went to the polls and voted for Reagan in the South. That is a kind of media censorship. Call it "taste." Call it "intellectual prejudice."

The truth is that a lot of people didn't know what to do. But one thing they knew: they did not want their tentative minds insulted, and this is something that we have to watch for all the time, in aesthetic censorship. How many of you who would never say the words "dago," "yid," "nigger," will speak quite calmly about a "redneck"? Do you know that "redneck" is a pejorative term that has gotten people shot in my state? This is the kind of aesthetic censorship that is a danger in our country. We simply must go out to meet those who are less articulate than ourselves.

Now I've told you how to get over three kinds of censorship. You're on your own, and I'm going to go home when this is over and go back in that room where I can write the truth as arrogantly as possible.

Session IV:
Questions and Answers

AUDIENCE: Isn't there an implication that if I say, "Oh, you ought to read this," that what *you're* reading is not as good as this. Otherwise, I wouldn't suggest it.

SETTLE: No, just leave it around. You know if the title can't hook him, then it's my fault. I've often been asked who I write for. Of course, that's an unanswerable question. But I do have an answer for it, and it has to do with Chicago. I once gave Max Steele a copy of O *Beulah Land*, and he lent it to his brother, who was coming on a business trip to Chicago. He left it in a hotel room, and somebody came in and stole it. I was never more pleased with a story in my life. I mean here's a guy who's read the Gideon Bible one too many times. He hasn't got anything to read, and he goes in and cops a book and it's mine. Isn't that wonderful? There are more ways than one to get other people to read. Brag about it.

AUDIENCE: The only thing I would say in response to that is that I feel like I have had people damn my tastes, condemn what I was reading, and have found out that, in fact, they were right. I agreed with them after they said, "You know, instead of reading *this*, you ought to read *that*."

SETTLE: Well, why can't you say, "When you finish this, why don't you read that?" That's less pejorative. Aesthetic censorship came up the other morning with the Virginia Librarians' Association. You think you've got problems. To be in a small town in Virginia with Jerry Falwell breathing down your neck, when you're a librarian, is not easy, and they're a gutsy bunch, let me tell you. But one lady said, "Now do you

250

think that we ought to just give the people the books they want? Why don't we make them read the books that are good?" And I said, "That's exactly what aesthetic censorship is. We have no right to do that. There is a balance all the time."

AUDIENCE: Grace Paley was talking about how the poet should be a woman. What about being a man? Should a woman be a man?

PALEY: No, I mean the poet has been a man for such a long time, so it's for the woman to be a woman, and the man to be a woman.

SETTLE: Teiresias was both.

AUDIENCE: Bob Stone was up here a while ago, and I don't know if he worries about something like that but—writing has a way of affirming whatever it talks about, and so if you write a very believable scene of horror, maybe it's inspirational to all the serial murderers out there.

SETTLE: I know what you mean. I doubt if anybody, for instance, ever had a love affair because they read *Madame Bovary*, but they may have had a quickie if they saw *Deep Throat*. It's the difference between art and pornography. There is plenty of killing in *War and Peace*, but there's not the gratuitous violence that there is in a Sam Peckinpah obscenity of a movie.

AUDIENCE: It sounds like you're only talking about the difference between literature and popular literature.

SETTLE: Maybe I am. I don't think it has to do with subject.

AUDIENCE: If you write for a lot of people, you'd better be careful, but if you write for literature classes, you don't need to worry about it.

SETTLE: Who writes for literature classes?

AUDIENCE: Well, frankly, who else reads *War and Peace*?

PALEY: Could I say something? You know, when Bob Stone described what happened to him on that ship and when he looked out at that sea, I don't think anybody would say, "Boy, that's groovy, I mean that is great, I can't wait until I see a sea of blood." When he opinionated about it afterwards, that's when things changed. I mean, that's when the description changed, and it became something entirely different; it became another story.

WILLIAMS: The idea that literature, writing, promulgates what it depicts is ridiculous. One of the main implements of fiction is irony; if you read Bob Stone's *Flag for Sunrise*, the brutality in it doesn't make you want to go out to do it. And I don't want to get involved in women against pornography at all—but I'm one of the people who believes that you can't say I'm going to censor my little razor's edge of *Deep Throat* and the rest will be all right.

SETTLE: I'm not saying that, you know.

PALEY: That's another subject.

SETTLE: I do think, though, that you can have the opinion that one is evocative, and the other is not necessarily so.

AUDIENCE: Now that women have positions of authority, we have Maggie Thatcher and Golda Meir, two women who sent their countries into war. And if Jeannie Kirkpatrick has her way, we'll be involved in a war in Central America.

PALEY: I agree with you, you know, but in a way, that's sort of easy, because there's no question but that as we change culturally, and so forth, and as we grow in a certain direction, there's no question but that some women will play that role. And there are some women that play that role in their own home. But in general, and this is true certainly in all parts of this hemisphere, and in much of the world, the raising of small boys into warriors and into soldiers and into competitive killers and into people whose major excitement and aspiration is power and, from that, death, is a fact, and it can't be denied. And if a few women want to get into the act, you know, well, that'll happen. My hope is that men will improve faster than women get rotten.

AUDIENCE: My question is for Grace Paley, and the point you just made on power. It seems that power is wrong, but what are you going to put in place of power, or is there good power versus bad power?

PALEY: I'm not just talking about power. I'm really talking about domination, and that's a little different than power. And that again

252

begins very early. And you know, just to talk a minute about it, when you think about bringing up your children—I'm talking of men as well as women—you think *you're* bringing up your kids. I like to think the nice things in my children are a couple of things I put in there. A couple of injections of virtue, decency. But you don't really. The world is bringing up your children as much as you are bringing up your children. Nobody brought up their children to go to Vietnam. Nobody brought up their children, in my generation, to live through a period of such terrible drug abuse so that in my children's lifetime—and my children are around thirty or so—there are more dead people, there are more people who have been killed by cars, drugs, war, by all of that, than there are in my lifetime, and I lived through the Depression and the Second World War! I'm talking about this country only in this respect. But in other countries too, a parent does not necessarily bring up a child in that sense.

I've got the preface to a tiny story. I'm very fortunate to be able to go to the playground again now that I have a grandchild, and I always like doing that. And so I was out there when this little boy comes over to his mother and he says, "How come Laura can run so fast? She's a girl." Well, his mother is one of the real great feminists of lower Brooklyn, you know. So I think of the fact that when she heard this, she looked at him, and she said, "That's my Matt, you're talking."

Do you see what I'm trying to say? So that already at the age of four, with a feminist mother and probably an awful nice father—probably; well, why not?; let's say he's great—with all of that, this little boy has already been drinking out of this bottle of superiority and domination. I don't like to use the word "power" myself. I use it sometimes by accident. But what it is, is this child growing up in this already. Luckily, his mother said to him, "Girls can run as fast as boys." Which, of course, isn't true—but that's another story.

WILLIAMS: I've got to stir the hornet's nest a little bit, because although I like to think of myself as as much of a feminist as a man could be, and there's no one on earth who I love as much as Grace Paley, I think that you're leaving out a lot. When you were talking and I started to think of my own life experience, there wasn't at all this split between male/female in terms of the issues you're talking about. And if we're going to talk about intimate nurturing, it wasn't necessarily one's father who taught you that you had to be dominating and competitive or however we would define the malevolent aspects of masculinity. And neither was it only men who voted for Reagan in the election. In fact, one of our great disappointments was that women didn't enact what you're saying. And we can talk about women's consciousness, not having yet been touched by what it will be someday, but you're making it sound as though it's some intrinsic thing that can be healed just by sort of turning the things around. Perhaps there is an element to that, but there is more—it seems to me that it's a much more complex issue. Indira Gandhi was a quite beautiful woman when she was young, and quite a feminine woman, and I gather, that at the feet of Mahatma Gandhi, was quite the perfect gentle woman, but she had become quite a ruthless dictator, or wanted to be, at the time she died. So I don't know that this man/woman problem is quite so easily resolved. As I say, I'm serving up a little nest of hornets that probably—

PALEY: But you're right in that it can't be easily resolved. If it was, we would resolve it. It's historical, it's in our literature. Our great literature really begins with Homer—that's our great western literature—it's a murderous literature. It *begins* at that point, so how are you going to get rid of it? Of course, that's exactly the point I meant to make when I described this little boy. And as for the mothers, my mother raised me to do things that really were in some ways harmful, which she did to protect me—I mean she really did it to *protect* me. And you ask a black mother in certain parts of this world, of this country, why she's telling her kid to be quiet or to do this or do that. Well, there are these acts which are done to protect the child or to advance the child. You have a son, if you don't have the consciousness of this mother I described, Matthew's mother, well, you don't want that kid growing up with everybody laughing at him, for God's sakes, because of what they think are cockeyed notions. A woman will do the same thing. So it's historical, and it takes time, and if the world lasts, we'll make it.

SETTLE: I'm really going to put the cat among the pigeons now. There was one historic time in the twentieth century when the women of a certain country reached total equality with the men. It was in England during the Second World War, and there was total conscription of women at the age of eighteen. They could go into the land army, they could go into the women's navy, the WRENS, they could go into the women's army, the ATS, or they could go into the WAAF, the Women's Auxiliary Air Force. I joined the Women's Air Force in England with three hundred conscripts from the East End of London, all eighteen. In the whole experience that I had I never saw the feeling of power or the feeling toward war as a prerogative of either sex. It was individual with people. You've never seen a sergeant until you've seen a female sergeant full of a sense of domination over people. There's still one I'm after. She's out there somewhere. She's four feet, eleven inches tall, and she made me run behind her bicycle. It was the lowest moment of my life. Well, I've made her immortal now. But this is what I mean: I cannot enter this argument because I did not have the experience of these attitudes being sexual, ever.

There were sensitive pilots, there were bloody awful women. There were very, very violent women. I was thrown down a flight of steps because my accent was different, so they decided I was a "toffee nose" from Up West. (This means that I was a snob from the West End of London.) Therefore, they drank a lot of beer and grabbed me by the shoulders and threw me down the stairs. Well, I lay on the ground, and that's when I joined the WAAF, because I said to these ladies who were leaning over me, in the best Anglo-Saxon that I knew, where they could put their whole past and the whole war and the WAAF and the lot. After that, I was quite accepted. But then again, this crossed sex lines. It didn't cross them so much in the American army only because women weren't conscripted. If they'd been conscripted, if they'd been in the jobs that we were in, it would have been very much the same for them. The awful thing was that after the war, gradually and gradually, women in England went right back to what I call "the dropped-womb set." Trudging along with market baskets and being allowed to go to a pub once in a while and so forth. I'm talking about that awful phrase "the working-class woman," with whom I spent most of my time, thank God. I'm one American who cannot be a snob about England. And these people went right back often to what they'd been before the war, to what was expected of them before the war, and when *All the Brave Promises*, which was the memoir that I wrote about the war, came out in England last summer as a paperback, somebody went to the Imperial War Museum to find photographs of women in uniform to put on the cover of that book and they could not find them, because there was no record in the RAF part of the Imperial War Museum of the war duty of 180,000 women.

PALEY: That just seems to show exactly the way I feel about it. I mean, it's not that women were sent back in this country and went back to the kitchen immediately too. The same exact thing happened. As far as I'm concerned, I would not like to be equal with men in being enlisted. I wish that men would be equal with me in not being drafted, in not being enlisted, in not going to war.

255

AUDIENCE: I wanted to point the subject in a little bit different direction. Something that Mr. Williams said about Plato and banishing poets reminded me of when I was living in North Carolina. The *Asheville Citizen* had a policy against running poetry on the editorial page, but it would certainly run the television listings. I wonder if he doesn't feel that the poet has been banished in some ways from the society and replaced by the image makers, by the trendsetters of television. And how is poetry confronting that?

WILLIAMS: That's the question every poet obviously faces. There are all sorts of rationalizations that one can make for the utter argument of it. I think, in my own history, when I began to realize that poetry wasn't much read, my first impulse was to react in the way I try to to most problems I run across that touch me, which is to assume that I'm doing something wrong. So if there was something to be done, the first thing I thought I should do was to see whether there was any way I could change things myself—which, unfortunately, is of limited efficacy. The other thing is, I don't know how many people in history have ever read poetry, just as I don't know how many people have ever actually read the Constitution or the Declaration of Independence, even though they can be inspired by them. Then there's the old trickle theory, which is what Reaganism is based on: the idea that if you give the rich people enough money, some of it will trickle down to everyone else. Maybe poets like to think that there's a sort of percolation theory, which would hold that poetry, if you get enough of it around, will percolate upwards to where it can affect something. There might be something to that. I think I'm really groping, because this is something that I think about all the time, and I don't quite know how to introduce you to the argument.

I was at a high school in Houston the other day, and I met with two classes of ninth-graders, about eighty percent black, ten percent Chicano. I read them my poems, my adult poems—I guess I don't have children's poems—the poems I'd read to you if I were reading, and they were ready for them, they were responding. They asked just the questions I would have wanted anyone to have asked about the poems. So there is something that you begin to feel, that you *are* a part of what we call the culture of our society, whether or not everybody in the culture is actively participating or not. Another thing—this is a little axe I have to grind—about television, which you mentioned: I think that when we meditate, we meditators and thinkers, on television and on the people— always other people, of course—who watch television too much, we tend not to assume for them the critical apparatus that we have ourselves. I don't think that when people watch the situation comedies on television their souls are being destroyed. I think that they allow the stuff to enter into their souls at just the proper place. But—except in elections, which is another question, and the political parties—I don't think television is quite the tool for evil that thinkers think it is, because we don't have enough respect for the actual intelligence and critical acumen of the people who watch, who are offered nothing else, really.

AUDIENCE: Do you think that the educational reports by the government and some of the reform groups coming out right now do justice to poetry?

WILLIAMS: I don't think it matters that much. I'd like to believe that the reading of poetry is a sort of subversive activity that's available to people when they need it. When Terrence was talking yesterday about poetry in Central Europe dealing with issues of great moment . . . I think that poetry does that everywhere. Poetry is something that's available to people at times of crisis, and when they do find themselves, as for instance in America during the Vietnam War, in extreme social uncertainty, or extreme tension at least, then there's a great turning to poetry. During the war, when the people began to feel these things, they turned to poetry, and it was very gratifying to the poets. Then when the period ended, when the conflicts went back down into the unconscious again, we were a little bereft. But part of the business of writing poetry, I think, is that you want it to be *there*, it should be available for anybody in the culture when they need it.

V   Some Last Questions and Answers

Roundtable,
November 10, 1985

GIBBONS: Some of the participants in the symposium want to make some brief statements in response to other things that have been said. It's been very much a time for all of us to think about each other's words, as things have continued to echo each other and build. The first will be Michael Harper.

HARPER: I'm going to read a poem, and this is dedicated to Grace Paley. You know how she loves to talk about the feminine persona. This is for her. It's written by a man, but it's in a woman's voice. Keep your ears peeled for references to people like Pocahontas and to William Blake, who wrote the great poem about the chimney sweep. This poem is by Robert Hayden, and it's called "A Letter from Phillis Wheatley." The site is London, 1773, and Phillis Wheatley is writing to a woman of color in Boston, Massachusetts:

> Dear Obour
>   Our crossing was without
> event. I could not help, at times,
> reflecting on that first—my Destined—
> voyage long ago (I yet
> have some remembrance of its Horrors)
> and marvelling at God's Ways.
>   Last evening, her Ladyship presented me
> to her illustrious Friends.
> I scarce could tell them anything
> of Africa, though much of Boston
> and my hope of Heaven. I read
> my latest Elegies to them.
> "O Sable Muse!" the Countess cried,

embracing me, when I had done.
I held back tears, as is my wont,
and there were tears in Dear
Nathaniel's eyes.

   At supper—I dined apart
like captive Royalty—
the Countess and her Guests promised
signatures affirming me
True Poetess, albeit once a slave.
Indeed, they were most kind, and spoke,
moreover, of presenting me
at Court (I thought of Pocahontas)—
an Honor, to be sure, but one,
I should, no doubt, as Patriot decline.

   My health is much improved;
I feel I may, if God so Wills,
entirely recover here.
Idyllic England! Alas, there is
no Eden without its Serpent. Under
the chiming Complaisance I hear him Hiss;
I see his flickering tongue
when foppish would-be Wits
murmur of the Yankee Pedlar
and his Cannibal Mockingbird.

   Sister, forgive th'intrusion of
my Sombreness—Nocturnal Mood
I would not share with any save
your trusted Self. Let me disperse,
in closing, such unseemly Gloom
by mention of an Incident
you may, as I, consider Droll:
Today, a little Chimney Sweep,
his face and hands with soot quite Black,
staring hard at me, politely asked:
"Does you, M'lady, sweep chimneys too?"
I was amused, but dear Nathaniel
(ever Solicitous) was not.

   I pray the Blessings of our Lord
and Saviour Jesus Christ be yours
Abundantly. In his Name,

                        Phillis

   Derek Walcott's persona, Shabine, talks about his colonial education.
He says, as I remember Mr. Walcott's line, "I have no country but the
imagination." Then he goes on to say, "I got Dutch, Bajan white, and
nigger / I had a sound colonial education, / . . . so either I'm nobody, or

I am a nation." And with that, I'd like to pass the mantle to whoever is supposed to speak next.

GIBBONS: Do you wish to say anything, Derek, in reply?

WALCOTT: No, I don't want to say anything in reply. I'd just like to say, honestly, that one gets very cynical about conferences and so on, but I'm quite sincere about the fact that I'll be leaving here with two things, I think—however much you may wish to boo internally about what sounds fatuous. My admiration of the American conscience has been deepened by this. I think that not only among the writers, but among the people I've spoken to, the concern about responsibility is profound and admirable, and it's *there*. That's one. And the second thing is—I think it may happen to all of us here, however much we may hold an opinion of our own work and its defects or its possibilities—that one increases, in the company of other writers who have each had separate but equally important experiences, the feeling of how inadequate one's work is in terms of, in the widest possible sense—not in Yeats's sense—responsibility. Not only about party or country, but a deeper responsibility, something that's as deep as Blake and Yeats. Perhaps a further word than "justice" is "responsibility" (and that word that has been used a lot, "justice").

I think that there is a danger also, perhaps, in demanding of writers that they speak up. We have to watch out, for the democratic urging of writers to say something about things can be switched, because another regime might say, "Why don't you write about the revolution?" And one has to be careful that either system is not saying, "Speak up." I don't think it's as shallow as that, but I think it does say to one what one keeps forgetting as a writer, as a poet, or short-story writer, what Shelley kept saying (Hemingway said it, too)—really what one forgets that one is supposed to do is be aware of a *justice*—not only of injustice, but of the perpetual folly of a justice that is radiant. And that it is the writer who is stubbornly insistent, and has to be insistent, and to believe that such a radiance is possible. That even if it is clouded, and one lives in darkness, it has to be believed in. And I think that *that* responsibility, in however casual a gathering this may have been throughout—that's what I'm leaving with. It doesn't mean that I have to go back and feel, well, I've got to write a political poem or something. But one just feels a little ashamed of not remembering, outside, a little more deeply.

DES PRES: By way of a footnote I'd like to add a comment about Robert Stone's impassioned description of what I would call the vision of evil. I confess that I believe what he says, or at least I cannot find it within myself to moralize against that kind of fascination, if that's what he means, with moments of terror that seem so keenly real as to cut off doubt—moral, metaphysical—of any reasoned kind. If Stone is right, such moments come at us with disarming force, pressing upon us the excited sense that, as Stone put it, *this is it.* It's as if we require to know, or needed the world to confirm, the worst that's "always already" imagined. Listening to Stone's account of what he saw and how he responded, it's easy to sit here and assume that we would react more nobly than someone in a gunboat, beneath the strafing planes, watching the water clot and redden with human debris, someone seeing it not as cause for outrage but as visionary evidence of how, at its terrible limit, existence is. It's important, too, to keep in mind that Stone was mainly a spectator, not unlike the literary artist. And then I begin to wonder if our yearning for, perhaps even our envy of, such experience—evil beheld and frankly known—mightn't be a kind of key to the authority that poets who do behold, who do frankly know, exercise over us.

Let me back up and recall that William Blake (since we've already invoked him) said that Milton wrote best in *Paradise Lost* when he was mapping Hell's streets. Blake said that the upright puritan poet was of the Devil's party without knowing it, and by this he meant that there is more energy, more excitement in Milton's language when he is portraying evil than when he gets around to God. A little later Hazlitt, in one of his essays, made the same point about Shakespeare, whose language comes most alive when he describes characters like Macbeth, a figure the more splendid the more destructive he becomes. I think we feel a real fascination with power and with images of ruin, and when poetry has the guts to confront this matter we are no longer dealing with the beautiful but with the sublime—the sublime as people like Kant and Burke defined it, something vast beyond human norms, something terrible and overwhelming, but also, for the viewer safely distant, something that in its terror leaves us exalted.

To make remarks like these is more, perhaps, than decency allows. But thinking about literature in relation to politics has tempted me to speculate upon our hunger for art that does not back down, for poetry that takes on the darkness of our time and frankly confronts the problem of our response to power and the sublime. For me, the prevailing image of the sublime, and maybe our era's truest emblem, is one we all see often, and one I just had a chance to see again the other evening in a satiric film called *Atomic Cafe*, which maybe some of you know. The film contains lots of documentary footage of atomic explosions, and there it is—the famous mushroom cloud, some shots incredibly beautiful, if that's any longer the word. In image after image the fireburst spreads upward and out, the thermonuclear dome expands, inscribing its dominion. And as I remember watching this thing, I couldn't but be impressed by its visible magnificence, its exceeding brightness, its power to seduce, as monstrosity always seduces, by the eerie glamor of spectacular show. Maybe it's just me, but when I consider the relation of beauty to political atrocity, I think that artists, poets especially, are facing big trouble. When at Alamogordo the first of the great bombs went off, Oppenheimer had it right. He felt terror but also exaltation, and instinctively he turned to poetry.

EPSTEIN: I had no idea I was opening this can of worms with my little talk about the imagination, but here it is. I'm not *in the least* seduced by the beauty of the atomic bomb. I mean, I don't find it beautiful at all, do you? I see this thing going off, and I shudder. There's not the least sensation of any aesthetic dimension whatsoever to me.

PALEY: It isn't even pretty.

EPSTEIN: It ain't even pretty. I don't understand that, but that isn't the point I wanted to make. I seem to be locked into a conflict, or perhaps a pseudo-conflict, with Bob Stone about this, this question of the beauty of atomic bombs, and the corollary of whether we all have D'Aubisson or Hitler or whoever you like within us. I suspect we do not. But to be the devil's advocate, or simply to grant the point, maybe we do all have that potentiality within us. I think the point is that we *not* succumb to it, that we *not* become the D'Aubisson within us. Which raises the question of art and the craft that we practice. And I did think of one example that I wanted to give in favor of my argument of—I suppose you can speak of two imaginations, a healthy and a diseased, and that is—and this name has come up often in the last two days as well—Joseph Conrad.

The example I thought of was *Heart of Darkness*—*Heart of Darkness*, on the one hand, and *Apocalypse Now*, the film made of that, on the other. Now, I think that you at least know the film, if not the novella. I think the task is—how shall I really put this? In Conrad's work, Kurtz is seduced by evil, by "the horror, the horror," and Marlow struggles with it. And there's a wonderfully complex and ironic, but—finally, I think—

rather firm separation of Marlow from the horror. Conrad earns that separation—the word "transcendence" was used before—in that small, beautiful novella. However, in the film that was made of Conrad's novel there isn't any separation at all. The images—I suppose there was an intention to show the horror and a way of transcending it, but as I argued in my talk yesterday, there is a way in which Coppola himself, and perhaps his audience, becomes seduced by the very images of evil that he presents, the way the camera lingers on the scenes of battle, and indeed tries to make them—not for me, but I suppose for many— beautiful. The helicopters coming out of a Wagnerian sky playing *Die Walküre*. That's as close to a Nazi image, or a fascist image, of the imagination as I've seen in a long time. But even more, what happens not only to Brando, but—is it Martin Sheen who plays the part of Marlow?—the way in which they are overcome by, seduced by, fall in

Leslie Epstein

love with, the images of death and evil in that film, with no hope finally of escaping, no convincing transcendence at all. So I think it's simply the duty of the artist to be Marlow, rather than Kurtz, in a nutshell. And maybe Bob can respond to that, if it so pleases him.

STONE: I hadn't intended to respond, but I will respond. What comes to me most immediately is again something from my experience. *Art and Architecture* magazine was sent, by a mysterious donor, a series of pictures taken at Los Alamos and the various testing grounds, White Sands and Los Alamos, during the late forties and beyond into the fifties, while they were developing the hydrogen bomb. Now, I described illumination rounds as beautiful—which, in their way, they are. These pictures were sent to *Art and Architecture* because they were exquisite. I mean, they were freakish! But they were—I mean, there was no way to call them beautiful. They were cloud formations contorted into the most exquisite and unimaginable shapes. They put one in mind—I mean, we were speaking of other cultures, and in the United States and the West we're always looking for this other culture that is better than ours, the eternal pursuit for the noble savage, the culture that Grace talked about that says "we," the culture that says, you know, "No, here, take my beans. I don't want my beans, you eat them. I'll starve to death."

PALEY: That's just the culture I'm talking about.

STONE: These pictures were very beautiful, but they were also absolutely freakish and deadly, I mean, because anything that color has got to be poisonous. They were these enormous poison clouds. They were out of the *Bhagavad-Gita*. You understood why Oppenheimer said, "I am become Death, the destroyer of worlds," and the whole, I think, sutra of that part of the *Gita* that goes, "Behold . . . I am the dice-play of the cunning . . . I am come as Time, the waster of the peoples," and it ends with his saying, "Behold me in all things, and fear not," which is rather a turn.

But these were totally terrifying, so I thought I would write—you know, the only thing to do with this stuff, I thought, is laugh at it. So I wrote a little text, which it was my job to do, and it was titled "All Right, You Shit-Birds, I'm Not Up Here to Play Fiddle Fuck-around," in which I impersonated the Instructor in Experiential Cosmic Death, who was instructing the readers of *Art and Architecture* as to what it would be like. In my little text, I informed the readers of *Art and Architecture* that a very high-class person, Dr. Oppenheimer, having seen an explosion such as the ones that the readers were witnessing, permitted himself a very arcane and high-class remark, "I am become Death . . . " We said we expected the same kind of response from the readers of *Art and Architecture*. We said to them, in this little text: "This isn't *People* magazine, this is *Art and Architecture*. So, you shit-birds, I'm not up here to play fiddle fuck-around. When you see these pictures, I want a high-class response, I want a profound response." *Art and Architecture* sent my little essay back to me, saying, "It's very funny, but we can't put this in *Art and Architecture*," whereas the ten pages of nuclear explosions that would make your hair stand on end, if you thought about it right, they were quite ready to put in *Art and Architecture*. There's a moral in that which I, who have been drawing morals, will leave to your capacity to draw.

EMERSON: Nelson Mandela, the most powerful man, a black, in South Africa, has been in prison since 1964, and in prison he is still an awesome and remarkable power, as none of us out of prison will ever be. Why is that? One of the things that Archbishop Romero said before he was shot in the cathedral in San Salvador—he was pleading for the violence to end, and he was calling upon the army and the police and the national treasury to stop the killing—he said, "Brothers, we are the same people. Each one of you is us." What have we got to do, sitting on this platform, with any of that? I suspect, very little. The trouble with the most brilliant people in America, and some of them are here with you tonight, I not among them, is that things don't happen to them. They happen to other people, and then they discuss what has happened. I would give up writing every day in my life to stop the war in El Salvador for fifteen minutes. I would close every museum if every Vietnam veteran could have a job. I would close every art gallery, shut every bookstore, if war could be stopped. I am a subversive, not by choice, but perhaps by lack of intelligence. Lillian Hellman once said to me, "A most astonishing thing happened in America—it never happened before, and I can't believe it." The students, the American students, who had no history of dissent, rose up in the sixties, failed, rose, made mistakes, pushed, hollered, as European students have done. And so I've talked about Nelson Mandela, Archbishop Romero, who, before he was shot by the henchmen of Roberto D'Aubisson, said, "Stop the killing, brothers, each one of you is us, or each one of us is you." I've told you that Lillian Hellman said that she had seen the students, the privileged class of America, rise up in the 1960's and say "no." And I draw no conclusions, except that in this room, somewhere, there must be someone who does not want to be us here on this stage, but who wants to bring about change, not to talk about the people who effect it. I hope that someday we will be in the audience, and you will talk to us about how you did it.

FORCHÉ: I'm not sure that maybe what I had decided to say up here hasn't already been said, but I have three little stories. They're very small, I'll try to make them even smaller. They have to do with this whole idea about aethestics, and the imagination, and empathy. I got back from Hiroshima one week ago, a place I had visited once before. If you go to the transcripts of the cockpit of the *Enola Gay*, you will find comments after the bomb was dropped describing the cloud and the light. It is called "beautiful" in a number of different ways by those in the cockpit of the *Enola Gay*. But in my time in Hiroshima, both in '83 and '84, in speaking with thirty-seven survivors called *hibaksha*, who told me in great detail, and most of the time crying, about what happened to them, beginning the story of their lives at 8:15 a.m. on August 6, 1945, and ending the story of their lives in the months that followed, not one of them mentioned, ever, any word that had anything to do with beauty. And so I think it depends on your point of view.

And I also want to say that, in terms of empathy, I had a lesson once that I want to share. In El Salvador, I was working as a woman named Louise for Amnesty International, and I was very concerned about political prisoners and their whereabouts. I didn't know that at that time most of the people who had disappeared were already dead, but finally my friends and mentors told me that this was the case. However, if there was something that I would like to do about people who were in prison, there was something that they would offer me to do. They wanted me to go inside a prison and they wanted me to visit someone in the prison there, as if I knew him before. And they wanted me to spend half an hour inside the prison. And they told me there was something inside that they wanted me to see, and they thought maybe my friends in Amnesty International would be interested in it. And they said, "You can't take any paper or camera or anything, you have to memorize." Then they said to me, "We give eighty percent chance that everything will go O.K." And I thought, eighty percent? And they said, "Oh yes, that's very good odds. We think that everything will be fine." But I was thinking, of course, about the other twenty. So I said finally—because I had an agreement with my friends that I would do what they wanted me to do and learn what they wanted me to learn, and if I came to something that I didn't want to do or felt tired or felt bored, I would just go home—I decided to go into the prison rather than go home.

And in the prison there were men being kept in small wooden boxes. I was able to see this by the man who was taking me around when I was first going in—I should describe just a little bit to you. It was a four-sided structure with an open courtyard, and when I was brought into the prison, a prisoner brought me an Orange Crush and handed it to me so that—I didn't know why, and I protested a little bit, but he said, "No, you're going to need this." So I walked in with my little Orange Crush and I had a sweater over my arm, because it had been chilly but now it was hot, and when they opened the doors, I nearly fell over from the stench of shit and piss and vomit. And there were maybe four hundred men in there, and I had been told that some were criminal prisoners and others were not, but they were all in there. And the man walked me around, and the guards had their G-3's, standing around—that's an automatic weapon. The guards were about seventeen, eighteen, nineteen years old, and they were very interested in me at first, and then sort of lost interest and got interested in a little game with dice.

And when that happened, my friend said to me, "You see that dark open doorway in there? I want you to go through that doorway, that's what you want to see, that's what we brought you in here for." And he said, "Try to see what's in there, but only stay one minute, no more. Don't stay longer. Count." And then he said, "When you come out, if

Leslie Epstein, C. K. Williams, Carolyn Forché

270

they see you come out, make a face like an absentminded North American lady," and he made an absentminded-North-American-lady face for me, so I would know what it looked like. And he said, "Just–you don't know where you were going, you got lost, you didn't see anything." So I said O.K., and I went inside, and inside there were six wooden boxes, three across and three stacked on top of them. They were about one meter by one meter by one meter, and they had openings in them the size of a book that were covered with many layers of chicken-wire mesh, and they were padlocked. And I thought it would be impossible, when the boxes started to move, for someone to be other than completely crouched inside. And I counted them, and I made a mental map–this is everything automatic, I was supposed to do this. I was supposed to walk out and take the map and send it to Amnesty and the International Commission of Jurists in Geneva. So I did it.

Maybe I have them now, I don't know, I had them earlier today, but I got hives while I was doing it. And I counted, and I walked out, and I made my face blank, and I was a little panicky, and he told me to tie my sweater around my neck to cover these up, and he said, "That's called *el oscuro*, the 'darkness solitary.' Sometimes men are kept in there one year and can't move when they come out, because of the atrophy in their muscles." And so the rest of it is kind of a blank for me.

I know I was in there about ten more minutes. I know I went out and talked friendly with the soldiers. I know I got in the cab of the truck. I know I was driven away, then all of a sudden I really became sick and vomited all over the inside of the truck and started to cry hysterically. And the man who was with me, who was my friend, a Salvadoran who had led me through many things, stopped the truck and yanked on the emergency brake, and he said–I thought he was going to pat me on the shoulder and say, "Oh, poor North American lady, we will take you now to the hotel for a drink or a nice meal, and you can go to bed, and we are very sorry that you feel so bad." That's what I expected, really, that's what I expected. And instead he folded his arms, and he got a very stern look on his face, and he said, "O.K., you go ahead," and he said, "You pay attention to what you're feeling right now." And I thought he was hard, you know. And he said, "Because this is what the oppression feels like. And if you can imagine this now and hold it in your imagination and keep it, then you're going to understand what these people who live in shit shacks and have no place to shit in the morning feel like every day, and that is the condition of depression and anxiety and fear and revulsion out of which they have to form some sort of sense of communion with each other."

So he said, "Pay attention, because this is important. This is the most important thing you're going to learn here." And I was pissed off at first, really angry. And then a little light went on in my head, and I realized that he was trying to teach me something, how to—and this is a hard thing for us to learn, I think (by "us," I mean our nationality here in this country)—how to get inside another human being who isn't one of us. And that's what the imagination is for. And that's what other people up here are saying. And that's why I thought I was saying it twice too much. But that's what's important, and weapons are only beautiful if you're not wounded, or it's not your country, or you're far enough away, or if you're not making any connection between the light or the glowing white plumes of a phosphorus bomb or the little tiny red stars of tracer rounds and what they *are*. So you have to make the connection. That's what's important. It's only "beautiful" if you are being vacant about that connection, or if you're safe. That's all.

STONE: In order to provoke a question, I'll say something briefly. It may get worse, it's going to get worse than this. If it gets down finally to two superpowers, as it seems to be doing, then morality is going to get very scrambled, and respective cruelties, the aesthetics of violence, the spectacle, the living that we writers have been making, it seems, for a large part of the century by chronicling inhumanities—I mean, which is not dishonorable; it is right to chronicle inhumanities—and what is important—

EMERSON: Only—if you wait until they happen to other people and never expose yourself, then that is the ultimate indecency.

STONE: If you can't write about them if you don't expose yourself, that's dishonorable. Well, I never write about inhumanities, Gloria, that I don't expose myself to, that's a rule of thumb with me.

EMERSON: Yeah, but there's a difference between a famous writer and an eighteen-year-old draftee and a Salvadoran—

STONE: I wasn't a draftee.

EMERSON: There's a difference between the writer seeking it, the photographer seeking it, and the kid from Tennessee who's there who never had a choice. That's an obscene difference. Don't be like that.

272

STONE: Anybody who goes out looking for atrocities in order to collect a catalog, you know, is in real trouble and will carry within themselves their own punishment. We don't have to worry about such people. But the thing is that things may get worse in this battle between superpowers, both of whom claim absolute morality and both of whom cause little other than suffering.

EPSTEIN: I just want to say it's not at all obscene to write about things that you don't see directly and expose yourself to. It's just imaginative. There's nothing obscene about Proust writing about Dreyfus from a cork-lined room, whatsoever.

SETTLE: Especially since he—I want to answer that. Proust, who was known as such an aesthete, was one of the first people to put his raw material for his work in jeopardy by going around and starting the first petition for Dreyfus. So he was very much the kind of person who should have written about it.

STONE: It is out of moralizing—I mean, beware also of moralizing, because it is out of moralizing that all this, all this agony comes. When you begin to moralize, when you begin to draw morals, be very, very careful as you draw them, because the people who are inflicting this pain, regardless of ideology, are all people of conviction. Don't consider lack of conviction as the worst of evils in the present world. All these people believe very strongly in what they believe in.

HUGO ACHUGAR (FROM AUDIENCE): I was moved by what Carolyn Forché said. I am wondering if I was moved because the reality she was describing was so horrible, or because she did it with art; she was persuasive, she was a poet, speaking about that. I don't believe that just telling atrocities is enough. Sometimes you need a special language to get through. One of the problems of the Left in Latin America—and, from what I know, in the States it is almost the same—has been clichéd language that moves nobody. Also, I am a little bit skeptical about some of this concern, liberal concern—I am not allowing anyone to pass as liberal, I was one—this liberal concern in the United States about in Ethiopia there is famine, in Central America they are being tortured, we're going to protest or we are going to sign or we're going to demonstrate, or whatever. And I distrust that discourse which supports war or this fascination with machine guns, etcetera. Why? Because there *is* an aesthetic discourse of war. During the sixties, poets in Latin America, and not only in Latin America, would try to move their audience to provoke a kind of support for the arms struggle. It was supposed to be wry, to be something not so clichéd as the Red star of the revolution or the victorious machine gun of the revolution, but there *was* that kind of discourse. And it was right to have that kind of discourse. Now that the times have changed and social democracy is a kind of ideal all over the world, the armed struggle is ended as an ideal, and that kind of a discourse has disappeared.

AUDIENCE: This is for anybody up there. As chroniclers of inhumanity, all of you, or many of you, seem to have a special relationship with events in the Third World, which makes you very unusual among Americans. It makes you unique also among your fraternity and sorority of writers. Do you feel that at the present time people are paying less attention to that kind of chronicling of inhumanity, that you are losing readers in a Reagan era? Not that you are losing only people who are going out and voting for Reagan, but also many of my own contemporaries who were riveted in the late sixties by Third World concerns when they were students, and are now partners in law firms, etcetera, and seem to have lost interest in that kind of thing. Do you feel that this is not a good time in this country for chronicling Third World inhumanities?

WILLIAMS: I've been away for a few months out of America, and in coming back and beholding the election—I know many people felt this—probably the most upsetting thing about the election was the fact that the young people were supporting Reagan apparently, according to polls, according to the voting. But the constituency that you're speaking of for the sixties did support not simply Third World concerns—it's important to remember that. We tend to define the sixties in terms of the Vietnam War, and one of the most important things about the sixties was that everybody was beginning to be aware that it was the same struggle in America as in Vietnam, as in Central America. And the thing that I tried to address in my talk, and which I really obviously didn't solve, is this enormous illusory structure that's being put up about what America is and the image of the American empire. But people are rather glib in saying why so many voted for Reagan. People tend to dismiss it as—well, he stopped inflation. It almost reminds me of Hitler building the autobahns. Yet apparently most people in America aren't better off than they were four years ago. Apparently, unless you're in the really higher brackets, you're not in a better economic situation, so something much deeper is happening.

The question that you're asking implied, I think, an accusation about what's happening here. And I think it's something that we all feel, and I think we're all—*I'm*—very, very puzzled by. It's as though the ground were taken out from under me. And obviously the key question in America is racial—racial justice. But it's as though the issue were sort of absolutely obliterated in some sleight of hand.

ANGELA JACKSON (FROM AUDIENCE): Ronald Reagan assured white America that to be white was to be privileged again, because the rest of the world was beginning to tell white America that to be white was not to be privileged, that you had to give up that privilege. So he has assured white people that to be white gives you the right to stomp a little black island, to ignore questions of any social inequality or self-determination within the United States and around the world.

WILLIAMS: I think I might be posing a bunch of questions in the guise of a statement. How is it that, for instance, a generation of college students have accepted that argument, when in fact they aren't benefit-

Angela Jackson

ing in any way? In fact, many college students say, "Well, in fact, it's harder to get college loans for your education now, but I'm still going to vote for him." In other words, that would be the argument against him — but there's a level missing that I don't understand, about what's happening in America.

JACKSON: It's the national restoration of the national ego. If you see that glory in war and stomping on somebody else, of color usually —

STONE: But that's not what elected Reagan. There's only one issue in bourgeois parliamentary democracies, and that's the economy. That's the only issue that the electorate votes on.

SEVERAL (IN AUDIENCE AND ONSTAGE): No.

STONE: I don't think it's wrong in any election since 1905.

PALEY: I don't think so. No, I think it's what they *think* they're voting on. I think it's what they're *told* they're voting on.

STONE: What they think they're voting on is what —

PALEY: No, it's what they're *told* they're voting on, but deeply they're not voting on it, they're really voting on what Angela is talking about, and to see that — I'll tell you, when you're talking about what's happening in the country, I don't worry so much about the college students. They weren't so hot in the beginning of the Vietnam War either, you know. It took them a while. But all the energy that's going to come from the students, eventually it comes, you know. You talk to them long enough.

STONE: Then they get drafted.

PALEY: Eventually, they wake up to the fact. But it isn't a God's truth that all energy comes from them, I don't think so. I think a lot of energy really comes now from race and from women. That's where the energy is going to come from, and that's where the leadership is going to come from. It's not going to really come from the kids. They'll come, they'll be the *followship*, and they'll get nice and active after a while. I just also want to say that more is happening in this country, really, than you realize. Don't be so totally, absolutely — on account of this rotten, terrible election — so absolutely discouraged. There are things happening in different local parts of the country which are really very exciting and which have nothing to do with the electoral process. The electoral process is there, it's horrifying, and we've all been hit on the head—ouch!—by it. But it's not the beginning and end of the thing. Where I live now the Central American Committee is very big. I mean, it's enormous. It has tremendous meetings, they're always crowded, it covers two states, one of which voted entirely Republican, and they sent lots of people to Nicaragua. That's just one thing.

But now I just want to say one other thing. As important as the fight on the Central American issue is, as important as that fight is, for me, I really want to talk about how this country is being militarized. This is an argument I have with some of my friends who want to put all—every bit of their energy—into the Central American area, which with my whole heart I know is important. But the country is being militarized, the high schools are being militarized, and as long as those schools are being militarized, they're sending recruiters into those schools, that's where it seems to me we have to be doing a lot of work. We have to be sort of going back in there again, and—I mean, here I am sixty years old, and I'll start all over again!—we've just got to keep going, doing the thing over and over again. It's the militarization of this country which is one of the most terrifying and horrifying things, because we really got rid of a lot of that, you know. I feel we really, really changed things for a while. It's coming back, like that.

STONE: These varieties of liberalism confuse me.

PALEY: Are you referring to me? Well, you're dead wrong, baby. Try dealing with my liberalism.

STONE: I mean, I—

PALEY: Now.

STONE: I have always thought that you have to make a final decision that either power will reside in the working class in the United States or we will continue to have what we have, which is a half-step slightly turned around, occasionally malicious, depending on your point of view, from parliamentary government like France has had, and England has had, and all these other half-step countries like our own have had. And I don't believe, and what I most importantly don't believe, is the idea of interpolating the Third World that the deserving-America has. One of the things that has been going on in America is this endless search for the deserving poor. Where are they? I mean, all we've got are these squareheads, Polacks, jerk-arounds. I mean, where are the deserving poor? We've got to find the deserving poor.

JUST: They're right on this stage, Bob, right here.

STONE: If we cannot build on the American working class, a working-class society, then we might as well shut up, you know, about playing around with a Marxist or Marxoid kind of game. We build it on the American working class or we build it on nothing. And I don't know, Marcusian, or substitution—let's have a *substitute* working class! Let's bring in a singing, dancing working class! So we can have a really groovy American revolution. No—we build it on the American working class, or we don't.

EMERSON: They're our surplus. The reason we don't have one is we're always getting rid of them. You know what they used to say about Vietnam: clean up street corners. Send the kids off who stand on the street corners. It's called "Beautify America" campaign. We took out a whole economic class in Vietnam.

I want to tell a story and then we can go on. I may have been misunderstood, as I often am, when I said, and I didn't mean it of certain people on this panel, when I said that people exploited tragedies. They dashed in and out of a hot story in El Salvador to write for *People* magazine, or the television reporters say, "Gee, Mr. Jenkins, how do you feel about your kid being killed in Beirut?" It shouldn't be tolerated, especially what's done on television. A recent conference at the University of Southern California (which was quite worthless, really only a promotion for the university) was called "Vietnam Reconsidered," and I had the bad luck to be chairman for the veterans' panel, because after all, *I* wasn't famous, but I was sure better known than *they* were. I had lots of friends who were veterans and I could be trusted—you know, a nice middle-class lady who worked for the *New York Times*. Who knows what one of those freako combat vets might say? But little did they know! And as chairman of the panel, I discovered that we were on the third day; we had had a panel discussing antiwar posters before the veterans, and we had had a discussion of the petitions that the intellectuals had drawn up, and we had had antiwar art. But the participants in the war were the last to be heard. I got up to start this little panel, which was doomed from the start. And afterwards a veteran got up, and said:

"Beware of famous faces." All I am trying to say to you was what he said. He looked around the room, and I remembered during the war how many soldiers hated the correspondents, hated us, wished us all dead. And they were right. We were among the real war profiteers. They did the dying, we got the story. They got wounded, we got the prizes. And they're not dumb, they know it. And we built our careers on their corpses. So they can recognize real war profiteers, and that's what correspondents are. Not novelists, but correspondents.

STONE: No, but even more, one of the reasons that the war—

EMERSON: Who's telling this story, you or me?

STONE: I guess it's you, Gloria.

Terrence Des Pres, Gloria Emerson, Robert Stone

EMERSON: And the veteran turned around and said to the audience of men who already knew, "Brothers," he said, "never trust the famous faces." And don't you guys, either.

ALAN SHAPIRO (FROM AUDIENCE): I have a question for the whole panel. I'd be curious to know if anybody on the panel has read James Baldwin's essay on "Everybody's Protest Novel," *Uncle Tom's Cabin*. In this essay, he argues for a moral literature, and distinguishes that from a moralistic literature. He criticizes *Uncle Tom's Cabin* as being moralistic, full of sentimentality, which he defines as "the ostentatious parading of excessive and spurious emotion." Sentimentality is "the mark of dishonesty, the inability to feel; the wet eye of the sentimentalist betrays his aversion to experience, his fear of life, his arid heart; and it is always, therefore, the signal of secret and violent inhumanity, the mask of cruelty." What he dislikes about *Uncle Tom's Cabin* is that it assumes that the slave owners are monsters, moral monsters, motivated by a kind of unexplained malignity. And he argues on behalf of a novel that would try to understand what it's like to be a slave owner, what it feels like, what kinds of psychological questions enter into it. In that sense, you can describe Robert Stone's novels, *Dog Soldiers* and *A Flag for Sunrise*, as extremely moral, fascinated by violence without being seduced by it. And as you read those books—as I read them, anyway—you enter into the minds of horrible people. They don't become less horrible, but you do establish the basis for some kind of empathy. And so you understand what it's like to be evil. Understanding doesn't mean that you can necessarily make yourself less evil, but certainly making yourself less evil requires understanding. Understanding's not power, but power requires understanding. In that sense, I think, literature is moral. To go back to what Mary Lee Settle was talking about earlier today—why bother criticizing someone who reads Judith Krantz?—I think you *can*, because she invites us to bathe in a kind of moral self-righteousness, a kind of sentimentality, a corruption of language, a false conviction that evil is the other and not also ourselves. I regard a Judith Krantz novel, or a novel like *Uncle Tom's Cabin*, or a statement from the Defense Department that describes initiating a nuclear holocaust as "preemptive deterrence," or a resident of Marin County describing adultery as "polyfidelity," as a corruption of language, which it is one of the tasks of literature to resist.

SETTLE: May I answer that? It's curious to find oneself defending Judith Krantz, whom I haven't read.

STONE: But if you'd read her, Mary Lee, you wouldn't defend her quite so vigorously.

SETTLE: My point is that we all know not to dictate to other people, but to allow them to find out for themselves. What I would like to answer is the thing about *Uncle Tom's Cabin*. Having written a five-volume novel which has hundreds and hundreds of people in it, one of the worst times that I had with that necessary empathy that you have to find—I don't care if somebody walks into a novel for two paragraphs, there still has to be empathy with them, or they're not alive—was in the pre-Civil War novel, about a slave-owning family and their people, their slaves. And the worst moment of the whole lot was to become, for the time, a man and his wife discussing selling another human being because cholera had broken out in the valley and they needed money to get their children up to the spa to get out of the cholera. In those novels, I wrote about five battles, but never in writing about battle did I have the psychic dilemma of forcing myself into that empathy. So he's right about that.

I once taught a course not by saying you can't read *Uncle Tom's Cabin*, but I said, "Read this, and read Turgenev's *Sportsman's Sketches* at the same time." My point was that Turgenev, with the *Sportsman's Sketches*, was very much responsible for the freeing of the serfs in Russia, and they were freed without a war, whereas isn't Harriet Beecher Stowe the one of whom Lincoln said, "This is the little lady that started the Civil War"? Mark Twain said *he* started it. He said that if he'd have been there, the war would have stopped dead. And if you want to read of the seventies, try Walter Scott.

Now that I've got the microphone, I have something to say to everybody. I've been listening to the moral dilemma of the United States right now, and a great deal of it in terms of its extremes—someplace else, some other time, some other death. I would ask us not necessarily to be kinder to ourselves right now, but to understand in the terms of our history—and some histories are like other histories—that we're tired right now. We are ten years from a very bad and very unjust war, in which we, the good guys, turned out not to be. Psychically, we have to get used to this. It seems to me that we've been doling out an enormous hangover. This conversation should all have been had when Nixon was president. Because that's when it was new, and that was the most dangerous time in this country. Does everybody know what the time of Thermidor was? It's the time that comes after revolution when everybody gets tired, and when a dictator takes over. It was the time of Thermidor when Napoleon took over from the Triumvirate and became the dictator of France. It was what Trotsky called the time of Thermidor when Stalin took over. We've very nearly had our time of Thermidor in this country, and, after it, as in both the other countries and as in England, when its time of Thermidor happened after the English revolution (in the mid-seventeenth century, when Cromwell took over and destroyed the Left, which we've all forgotten)—after these times of Thermidor there has come, every time, a deep national psychic fatigue. And just maybe we'll feel a little bit better by realizing that we have now four years of stale-mate. We don't have a disastrous Hitler. We have a President Ga-ga, Ga-ga. And a Congress that he can't control, with congressional elections coming up in two years, and we're tired, and maybe we need that four years. Historically other people have needed it, and had it, and come out of it. So don't go home feeling too badly this evening.

HARPER: I'd like to respond because one of the things that I'd like to share with you is something that happened to me a while ago, and that's taken me a while to absorb. I'm going to do it in two parts.

There was a war called the Biafran war, which I lived through, because I taught Nigerian students in California. This was the time when Reagan came to power as governor, and I got a certain kind of lesson about politics in this country then, which was the good old days of the "War on Poverty." Do you remember that? Some of you don't. Some of you were probably not born then. But that was my first initiation, and one of the things about Americans is that they have to be initiated quantita-tively and often. Otherwise, amnesia sets in. So I just want to share with you a little dialogue. This happened to me in an automobile.

We invited—when I say "we," I mean a committee of people who had the job of spending the university's money on the university lecture committee. I had the job of inviting Chinua Achebe, the Nigerian novelist, to campus. And he agreed to come—he was then teaching at the University of Massachusetts at Amherst. We were driving the car—I think I was taking him to the airport—and I made the mistake of asking him about the Biafran war, in the childish way that most Americans ask silly questions. He knew, of course, that I'd written poems about it, and he knew a great deal more about my work than I thought. And he said to me, "Michael, I can remember driving around in a car very much like we're driving now [we were on the freeway]. And Leslie Fiedler was in the car. He and I were talking about trying to raise money for the Biafrans. And Fiedler said, 'I think I'll call my old college roommate and ask him for some help. He and I went to school at Harvard.'" And

Michael S. Harper

Achebe said, "Oh, who was your college roommate?" And Fiedler said, "Henry Kissinger." And Fiedler did what he said. He got in touch with Kissinger, and Kissinger said, "I'll get back to you soon." Then Achebe stopped for a long time; we rode for about two or three minutes. And he said, "The word came back from the administration, which is to say that Kissinger had an underling get back to Fiedler: 'This is not in our sphere of influence.'" And then Achebe said, "And I knew that millions would die." That's the first thing I want to say.

The second thing is to read from a book that I coedited, because I think that we need to get out on the table something that's very difficult for people in this context to deal with, and that is race relations, which I call "race rituals," and which James Baldwin wrote very eloquently about. Baldwin *keeps* writing about race rituals, because he just can't believe that we can ever get to race *relations* until we can get through these race *rituals*. And we've got them, and we keep playing these games, and black Americans do too—they're so often so wonderfully euphemistic that they don't tell the truth either.

So I'm going to read from Mr. Achebe just shortly, just to put some things on the table, because this has to do with aesthetics, it's got to do with Conrad and *Heart of Darkness*, and it's got to do with continuing and prevailing incompetence in seeing the world.

> It might be contended, of course, that the attitude to the African in *Heart of Darkness* is not Conrad's but that of his fictional narrator, Marlow, and that far from endorsing it Conrad might indeed be holding it up to irony and criticism. Certainly, Conrad appears to go to considerable pains to set up layers of insulation between himself and the moral universe of his story. He has, for example, a narrator behind a narrator. The primary narrator is Marlow but his account is given to us through the filter of a second, shadowy person. But if Conrad's intention is to draw a *cordon sanitaire* between himself and the moral and psychological malaise of his narrator, his care seems to me totally wasted because he neglects to hint however subtly and tentatively at an alternative frame of reference by which we may judge the actions and opinions of his characters. It would not have been beyond Conrad's power to make that provision if he had thought it necessary. Marlow seems to me to enjoy Conrad's complete confidence, a feeling reinforced by the close similarities between their careers. ("An Image of Africa," Chinua Achebe, from *Chant of Saints*, ed. by Michael S. Harper and Robert B. Stepto [University of Illinois Press, 1979], p. 318.)

Now, I won't go on to badger you with other excerpts from this essay. It's called "An Image of Africa." Achebe goes on to speak to *his* audience, who are the people who actually lived in the place that Marlow fantasized about. You know who they were. He gives you their names. And if you need a literary lesson, and I think all of us do—it was given to me the hard way—sit down and read Mark Twain's "King Leopold's Soliloquy" and read Conrad's *Heart of Darkness* again, and then read Mr. Achebe's essay, and you will get some of the imagery to which I tried to allude yesterday, in talking about our need for a real complex of the insights necessary to understand the world in terms of a comparative humanity.

I was not playing games. I was being dead serious. I have great fear—I will say this openly—I have great fear of the moral will of Americans to do anything that requires more than a *week*, O.K.? They begin to forget in about a week's time. Their moral vision can be sustained about that long, you know. And I don't by any means put myself in any category apart from that, all right? One of the contradictions about black Americans is they are American as apple pie. That's one of the contradictions. And we have the numerous examples of the Vietnam veterans. I wrote in 1973 a narrative which I thought made it pretty clear how the option given to the poor—which is to say, working class, black and white, Chicano, whatever—was to be either a victim or an executioner, and I don't think either one of those options is a good one. We have to figure out a way not to repeat these mistakes, and I think it's going to be difficult, because I think we're too comfortable. And I don't take any more responsibility than I have to take, but I have got two sons who are going to be in the military if I don't make sure that they don't go.

EMERSON: That whole fourth row will be in the military.

PAUL BRESLIN (FROM AUDIENCE): As I've been listening, I've been thinking that perhaps one hard thing, as several of you have said, is to get clear and present in your mind what's happening to people elsewhere whom you can't see directly. But one thing that troubles me is that it's hard to get from that to a clear sense of what to do beyond the personal things that come up in everyday behavior. For example, a few years ago Northwestern decided to host a Midwest conference on defense research, war research. And at the time I wrote a letter to the student newspaper protesting this, and participated in circulating petitions against it. That was very easy to do. But then you think beyond this—do I, for instance, favor unconditional unilateral disarmament at this time? I think if I really got honest about that, I'd have to say, no. I mean, I don't think that the Soviet Union, for example, is entirely a scare, is entirely invented by right-wing propaganda to get us all scared. Of course, it's certainly been blown out of proportion. But there are some rather nasty people over on that side, also. Well, if I don't favor unilateral disarmament, where do I suppose that this war research is going to get done, if not in the universities? In other words, I think it very easy to discover where my gut sympathies lie and to want to alleviate human suffering and prevent violence, but I find that the more I find out or think through the ultimate consequences of a particular gesture or action, the harder it is to see the way through.

Now to turn to something I know not as much about as I should—Nicaragua. A year ago, I would have thought that the United States was against any government that proclaims itself Marxist or communist, and they're just out to get the Sandinistas for that reason, and would support any kind of brutal regime as long as it claims to align itself with us. But then you start reading that the Sandinista revolution has become very corrupt, and that most of the old Somoza people are now turning up in Sandinista government, and it becomes—

AUDIENCE (SEVERAL VOICES): What? No!

BRESLIN: I've read in *New Republic*.*

AUDIENCE (SEVERAL VOICES): No! *No!*

AUDIENCE: I don't want to be rude, but most North Americans don't have any damn sense of geography anyway, first of all. Because of that geographical, ethnocentric, white-man's-God complex that enjoys atom bombs falling in bliss, the Virgin being seen in the mushroom cloud. It's amazing. It shocks me, but you know, I'm a technological primitive. I belong to the Mestizo people. I'm Indian, going back thousands of years, and I'm Spanish. And we're just amazed, with Red Cloud saying, "I can't wait until the earth rolls back on these people." You know, I just can't wait. You know, Vine Deloria says, white people don't give a damn about nuclear reactors and about nuclear war until *they* are the corpses strewn across the earth. But we were butchered in the valleys of Texas in 1842 and 1848. Samuel E. Chamberlin, in his confessions about the Mexican War, will beat your novels out about the howling fiends as they deboweled women and children of the sovereign nation of the Republic of Mexico. And Walt Whitman applauded it. And don't make excuses for that son of a bitch.

EMERSON: Not me.

---

*Mr. Breslin offered the following citations as evidence of what he had intended to say. The article in question is "Nicaragua's Untold Stories" by Robert Leiken, *New Republic*, October 8, 1984. Two relevant excerpts:

> In the village of El Tránsito, two hours northwest of Managua, most of the people belonged to the C.D.S. [Sandinista Defense Committee] at the outset of the revolution. Now there is but one member, the coordinator, formerly the village's leading Somocista. (The transformation of Somocistas into Sandinistas and of Sandinistas into oppositionists is very common. In every town we visited we were told that former Somoza officials are now running C.D.S.s) (p. 17)

> We spoke with two organizers—middle-class, professional women who had belonged to the F.S.L.N. before the revolution. (According to one, "the F.S.L.N. says that the opposition is Somocista. But most of the old Somocistas are working with the government. The opposition has remained the same.") (p. 21)

AUDIENCE: No, but some people do. Now, the judgment will come, not because I say so, but because that's what will happen, based on action, reaction and history, which you'll see. It's going to come. Reagan's terrified of it. And people like Larry McDonald, who got bopped out of the sky in the Korean airliner, made it a point before he got killed to investigate people, my people, the Chicanos, who are writers to one another, who decided to inscribe at the bottom of their letters the words A-Z-T-L-Á-N. There's a piece of geography for you. Where the hell is Aztlán? Anybody know? Raise your hand. That's Texas, Colorado, Arizona, New Mexico—all the land that was robbed by the son of a bitches. That's Aztlán. García Márquez says we're going to get it back numerically, because we're going to populate it and take it over once again. That's where we're going to get Aztlán from. But Larry McDonald said these people are the seeds of subversion in the United States, they are seditionists, the people who write, "Aztlán. San Antonio, Texas, Aztlán." And those people who write like that happen to be Chicano poets, they happen to be the people who are getting stopped by the Secret Service, who get bopped around, but you don't hear about

Terrence Des Pres, Gloria Emerson

them, because we speak another language. And we don't speak anything broken, we speak a language. It's not broken English, or broken Spanish, it's our language. Thank you.

EMERSON: I want to make a comment about Mary Lee's remarks, which I thought were profoundly intelligent. My only objection to her remark about the four years that are coming up and how tired we are, is that other countries are far more tired than we are, because of us. Vietnam is exhausted. I saw that country in 1956, two years after it won its war against the French, and when I left it in 1972, it looked like an ashtray. And many Vietnamese children will grow up impaired by malnutrition because the United States has a boycott against any group sending any nutrients or dried-milk powder.

I believe the defeat in Vietnam has led to our involvement in Central America. Other countries are more tired of us than we have ever been tired of ourselves. Yes, we need a rest, but they need a rest, too. I criticize America mostly on what it does to other countries, and I am speaking about the Reagan acceptance of a facist regime in South Africa, and that is the acceptance of evil. And I am talking about Reagan's turning Honduras into Danang, into a military base, so even those Hondurans who are trying to get more money are trying to protect themselves. And I'm talking about what's happened to Costa Rica. And I'm talking about Nicaragua, which had a national insurrection and is entitled to make its own mistakes, as we have made ours for hundreds of years. And their population is 2.2 million. That's one-quarter of Manhattan on a Tuesday! And I'm talking about the backing of the worst possible forces in El Salvador. Who do you think paid for the crates? And who do you think pays for the police advisors? And who do you think pays for that poor Salvadoran army, which will never win, because you can't *buy* an army, you can't inject motivation as you inject a vitamin. We tried that with the South Vietnamese. And you can't import revolution. It isn't a lamb chop, or dog food or a bandage. It must come from the hearts of the men who are willing to be killed. Castro is never as powerful as we make him. And I am tired of America, but God, millions of people are not only tired of it, but wait with fear to see what we will permit our President to do next. And that is the crime. And that is what you must be held to account for, all of you.

PALEY: Hear, hear.

288

EMERSON: It's awful, but it's true.

AUDIENCE: Someone mentioned the fourth row, and I'm pretty much of that age, and I'm in the first row. I'll speak just for myself and not my generation, my age group. I have a great fear, because I'm watching, before my eyes and before my ears, history repeating itself. And at the speed of technology, history is repeating itself even quicker. It hasn't been barely ten years since Vietnam. And here before me there's going to be another war. And I can still remember walking down Highway 53 in Du Page County the day the draft was ended, and I was old enough to remember, I was old enough to comprehend what that meant. Oh boy, I don't have to go to the army. And it was wonderful. And then I hit eighteen and suddenly they were talking about draft registration, and in order to continue my education, because I couldn't afford it otherwise, I had to register, I had to fill out that card and put it in. And I did it, and now I have a number. And I don't know, I honestly don't know if I will be drafted, if I will be called up or if there will be a draft. They're talking about that they have enough soldiers now. Enough people have been unemployed long enough that they had to do something.

EMERSON: The volunteer army—

AUDIENCE: So, I try to project myself into the future. I try to—what we're talking about here mostly was about Vietnam, and the new Vietnam is coming up, and I feel it, and I hate the feeling, I hate the thought. And it's coming up before our eyes, and nothing we say here, nothing you say up there, is going to stop it. Is it? Is it really going to stop this from happening? Reagan—his administration, his people—have been reelected through him, and they're going to continue their policies. The tribe is threatened, the American tribe has been threatened. Its zone of influence is threatened, and now they're going to go down there once again, to Nicaragua, and pounce on the little ones. And they're going to ask my generation to do it for them. And someone mentioned earlier today the poor boy fighting the rich man's war, and once again, history is going to repeat itself. Unemployed boys who are now in the military are going to go fight the employed boys' war. And the boxes will come home. I try to put myself into the future and think, in 1997 I'm going to think about this, if we make it to that year. I'm going to be sitting somewhere, hopefully, and I'm going to think about this night and about the discussions of Vietnam and how there's going to be discussions about Nicaragua and Central America.

WALCOTT: I just want to say something about what someone on the floor who described himself as a Mestizo imagined. No writer—not even of the Bible, in which the Philistines, or whoever, smashed children's heads against stones—no writer is, has been, can be, "stupid," right? That includes Whitman. So to call Whitman a son of a bitch in the heat of your historical anger—that's the mistake which I was trying to talk about. Your historical reaction to Whitman is in error, but it's because you're thinking history, you're not thinking Whitman, in which the truth in Whitman has no history. You're reacting, you're getting the reaction that people want you to get, which is a historical reaction to journalism, not to poetry.

Pound was also a damn fool when he wrote about the Jews; all right. The fact that he became penitent at the end is a matter of luck for Pound—that he could repent. And he could have died without the repentence. Faulkner, for all his alleged compassion about the black man, is still a literary person looking at a black man. And you'd have to say that all writers are hypocrites, which for most of the time we are. Out of our lives, I would say, for three percent of our lives we speak the truth. It isn't that we want to lie, but that we prevent ourselves from the complete truth, for some reason, either for race, for history, for anything, nationalism, anything, style, fame, anything.

So basically, if we are judged, yes, we are liars, O.K. But that doesn't mean that, ultimately, there's no will to talk the truth, when that does happen as it does in poetry—otherwise, if there isn't, then there's nothing. There's really nothing, if there isn't in poetry, right? And this means not just religion; I mean poetry.

Another thing bothers me a little, or considerably—when people say "It bothers me a little," they mean "considerably." There are two quotations that I remember about truth, which are clichés that everybody knows. One is, of course, Pilate's answer, or question which is an answer. "What is truth?" said Pilate, or asked Pilate, and wouldn't wait for an answer. Well, because nobody had an answer, he walked off, and then some cockney guy said a few years later, "Truth is beauty, beauty is truth," and Pilate wasn't around for that, but he would have said, "What's this crap?" When we use the word "beauty," we're using it here in a malign sense. In other words, we're making personal assessments of what is supposed to be beautiful, and that is also hypocritical, in the sense that we are claiming truth, just through our reactions to what we think—that's the height of the sentimentality Baldwin is talking about. When Keats says "beauty is truth," he's not saying "beauty is fact." He's saying it *is* truth. (Eliot, in one of his usual moments of self-advancement, said, "I don't understand what that means because it doesn't have another verb." You know, beauty is truth, truth beauty. That's not English, right?—Maybe American, but it isn't English.) And I think that to use these words, like "beauty," and to say "this is beautiful," is only a very superficial patter about something in the eye. But in what is supposed to be the human soul, there is such a thing. It is not about being "beautiful."

The thing about good, I think, is we feel it can't do anything, whereas evil is active. You can see what evil does. It gets results. Good doesn't seem to get results. But that's typical of what good is not supposed to do,

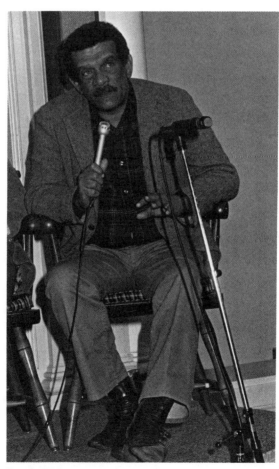

Derek Walcott

get results. And I think that when you encounter the terrifying kind of almost amorality that appears to be in Stone, you have to remember that what has to be done is to push the habitual concept of what is comfortably evil into another dimension, which is uncomfortably evil. And I think that that has to be respected. I agree that it *should* illumine, but in any case it needs doing, and the deeper the fear is, the deeper one must push into the discomfort.

EMERSON: I applaud what Mr. Walcott has just said. But I found it thrilling that this remarkable man called Walt Whitman a son of a bitch, because it meant he's read him. And I don't think Walt Whitman would mind, he would be honored to be called that, and we could talk about Hawthorne criticizing Emerson, the bishop of our possibilities, and we could talk about Emerson's loss of nerve, and Emerson and Thoreau. We have the right to call Whitman a son of a bitch if we've read him and we remember him. I disagree profoundly on the power of good. I'm thinking of Gandhi, I'm thinking of Rosa Parks, I'm thinking of Nelson Mandela. I'm thinking of many people. Evil is active, but good can change rocks into water and make us something that we are not. And it is within our grasp, and it's very hard. But good is infinitely more active than evil. One just has to hear the voice inviting you to join them to do it. That's all.

STONE: To speak so, which is nobly spoken, is almost as though to say that if we wait long enough, we will see the outcome. Do we really believe that we are going to see the outcome, that the world will see the outcome, of the struggle between what we call good and what we call evil? And we have always to guard ourselves in terms of how we define it. For example, anger, pure anger, can assume the cloak of virtue by nature of itself, so that to be angry, only to be angry, is to be right, and to be virtuous. We have forever to keep redefining the "good." Are we going to see the end of this struggle between good and evil? I mean, we have got to continue trying to combat. But I think if we really look for an end, we might as well be up there with Reagan and Jerry Falwell on the rafter. Is good going to triumph? I heard that when the end of the world was coming, people would be going around saying they were God! And I thought, that's going to be really strange. Will Jerusalem be builded here among these dark satanic mills? I mean, are we going to see the triumph of good over evil? I have a lot of trouble believing that.

PALEY: We might get rid of the dark satanic mills, at least —

STONE: That would depend on the demand for what it is that the dark satanic mills make.

PALEY: —I mean, he had that in mind, for Christ's sake!

At this point, discussion was brought to an end, and with it, the symposium.

Robert Stone, Grace Paley, Stanislaw Baranczak

Contributors

Terrence Des Pres is the author of *The Survivor; An Anatomy of Life in the Death Camps* (Oxford University Press, 1976). He is working on two new books, on contemporary poets who write about politics and on writers in extreme circumstances. He teaches at Colgate University. ★ ★ ★ **Carolyn Forché**'s first book of poems, *Gathering the Tribes* (Yale University Press, 1976), received the Yale Younger Poets Award. Her second book, *The Country Between Us* (Harper & Row, 1982), won the Lamont Prize. ★ ★ ★ **Leslie Epstein** has published two books of short fiction, *The Steinway Quintet Plus Four* (Little, Brown, 1976) and *Goldkorn Tales* (E. P. Dutton, 1985), and three novels, *P. D. Kimerakov* (Little, Brown, 1975), *King of the Jews* (Coward, McCann & Geoghegan, 1979) and *Regina* (Coward, McCann & Geoghegan, 1982). He directs the Creative Writing Program at Boston University. ★ ★ ★ **Michael S. Harper** is the author of seven books of poems, including *Dear John, Dear Coltrane* (University of Pittsburgh Press, 1970; reprinted by the University of Illinois Press, 1985) and *Nightmare Begins Responsibility* (1975), *Images of Kin* (1977) and *Healing Song for the Inner Ear* (1985), all published by the University of Illinois Press. Harper coedited, with Robert B. Stepto, an anthology of contemporary Afro-American writing, *Chant of Saints* (University of Illinois, 1979). His autobiographical essay, "Why Don't They Speak Jazz?," appeared in *TQ* #55 and in *TQ 20* (the twentieth-anniversary anthology, which itself was issue #63). He is the Israel J. Kapstein Professor of English at Brown University.

Stanislaw Baranczak has published six books in Polish and is preparing a collection of his poems translated into English. Some of these appeared in *A Window on Poland*, *TQ* #57, Volume 1, and in *TQ 20*. He is the Alfred Jurzykowski Professor of Polish Language and Literature at

Harvard. ★ ★ ★ **Derek Walcott** was born in St. Lucia, Windward Islands, the West Indies, and maintains a permanent residence in Trinidad. He has written several plays, including *Three Plays: The Last Carnival; Beef, No Chicken; A Branch of the Blue Nile* (Farrar, Straus & Giroux, 1985) and *Dream on Monkey Mountain* (Farrar, Straus & Giroux, 1970), which won an Obie Award as a distinguished foreign play. His seven books of poems include *The Star-Apple Kingdom* (1979), *The Fortunate Traveller* (1982) and *Midsummer* (1983), all published by Farrar, Straus & Giroux, which also released Walcott's *Collected Poems* in 1985. He teaches at Boston University. ★ ★ ★ After a career as a foreign correspondent for *Newsweek* and the *Washington Post*, **Ward Just** turned to writing fiction, and has published six novels and two collections of stories. His books include *A Family Trust* (Atlantic-Little, Brown, 1978), *Honor, Power, Riches, Fame, and the Love of Women* (E. P. Dutton, 1980) and *In the City of Fear* (Viking, 1982). His latest novel, *The American Blues* (Viking, 1984) was excerpted in *TQ #59*, a special issue which took its title from that book. A short story, "The North Shore, 1958," appeared in *TQ #62*. ★ ★ ★ **Gloria Emerson**'s book, *Winners and Losers: Battles, Retreats, Gains, Losses, and Ruins from a Long War* (Random House, 1976; reprinted by Penguin, 1985), received the National Book Award. Her latest book is *Some American Men* (Simon & Schuster, 1985). She has been the Farris Professor of Journalism at Princeton.

Robert Stone is the author of *A Hall of Mirrors* (Houghton Mifflin, 1967), *A Flag for Sunrise* (Knopf, 1981) and *Dog Soldiers* (Houghton Mifflin, 1974). His new novel, *Children of Light*, of which an excerpt appears in this volume, was published in spring 1986 by Knopf. Stone's fiction appeared in *TQ #50* and *TQ 20*; there was an interview with him in *TQ #53*. ★ ★ ★ **Grace Paley** has published three volumes of stories, *The Little Disturbances of Man* (Doubleday, 1959; reprinted in the Penguin Fiction Series, 1985), *Enormous Changes at the Last Minute* (Farrar, Straus & Giroux, 1974) and *Later the Same Day* (Farrar, Straus & Giroux, 1985). Her book of poems, *Leaning Forward*, was published by Granite Press in 1985. ★ ★ ★ **C. K. Williams** is the author of four books of poems, *Lies* (1969), *I Am the Bitter Name* (1972) and *With Ignorance* (1977), all published by Houghton Mifflin; and *Tar* (Random House, 1983). He is the co-translator, with Gregory W. Dickerson, of Sophocles' *Women of Trachis* (Oxford University Press, 1978) and has prepared a translation, with Herbert Goldner, of Euripides' *The Bacchae*. He teaches at George Mason University.

Mary Lee Settle's novel, *Blood Tie* (Houghton Mifflin, 1977), received the National Book Award. Her other eight novels include O *Beulah Land* (Viking, 1956; reprinted by Ballantine, 1981), *The Scapegoat* (Random House, 1980), and *The Killing Ground* (Farrar, Straus & Giroux, 1982). Her latest novel, *Celebration*, is being published in fall 1986 by Farrar, Straus & Giroux. ★ ★ ★ **Angela Jackson**'s collections of poems include *VooDoo/Love Magic* (Third World Press, 1974) and *The Greenville Club*, in *Four Black Poets* (Book Mark Press, 1978). Another excerpt from her novel, *Tremont Stone*, appeared in *Chicago*, TQ #60. She is writer-in-residence at Stephens College, in Columbia, Missouri. ★ ★ ★ **Bruce Weigl** is the author of two books of poems, *A Romance* (University of Pittsburgh, 1979) and *The Monkey Wars* (University of Georgia, 1985). Poems of his appeared in *TQ #55* and *TQ 20*. He teaches at Old Dominion University, in Norfolk, Virginia ★ ★ ★ **David Lloyd** teaches at LeMoyne College, in Syracuse, New York. His poetry and criticism have appeared in *Ariel*, *The Anglo-Welsh Review*, *Poetry Wales* and other journals.

*   *   *

Barbara Foley is a member of the English Department faculty at Northwestern. Her book, *Telling the Truth; The Theory and Practice of Documentary Fiction*, is being published by Cornell University Press in spring 1986. ★ ★ ★ **Cornelia Spelman**'s pamphlet, *Talking About Child Sexual Abuse*, was published in 1985 by the National Committee for Prevention of Child Abuse. She is in the M.S.W. program at the Loyola School of Social Work, in Chicago. ★ ★ ★ **Hugo Achugar**, originally from Uruguay, has taught in Caracas and now teaches at Northwestern; his most recent book of poems, *Las mariposas tropicales*, was published in winter 1986 by Ediciones del Norte (Hanover, New Hampshire). ★ ★ ★ **Alan Shapiro** and **Paul Breslin** are members of the English Department faculty at Northwestern. Shapiro's books of poems are *After the Digging* (Elpenor, 1982) and *The Courtesy* (University of Chicago, 1984); he has contributed poems and essays to *TriQuarterly*. Breslin is the author of *The Psycho-Political Muse*, to be published in 1987 by the University of Chicago Press.